MEET ME
IN THE
IN-BETWEEN

MEET ME
IN THE
IN-BETWEEN

BELLA
POLLEN

MANTLE

First published 2017 by Mantle
an imprint of Pan Macmillan
20 New Wharf Road, London N1 9RR
Associated companies throughout the world
www.panmacmillan.com

ISBN 978-1-5098-2896-8

1 3 5 7 9 8 6 4 2

A CIP catalogue record for this book is available from the British Library.

Printed and bound by CPI Group (UK) Ltd, Croydon CR0 4YY

Visit **www.panmacmillan.com** to read more about all our books
and to buy them. You will also find features, author interviews and
news of any author events, and you can sign up for e-newsletters
so that you're always first to hear about our new releases.

Illustrations

KATE BOXER is a British artist and printmaker whose
unique and idiosyncratic body of work defies categorization.
Her most recent show, 'I Won't Eat You', was held in 2016 at
Cricket Fine Art, London. info@cricketfineart.co.uk

More of her work can be seen at
www.kateboxer.co.uk

Calligraphy

AMY GADNEY is a multimedia artist and writer. Winner of
the 2011 GAM prize, she has exhibited her work in both
Europe and America. Her first solo show, 'Ghost Load', was
staged in 2015 at Cecilia Brunson Projects in London.

More of her work can be seen at
www.amygadney.com

Design

DAISY SWORDER is the self-taught design whizz
responsible for taking the illustrations and calligraphy and
breathing story through them. *Meet Me in the In-Between*
is her first publishing project.

To my mother
for her wisdom, her love, and her lion's heart.

MEET ME
IN THE
IN-BETWEEN

DEMON

The demon came as demons do, during the faithless hours of early morning. I'd been ascending through ever-shallowing layers of sleep, when finally I breached the surface, stretched for my phone and groaned.

Four a.m. is a brutal time to wake. Too late for a sleeping pill, too early for a new day. I shut my eyes again, but almost at once the worries began crowding in, quickly magnifying from the banal to the overblown.

What if the accumulation of everything I've learned adds up to nothing?

What if the story I've sold myself about life isn't the real story?

What if I'm dying of that rare kidney disorder I read about in Time *magazine last week?*

4:02. A branch tapped against the curtainless window. Outside it was wintry black. The night had a picture-book quality to it: a waxing gibbous moon, spores of mist seeded through it. The air became eerily still, and for a moment I felt dislocated, suspended in time. My insomnia makes me vulnerable to the tricks night plays so I wiggled my toes under the blankets; then, reassured that I was awake, resolved to count my way back to sleep on the rhythm of tiny taps and creaks generated by the silence. I was close to succeeding, too, when I heard something. At first faintly, then increasingly clearly—the tread of footsteps coming up the stairs.

My eyes snapped back open. Alone on the property; this was the first night I'd slept here. The grounds were still a building site. My bed, the only piece of furniture in the house.

Mac and I had bought the place two years earlier and immediately begun renovations. The project nearly did us in. It was as though the house had been storing up its grievances for centuries and now, with every brick pulled, was releasing them back upon us. Bats, rats, floods, rot. One by one they came, the seven plagues of the English countryside. The house was an old rectory next to a Norman church and graveyard. There was a sense of unrest about the graveyard's higgledy-piggledy layout, as if bodies and bones had been shifted to make room for newcomers, and now the original occupants were muttering like angry commuters on a packed train. It was possible, I suppose, that this honey-coloured village had been an idyll for milkmaids marrying their farming loves, but it was equally likely that it had been a finger-pointing, witch-burning community, meting out innovative torture in the name of God. Long before the footsteps stopped outside the door, I'd wondered whether the place might be haunted.

Transfixed, I stared at the door handle but too late. The presence was already in the room.

The side of my bed dipped, as if someone had sat down heavily. Covers began pulling away from me like waves receding off a shore. I felt the embrace of pins and needles as a body pressed against mine.

It seemed to be made of iron filings—millions of them, detached, free moving, yet somehow magnetically drawn together into the shape of a man.

I would never see it, but this was the image that developed in my head as the arms gathered me in. Dear God, was it spooning me? For the first time in a long while I felt cherished and safe. Tears blurred my eyes. I was exhausted, demoralised, struggling to finish a novel. The renovation work had caused so much antipathy between Mac and me that we'd barely been speaking, let alone spooning. I sighed. The arms tightened in response, as if aware of the comfort they were giving. My every muscle loosened. Again the arms tightened—the iron filings moving fluidly into the gap left by my exhalation. I pushed out against my diaphragm, but once again as my lungs deflated the space was stolen from me. I began to panic. Whatever this thing was, it was not benign. I tried to call out, but no sound came. I strained to break free, but found I could no longer move my arms or legs. Soon I could no longer breathe. Pressure rose in my chest, but just as my mind started to close I saw a memory, flickering like a pinprick of light through the darkness. I'd experienced something like this once before, during the delivery of my first child by Caesarean. Something had gone wrong while they were stitching me up, and the pressure had built, culminating in a tremendous burst of pain in my heart. Simultaneously I'd heard the beep of the monitor flatlining. As medics pounced, some misplaced survival instinct told me they were trying to kill me and I'd fought them with the last of my strength. Now I did the same, mustering something internal, something almost telekinetic. My limbs spasmed. I felt the violent throwback of an explosion, and suddenly I was free.

*   *   *

In the bathroom, I splashed cold water onto my face. I've always suffered from nightmares. I can't tell you the multitude of ways I've watched my family being dispatched to their graves over the years. My brother hanging from the mouths of monsters. A faceless woman leading my mother away. My son waving at me, then turning to jump to his death down a bottomless black hole. Nor am I merely a spectator at the horror show of my subconscious: my hands have been chewed off by creatures of the deep, my eyes prised from their sockets by gelatinous fingers. In one of my cheerier recurring dreams I am forced to walk down a narrow corridor whose walls are a pulsing lattice of serpents, some oily and brown, others speckled and wickedly fluorescent, all with tongues that flick out as I pass. As if in a video game whose next level is unattainable, I am invariably struck before I reach safety.

Something grisly in childhood is supposed to account for adult phobias. My mother grew up in Africa, and certainly her stories of being chased across the plains by the black mamba were the stuff of bedtime legend. Closer to home, I remember running barefoot through the long grass at my grandmother's house and seeing the coils of mating grass snakes below me. In one airborne second, I managed to adjust my trajectory. Grass snakes are harmless, amiable creatures; nevertheless I later felt sick at how close I'd come to landing on that foul, writhing mass.

Further back still there had been a strange incident at the Bronx Zoo. A cobra, demented by captivity, had repeatedly bashed itself against the glass of its enclosure. Even as my mother tried to pull me away, I'd stood my ground, as fascinated as I was repulsed. So, snake nightmares I could account for—as for the rest, who knew?

"Fuck," I said to my reflection. "Fuck, fuck, fuck."

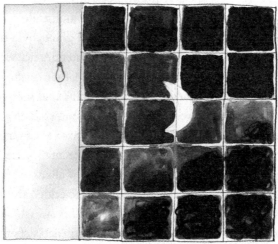

4:20am. No possibility of sleep now.

Back in bed, I tried to regulate my breathing but after a while became aware of my body feeling fractionally out of sync with its surroundings. The branch scraped against the window—a Maurice Sendak world of moons and fairy tales knocking to come in. Again the air stood still. My mind began to separate. *No*, I thought, *no*.

I scrunched my toes under the covers and looked around the room. Everything was as it should be: the edge of the mantelpiece, the tissue I'd dropped onto the splintery floorboards, my hand raised in the gloomy light.

This time when the bed dipped, something whispered in my ear. My skin began to burn. Arms closed around me. I heard a guttural noise and then realised it was the sound of me choking—choking on nothing. Pressure began building. Quicker this time, more urgently. Suddenly, spuming up through my terror, I felt a savage, primordial arousal, then the sensation of being penetrated, utterly possessed, before the unstoppable rush to orgasm, as intense as it was short, after which, spell broken once again, I found myself alone.

I curled into a ball. What was happening to me? Nightmares I could deal with, but this was no nightmare. This had happened while I was awake.

Everyone relishes a good haunting story. *Bella has a sex ghost.* The delighted whispering circled back to me within the week. Suggestions poured in. I should approach the local priest; hire a ghost buster. Friends recommended their latest psychic in the same casual manner they might have passed on the number for their plumber.

"Ask it to leave," Mac advised unhelpfully. "Unless, of course, you prefer it stays."

By the time my dentist, who'd recently completed a course in hypnotherapy, offered to cure my insomnia in between fillings, I was so unsettled that when he told me to relax and find a happy place, the best I could come up with was the chocolate croissant display in Prêt à Manger.

During this period, I suffered two more visitations. Both came at four a.m., both while I was awake. Before going to bed I had shut windows, jerry-rigged a bedside light, tuned the audio of my hearing to its most sensitive frequency for signs of unlawful entry. Nothing worked. Each time, the *presence*, as it was now officially known, returned a few minutes after I initially broke free to push into the empty crevices of my body, take me to the edge of the sexual abyss, and then carelessly drop me over, adding a frisson of shame to what was already a profoundly frightening experience. I was being defiled, brutalised. The creature had worked its full will upon every inch of my body, and yet, yet . . . I was taking pleasure in it?

It was a friend, a journalist and polymath, who identified the problem. "What you've just described," he told me over dinner, "is a classic visitation from an incubus."

"A what?"

"A demon who lies upon women in order to engage in sexual activity with them."

Terrific, I thought, picturing the reluctant old lady from whom we'd bought the house. Seemed she'd gifted us with something a little extra alongside her already generous endowments of mould and woodworm.

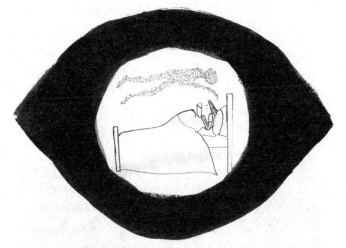

Must you stay? Can't you go?

Back home I hit Google. Attributed to everything from incest to the slovenly habit of eating in bed, the visitation of an incubus appeared to be a phenomenon in every corner of the globe. Cultural and mythological variations aside, all came with the same dread warning on the label. Under a helpfully graphic image of a satanic creature hovering over a prone unconscious female was writ: *Repeated sexual activity with an incubus may result in deterioration of health, possibly even death.*

Thoroughly spooked, I refused to stay alone in the house, shunting up the motorway to London on even the grimmest of nights. All of this produced a shimmering resentment, the full force of which I directed at Mac. The pull of his roots, this move to Oxfordshire, with its cultivated hedges and walled gardens, was his dream not mine.

~ *Fields and fields of boring* ~

Frankly I have only to look upon a flower for it to wither and die.

Now we'd lost so much money shoring up the place, it was becoming obvious we would have to sell before we moved in. All that agony for nothing, and as soon as my part in it was done, I bolted to the American West, taking my mess of a book with me. I wanted lions, not ladybugs. A bigger landscape, the sound and silence of wilderness. The West was escape, and escape was my oxygen.

Weeks later, having barely given the incubus a thought, I checked into a sweet roadside motel for the night. Four a.m. to the minute, I woke to a sense of heightened unreality and the presence between my thighs. I reached down in disbelief and felt the unmistakable iron fingers close over my hand.

By the end of that year, having received three more drop-ins—all in places I had gone to lose myself—I understood with a terrible clarity that I could not outrun this thing. Wherever I fled to, however far I travelled, there it would be, sitting next to me on the airplane, unfolding its iron-filing legs, reading the in-flight magazine and ordering the chicken or fish. This was no demon living in a house back in England. The demon lived inside me.

"You don't need a psychic," Mac said. "You need an exorcist."

In the panoply of the supernatural, possession is one of the more terrifying concepts: the idea of something lurking within you, something inherently evil, something that can't be controlled or killed off. *Poltergeist*, *Paranormal Activity*, *The Devil Inside*. Like everyone else, I tend to watch these horror flicks through spread fingers, laughing nervously at the pastiche of the girl in her white nightie—haunted, controlled, before finally being dragged across the bedroom, her nails leaving raw scratch marks on the wooden boards.

None of this exactly lulled me to sleep at night. It wasn't long before I found myself caving in to the self-pitying mantra of the victim: *Why me?*

I come from generations of pragmatic, no-nonsense copers, whose answer to almost every shape and size of dilemma is to tuck in our shirts and press on. I resolved to stop feeling sorry for myself. If the thing was feeding on fear, I would make light of it. Write the stupid thing clean out of me. I began working on a comic novel about a depressed obsessive-compulsive who falls in love with his succubus, as the female of the species is known. She was fleshy, voluptuous, and a marvellous cook, if something of a slob, who left crumbs in his bed and liked to gobble Viennese Sachertorte in his bath.

I couldn't make a single thread connect. Would my hero choose death and happiness with a figment of his imagination, or the misery of survival with his unloving, bloodless wife? No point asking me. Having ceded control of my own life, I seemed equally unable to puppeteer the lives of others.

The creative block that followed was both absolute and shattering. Day after day, I sat at my desk while the iron filings, like grain filling a barn, continued to pour into the empty store of my imagination.

"Repeated visits from an incubus can cause illness and sometimes death

CONFIDENCE R. I. P.

IDENTITY

SELF WORTH R. I. P.

But death of what?

Mac remained wearily patient, but I couldn't make him understand. I hadn't lost my muse. My muse had been destroyed by a ravenous pathogen. In lieu of working, I took up reading. Hefty tomes, dense, discursive. I managed about five pages before straying back to ghost stories, ones that freaked me out as a child. *The Turn of the Screw, A Christmas Carol,* Edith Wharton's "The Eyes." Patterns began to emerge. James's narrator was haunted by corrupted innocence, Scrooge by his greed and misanthropy. Wharton's egotist Andrew Culwin was tormented by the manifestation of his guilt and shame. So I wondered: *What if my ghost was also a metaphor for some buried, unexpressed emotion?* Forget the monsters, the rippling tapestry of serpents, the bottomless black hole. *What if the thing I was most frightened of was myself?*

"About that exorcist," Mac said. "I think what you really need is a shrink."

Er, nooo.

He persevered: "Has it not occurred to you that you might need to work through your past in order to move on to your future?"

No, it hadn't, and fuck that AA bullshit anyway. I was brought up to believe that talking about oneself was the height of boorishness. My family doesn't do shrinks. We don't do depression, body dysmorphia, or white-hot hysteria. We don't do alcoholism, chronic anxiety, or postnatal blues. Or, at least, when we *do* do these things, standard operating procedure requires us to do them in private. Even so, on the continuum of sanity, I've always considered myself closer to well-adjusted than to the twitchy loon of the asylum. So what if the inside of my head is full of politically incorrect gags, muddled ethics, and colourful flash cards of what to eat for my next meal? Nothing any doctor can say is going to straighten out the kinks in those telephone wires.

The very idea of finding a shrink raised antediluvian images of smoky rooms and Old Testament stares. You have only to look at my incubus to see I haven't always been the best picker of men. If the shrink I chose was subpar, he'd likely fall for my tricks and lies; if he was savvy enough to tap into the dark oily streams of my unconscious, chances are I'd be spending the rest of my days amid the whispery chatter and muted shrieks of the Hospice de la Salpêtrière. Were he to suggest there might be one or two things we could work on together—well, I know myself. I'd make up any number of deceits designed to show me in the best light, then I'd sleep with him. Seducing my shrink would prove he was a jackass and thus negate the need to listen to a single word he had to say.

"You could always opt for a female therapist," Mac pointed out.
"Now you're being ridiculous," I said, and flounced off to sleep on the sofa.

Later, blinking through the dust of insomnolence, it occurred to me that were I to ever commit to therapy—and the idea was making me more schizoid by the day—I would need a superior being, one free from the shackles of human fallibility. God, for instance, would tick a box or two. As the unseduceable, infallible, ultimate figure of male authority, he'd be a good fit for me, except for the fact that I don't believe in him. I don't believe in any kind of organised religion, but neither do I have faith in the process of therapy. Summarizing myself to some pen twiddler? Synopsizing my insecurities in the hope of extrapolating some life-changing realisation out of my own applesauce? I don't think so. Everyone walks through fear and pain. However crooked the journey that brings us here, here is where we are, and to trawl through the past looking to send your parents to the tumbrils for the way you turned out seems neither right nor fair.

So, lately I've been talking to "Sarah." Sarah is wise and statuesque, with grey hair streaked like winter marble. The fact that she has the exact same name and physical characteristics as my London literary agent is purely coincidental. Sarah believes that my brief dalliance with the idea of God was purely a frivolous mechanism designed to shift attention away from myself.

"Any excuse not to dig deep," she sighs. "And as for that infantile riff about sleeping with your shrink!"

"Oh, come on, how can therapy not be about sex?" I ask her. "Opening up to someone is the most intimate thing you can do. It leaves you far more vulnerable than taking off your clothes."

"This from somebody in sexual thrall to a ghost?"

"*Harrumph,*" I answered.

To begin with, Sarah appeared to me only at night, but recently she's taken to hanging around during office hours too.

"What are you doing?" she asks, swinging coltish legs off the edge of my desk.

"Working."

"On what?"

"A book."

"And is this book by any chance called 'Where to Buy High-Waist Jeans with a Pencil Leg'?"

I close the tab. See, this is the downside of virtual shrinks. They get into your head, they get into your hard drive, and soon there is nowhere to hide. The upshot is that the carbon footprint of virtual therapy is small. Recently, Sarah has taken to bringing an overseas colleague with her.

"Kim" is strong and fierce. The fact that she bears the same name and physical attributes as my American literary agent is also weirdly coincidental. Kim is spectacularly untroubled by any form of self-doubt, and for this reason alone I find her a little scary.

"Please," Kim says. "This self-deprecation/humble-bragging thing. It's not doing you any favours."

"I don't know why you're here," I grumble. "Either of you."

"Oh, we think you do," Kim says.

"I'm not blocked, if that's what you're thinking."

"Really? How long since you last published?"

"I've got tons of ideas."

"Show us one, then."

"Early stages," I mutter.

"Uh-huh." Kim gives Sarah a knowing look.

"Hasn't anyone ever suggested you might need to work through your past in order to move on to your future?" Sarah asks.

"Nope," I snap. "Never."

But after they leave, I dare myself to think about it.

Maybe at some point in life everyone comes to a full stop. A point at which people are forced to question who they are and what they stand for. *If the story I've sold myself isn't the real one, then what is?* Maybe the narrative of your past life can't be changed, but would it really hurt to check whether anything's been learned along the way?

"Memoir? That's what you're thinking?" At the first hint of literary productivity, Kim reappears, arms crossed, against my filing cabinet.

"It's not exactly my genre," I say.

"Rubbish." Sarah cleans her glasses. "Everything you've ever written is lazily disguised autobiography."

"That's because books are like nightmares," I say sullenly. "They, too, grow out of grisly past experiences."

"Don't be glib." Kim is already rifling through the box of old photos in the corner of my room. "How good is your memory, anyway?"

I clutch my forehead, wishing them both gone. I don't trust memory—edited footage run through the spool of sentiment and nostalgia. Memory is impure. It springs from the tiniest seeds of reality, and on the way to flowering it produces offshoots of nuance and tints of every colour. Memories are life as you choose to remember it. Life the way you wish it had been. Memory betrays us all; or maybe, in the end, we all betray our memories.

"Lighten up," Sarah says. "Nobody cares about the colour of the napkins."

A fantasy memoir, an unreliable narrator

"Christ, what does that even mean?"

"It means write about what's important to you."

"Though an overarching theme would make it easier to package." This from Kim.

I look from one to the other. "But where would I start?"

"At the beginning."

"Everyone has more than one beginning," I say. "One end but a thousand beginnings."

"This is no time to be pretentious," Sarah counters. "Keep it simple."

"What were you like as a child, for instance?" Kim asks.

"As a child?" I pluck a random photograph from the box. "Well, now you come to mention it . . ." I run my finger over the faded image. "Kind of adorable."

NEW YORK

VILLAIN BABY

The photograph was taken in the study of our New York apartment. On first glance it is a Hallmark tableau of a happy, close-knit English family abroad. Fear not, though—it is anything but.

The photo is originally intended for a newspaper—some odd publication whose name I can't remember—and for the purposes of artistic composition, we, the Pollens, have been arranged. Children centre forwards; parents at opposite corners of a linen sofa set against an intellectually abstract wallpaper that seems very much of its time.

Quizzical, a half smile on his lips, my father looks athletic in a grey suit over a pressed shirt. His cufflinks are enamel, his tie skinny, though not overly so. Dad's hair is bitter black, his skin pale, his nose from the Jewish side of the family. Heavily rimmed glasses lend him a bookish, if somewhat Clark Kentish, look—but this is just so. When at home, he is the English square, a true blue of Eton and Oxford. When away, however—and he is often up, up, and away—he is the superhero of the art world. Clues to his dual identity? The cowboy boots, the hair too long for his job, the gravitational force of his charm. Dad is the authoritarian but also the instigator of the Sunday-morning pillow fight. The president of the auction house bunking off work to take us to the movies. The aesthete who believes in the majesty of a hot-dog breakfast.

And my mother?

A Somerset Maugham beauty whose complexion remains English rose despite growing up under the blistering African sun. She wears a necklace of three jade strands and a wrap-around jersey dress whose psychedelic print is tastefully muted. When she laughs, and she's laughing now, her eyes crease to happy and her hair—rich as carob—swings under her chin. My mother, a volunteer teacher in Harlem, is 100 percent love and roast chicken picnics in the park. She is the draughtsman of boundaries, the rule maker, the advocate of a prettily said thank you. At home, where she is almost always to be found, she is the answer to every question, the entity around which our stratospheric demands orbit. Custodian of the bedtime story, coper, secret smoker, it is my mother who is the moral backbone of the family, then, now, and forever more.

But lo! What do we have here, perched so coyly on the sofa arm behind her? Eldest Child in her patent Mary Janes, so very clean and polished. Hair black as bog earth, complexion clear as water. Eldest Child is serious, clever, the prism through which every first-time parental neurosis has been filtered. She is neither smiling nor laughing. She is a million emotions away from joy, and though we are not done with her, not by any means, enough of the spotlight on sister Susie. It's time to pay attention to the photo's bottom right-hand corner, where little Marcus—that eminently kissable lambkin of God—is straddling a red plastic London bus, with the unquestioning delight for public transport that only a four-year-old can muster.

Apart from his pudding bowl of black hair—yes, again with the hair colour—there's nothing noteworthy about Youngest Child.

So what's noteworthy about the photograph in the first place, you might wonder. Why the inch-by-inch scrutiny, the wordy discourse?

Here's what's special about this New York Hasselblad moment.

I am.

I am what's special.

Me.

Right there, sitting between my parents on the sofa. *Between my parents.* See how I am the absolute focus of their interest? Note, if you will, that this very shutter second, recorded if not for posterity then certainly for the painful longevity of my siblings' existence, represents the outcome of a desperate and bloody battle.

In other words: it's the happiest moment of my life.

My sister, my brother, and I begin at the beginning, our ID cards clean and unstamped. Not yet nicknamed "Sticks" or "Froggins" or "Fish," we're bland and harmless—three little pastas waiting for sauces. We muddle through the honeymoon period of newborn without discernible stereotyping, but labels soon apply. Eldest Child is Numero Uno. Top Doggie, Head Girl. First to walk, first to talk, a pipper past every post. The whites of her eyes reflect nothing but gold stars and Best in Show rosettes. She is the Queen Bee, the Bee's Knees. She is brand-new clothes, later bedtimes, and the highest tax bracket of pocket money. Her position is unassailable; her ambitions are undetermined but lofty.

Baby brother is Dauphin of the Upper East Side, Caliph of our Ninety-Second Street apartment. The boy whose syrupy dimples make even the dourest of doormen smile. Marcus is First Caste Male, Man Cub, only and much longed for son, whose maggoty little penis carries the genus of the family name. Though currently the owner of no more than a handful of chewed and sticky baseball cards, he is heir to the glittering fiefdom of Pollen. Amenable, pudgy, he aspires to be a fireman but also sometimes a vet.

Then there's me. Tot Two, Second-Hand News, No Novelty, Replicant. I am Old Hat, Superfluous to Needs, a dreary amalgam of hand-me-downs and repeat-routine. Share the bedroom! Halve the space!

Sidelined and out in the rain, I am insecure and jealous, left to gnaw
on the entrails of exhausted parental affection. Pre-packaged to feel
hard done by, I am a spiraling vortex of need prepared to leech the last
dregs of unconditional love from the marrow of my mother's bones. I
am *Omen* clone, pedalling my horrid little tricycle across the family's
happiness and peace of mind.

I am Middle Child.

Plus, I am blonde, sort of.

"Adopted," whispers Eldest Child, before turning her soft-soaping
face to thank Mother for the baloney sandwich. "Thanks, Mumsie.
You're truly the bestest."

Not all talents are bestowed upon us at birth. The cutting snideness
and instant retort that will one day become my trademark have not yet
kicked in. Right now, brawn is all I have.

Middle Child likes to keep a metaphorical knife in her hand. To hell
with roast chicken picnics in the park. She wants roadkill, her sister's
carcass on a plate. Susie is her sworn enemy—for the homework she
completes, for the straight A's she achieves, for the shocking articulacy
she employs in the face of adult interrogation. See her—wearing her
gaudy Miss Diplomatic Immunity sash—adopt a world peace expression of enrichment. Watch her smile and feign thoughtful intelligence.
Later in life, when the difference in our hair colour is rendered unim-
portant, when we are inseparable, a witches' coven of two, I discover
that my sister is *genuinely* thoughtful and intelligent, while from my
own mouth will always slip things putrid and slithery. But for now, age
six to her seven and a half, my ambition is to slaughter her and keep
her head in a pickling jar.

Let the record show, however, that I have no plans to execute King
Baby. Oh, no. Him I will subjugate. Put a ring through his nose and

teach him to dance to my tune. I will bide my time, the puppet master behind the throne, and when he is finally crowned, the strings of power shall be mine.

One day opportunity comes. The entry-phone buzzes, the elevator rises, and Nanny opens the door.

"And how does nice Mr. Axelrod take his coffee?" she asks.

The photographer is professional, courteous. He remarks on the calm of the household, the children so tidy and well mannered. He sees only our surface, Lake Placid, but none of the currents roiling beneath. He begins arranging. A glass paperweight, art catalogues, the vase of flowers my mother has brought in from the bedroom. The photographer's concerns are the afternoon light and the paper's deadline. At length he turns his attention to the family, moving us here and there, in and out of frame, until quite suddenly the music stops, and I'm sitting where I'm sitting.

Between my parents.

Oh, the luck. I can scarcely believe it, for although I've always been told that the Lord giveth, let's face it, he often taketh away again almost straight after. *Our father who art in heaven*, I silently implore. *Please! Let me stay.*

"All right, everybody freeze!" Mr. Axelrod says drolly, and it is done.

The fists of Middle Child clench in triumph, a flame ignites in her heart, and as it catches and burns, the sky above the water tanks tinges red and a hot wind blows across the Hudson.

Now the photographer directs my parents to look at me. That's right—not at Eldest Child, not at King Baby, but at *me*. And because it is so unexpected and so thrilling, because it is the thing I want above all else, I panic.

In my embarrassment, in my agony, I blurt out something silly, accidentally witty. It is possibly the silliest, accidentally wittiest line anyone has ever come up with, and I wish I could remember it, but it's gone.

A flash of amusement crosses my father's face. He removes his glasses and pinches the bridge of his nose. My mother laughs and curls her hair around a finger. The invisible bubble coming out of her mouth says: *Oh my! We've been so foolish! It's been you all along, right under our very nozies!*

Why yes, my father's bubble concurs. *It is you, after all, Oh Favoured One, oh so very centred middling child, neither too tall nor too squat, too old nor too young, too near nor too far. Your very in-betweenness means you are ideally positioned to realise our every hope and dream. You and you alone shall be the carrier of the Olympic flame.*

And thus, the match flares, the baton passes, and Eldest Child's lips thin to invisibility. She has missed the writing on the wall. Too late she has understood that she is to be usurped, tipped off her perch, cut down in a hail of bullets. She is Queen Bee stung to death by the very colony over which she presides. The hare, fucked over by the tortoise. Perched on the arm of the sofa, eldest paws snatching at the grey linen, she gazes into the abyss. Sneak preview of Eldest Child's future? A cheerless meditation on the game of nepotism she has played and lost.

As for the Prince Regent? See the wheels on his bus go round and round? See that vacant expression on his face? Shock. For the first time in his toddly life, he has been rolled outside the magic circle. No longer warmed by the embers of favouritism, he must navigate the remainder of his life numb and alone: the shambles of adolescence, the bafflement of adulthood, the indignation of middle age, and the ignominy of death. Not even a fleet of red plastic London buses will palliate the horror of this journey to come.

Oh, Dear God, if this moment could only be set in concrete, snow-globed for eternity.

But wait.

It can.

It already is.

Because photographs are forever.

Farewell, sucker siblings.

The era of Middle Child has begun.

PIECES OF EIGHT

One thing I knew about my father's Sotheby Parke-Bernet job: it meant throwing a lot of cocktail parties. Women stood elbow to elbow, smoking, tortoiseshell bracelets chinking as they debated vital matters such as Lyrical Abstraction or the Paradigm of Cubism. Their sideburned counterparts, snug in black turtlenecks, nipped at martinis and leaned in doorways looking charismatic. These men smoked too, but then everybody smoked last century. Entertaining in 1960s Manhattan required imagination. No cubed cheese and pineapple on toothpicks for New York City's art elite, and so caterers were hired to produce trays of ingenious canapés that we, as the host's children, were expected to hand around. This duty required us to be formally placed on best behaviour, a state, as explained by our parents with their patented brand of loving sarcasm, a notch or two above our normally polite, helpful selves.

I had no objection to handing round food—any proximity to food was fine by me. It was the small talk I found galling. In the way that some people are socially hampered by lack of spatial awareness or a third nipple, I was born with zero talent for polite conversation.

Alcohol is not available to third-graders, even in measured calming doses, so I was soon labelled a disagreeable child, prone to bouts of idiocy. It wasn't fair. For instance, when my father's colleague Mr. Whipstein remarked, "Goodness, child, you've got tall!"

I, paralysed by self-consciousness, blurted back, "and you're fat!"

Both statements were equally true, but I'm pretty sure Mr. Whipstein's didn't cost him a week's pocket money and the mortification of

27

an apology. Still, I can't pretend not to know what my parents wanted from us at these parties: to scamper from guest to guest, bearing toothpaste smiles and crying, "Delighted to make your acquaintance, do try the shrimp," all the while parrying enquiries of a personal nature, if not with charm then at least with tact.

"How's school?" the interrogation would begin, and from there slalom viciously downhill to, "What do you want to be when you grow up?" And there it was. The dread question. How was I supposed to know? At eight years old, I'd barely worked out whether I was animal, vegetable, or mineral. All philosophical uncertainties are scary, but "Who am I?" has to be the most terrifying of all. I mean, is it really a matter of choice? Does the chicken actually *ask* to produce the egg? Conversely, I also resented the question for its implication that children were of no interest in their own right, but merely being kept in a holding pattern until they were old enough to pursue that mysterious trajectory known as a career.

At six, I was given a book called the *Big Bumper Book of Jobs*. It portrayed the daily lives of hard-working ginger cats outfitted as police officer, firefighter, nurse. Across terse double-page spreads, dedicated tabbies could be seen arresting loutish toms or saving sputtering kittens from flaming buildings. Other illustrations depicted attractive felines with curling lashes peeping out from under Florence Nightingale bonnets, while ripped-looking Manx cats in hard hats yowled orders across building sites. The book was inspiring. But I didn't want to be a civic, goody-goody cat; I wanted to be a different kind of cat. A fun, cool cat, like the fifteen- and sixteen-year-old Puerto Rican kids my mother taught how to read in her Harlem school. Like Bill Latimer, doorman of Parke-Bernet, "mayor" of Madison Avenue, and confidant of Eleanor Roosevelt. Bill was also a buddy of star quarterback Joe Namath and would take us to Shea Stadium to watch Jets games, always allowing us to eat hot dogs while hoisted onto his shoulders, irrespective of how much ketchup we slobbered down his neck.

"You can be anyone you want to be," was my parents' default line, but I was pretty sure I'd be laughed out of the party and sent to bed had I indicated a desire to be a six-foot-tall, fiftyish black doorman, so I kept quiet and proffered shrimp.

"Come, come," a Perspex bracelet insisted. "Everyone needs a passion—or if not a passion, at the very least a hobby."

Oh, I had a hobby. I liked to discredit anything my sister said and/or impose forced labour on my brother—a career that, in the unregulated market of sibling slavery, yielded unexpectedly high returns.

I also had a passion. In my free time I liked to torture dolls and stuffed animals. Run-of-the mill stuff really—singeing their hair, twisting off their heads. My parents encouraged it. No doubt they saw a future with Médecins Sans Frontières. *Right from the get-go it was obvious she wanted to help*, I imagined them saying. *You should have seen her, practise, practise, practise!*

And sometimes, so as not to arouse terror in their hearts, I'd pretend to do just that.

"There now," I'd say, zipper-stitching Teddy's severed head onto the ragged stump of his neck. "Those should stay in for a fortnight, but after that you'll be as good as new."

Truth be told, I wasn't the slightest bit interested in good-as-new teddies. As I joyfully dislocated Winnie-the-Pooh's shoulder or lit a match under Barbie's slender heel, I pictured them weeping—not from pain so much, but because they'd been betrayed by the very person who was supposed to love and protect them. Then, at the apex of their sadness and confusion, I'd turn it all around and comfort them, re-secure their love and forgiveness—until the next time.

I guess the calling I was loosely aiming at lay somewhere between Munchausen by proxy and Stockholm syndrome, but my parents' cocktail parties were hardly the moment to announce it. And thus the need for a more acceptable aspiration was born.

In her house back in England, our grandmother kept a dressing-up box, a beautiful red-lacquer Chinese trunk. Its contents were constantly in flux, but a rummage through them one summer yielded a pair of thick green tights, a suede tabard and a pointed felt hat. At eight, I had yet to pinpoint the difference between identity and career. It never occurred to me that the latter was something you stripped off at the end of the day. Robin Hood had potential. Years of filching quarters from the pocket of my father's tweed coat ticked the crime requirement, while running people through with a sword is one of those skills you're either lucky enough to be born with or not. I released Marcus from indentured servitude and promoted him to Merry Man, a role for which he dressed, somewhat obscurely, in a scarlet pirate's outfit. In her ruffled flamenco dress, Susie might have done for Maid Marian had it not been for her irritating habit of archly tossing her head and walking with elbow stiffly akimbo in the manner of a slutty Spanish infanta. For a while, "Outlaw, cheerful robber, Robin of Loxley!" was a crowd-pleasing answer at parties, combining altruism and political activism with a giant dollop of cuteness. Then, disaster. One day my mother seized my outfit and threw it into the washing machine, where it shrank fatally. To be Robin Hood, *garden gnome*, was not such a lofty ambition, and once again I found myself between careers.

The heroic age was followed by the cretinous. "I want to fence like Wellington," I announced to cocktail guests, "paint the birth of Venus, build a potato gun that can fire on the moon." Finally, one day when my guard was down, I blurted out the truth: "I want to be black."

The Lord John suit who'd posed the question snickered nervously into his whiskey sour, but the minute I'd said it, it seemed so obvious. My mother had been born and raised in Rhodesia. I lived in New York. *Could the term "African-American" have actually been coined for me?*

By the latter half of the 1960s, civil rights was an amorphous, dispersed movement being fought on multiple fronts across America. Malcolm X was dead. Martin Luther King's relationship with Lyndon B. Johnson's administration was deteriorating. It was the time of Huey Newton and Bobby Seale's Black Panther Party. Civil resistance and inner-city riots were raging every day on TV, but whatever it was about the cause that excited me had little to do with racism. I lived in my own bubble. I did not, for instance, take my favourite book, *The Story of Little Black Sambo*, to be an example of racial stereotyping with illustrations of "darky" iconography. Far as I could see, it was about a smart black kid with dubious taste in red shoes who outwitted a bunch of mean tigers. Little Black Sambo had been my mother's favourite book when she was a child and the copy she read to us was her own scuffed version with the original drawings. I never tired of it or its sister tale, *The Story of Little Black Mingo*, and even if I wasn't yet ready to apply their lessons—that courage was everything, while bullying and greed accomplished nothing—I took note.

I also had a golliwog family of whom I was very fond. Unaware that I was supposed to revile these as colonial caricatures, I made sure to subject them to experiments equally as sadistic as any endured by my white Ken doll. (It can't be denied, though, that Ken's muscular, tawny limbs were particularly delicious to melt.) But all that's beside the point. Privilege allows for multiple shades of colour blindness.

Then, as now, America's rage was fuelled by intractable and deeply rooted issues of class, bigotry, urban blight, economic deprivation, police brutality and wretched unemployment. I wish I could say I wanted to be black in order to whomp these, but in truth, I wanted to be black because I was a needy little ankle biter and most of the people my parents paid attention to were black—the activists they admired, the musicians they listened to, even the sportsmen they watched, from Bobo Brazil to Hank Aaron, whose giant baseball ad dominated Times Square. Black Is Beautiful was out on the street, and its energy crackled in the air. If you were born in the 1960s you didn't get to actually live in them—just watch them pass by in a series of vivid images. To me, black people looked like they were going somewhere and they were getting there in the best hair and the funkiest pantsuits ever.

"So," I asked my mother, "what do you think?"

"About being black?"

"You said I could be anything I wanted to be."

My mother considered me and I held my breath.

If ever a girl hankered after dark it was me, but I was born dishwater beige. This might not have been such an issue had I not belonged to a family of ink-heads. A drear little chiffchaff dropped into a nest of beguiling ravens. The blue eyes didn't help. Drama teacher after drama teacher cruelly stereotyped me in the role of jejune dimpled Gretel, while I ached to be the bony-legged witch. I wouldn't go so far as to say that my blandness got me bullied at school, but I've always had a thing about my colouring.

"I'm sorry, darling." My mother tucked a mousy tail behind my ear. "Maybe you should think again."

One day, strolling hand in hand along Fifth Avenue, the two of us chanced on a street stall selling wigs. All the big names were there, the Jackie O, the Catherine Deneuve, the Andy Warhol. I mittened through until I found what I was looking for.

In awe, I ran my fingertips over the Afro's kinked dome. Every tight coil was zinging with soul, the rhetoric of King, Satchmo's rasp, and the ball-bouncing skills of NBA champions.

"Please," I begged my mother. "I'll do anything."

My mother was sympathetic to the concept of wigs. She had, she confessed, recently bought herself an Elizabeth Taylor in which to meet my father at Kennedy Airport.

"And guess what?" she chuckled. "He walked straight past me, silly fool!"

Being black was a big decision, she counselled, as though I'd asked permission to marry a cult leader and raise quintuplets on his pig farm. "Wait a while. If you still feel the same at Christmas, we'll see."

Street Afros and other wig styles were available in a diverse range of female icons: the Kathleen Cleaver, the Billie Holiday, the Eartha Kitt.

"Get the Pam Grier," my mother advised in December. "It's closest to your skin tone."

The Pam Grier suited me. I have a preternaturally small head, but the Afro's radiant halo compensated nicely. I wore it to and from school, and though it tended to be itchy, particularly with the advent of warmer weather, I frequently slept in it too. As my confidence grew, so did my creative ambitions. Why the traditional orb? Why not shape the thing a little? I began to see a future for myself in Afro topiary. Scissors, a salon. It felt good to have a plan.

In those days we had a black cleaning woman named Lenor, who came three times a week. She arrived as we left for school and was often gone by the time we returned. I remember her as a scrupulous woman with a constellation of moles on her forehead and flat-ironed hair sprinkled with silver. At a guess, she might have been in her late forties, although a fondness for hatpins pointed to a more remote decade. She reminded me of a Beatrix Potter character, a wise and clever Mrs. Brock—the kind of upright wife who would never have allowed Tommy to topple into the moral abyss of bunny kidnapping. If Lenor thought it odd that I'd recently become black, she was elegant enough not to say so. The first time she saw my Afro she gave it a cautious pat, as though it were a small dead Pomeranian I'd taken to wearing on my head as a trophy. The following day she took a pick from her bag and instructed me in the art of back-combing. A week or so later, she pinched the curls and murmured, "You might want to use a little castor oil on Pam," producing a bottle of the stuff from her coat pocket. "Cost no more than a dollar," she said, waving away my thanks. "Keeps her soft, you know?"

It was around this time that Sotheby Parke-Bernet held the "Treasure of the Spanish Main" sale. A beachcomber in Cape Canaveral, Florida, had spotted something sticking out of the sand which turned out to be a gold necklace belonging to the admiral of the Spanish fleet. The necklace was made of links shaped like roses and had a clasp in the form of a dragon.

"You pulled the head off the dragon," my father told us, "and inside was a tiny spoon for clearing the wax out of your ears."

The ship carrying it, one of a fleet, had gone down in a storm in 1715, and when it was raised from the bottom of the sea, the treasure had been recovered intact.

A key part of my father's job, it turned out, was to liven up the stuffy world of the auction house. The sale he designed was an extravaganza. Before bidding started, lights were dimmed. Silhouettes of the stricken fleet, flung about by a wrathful sea, were projected onto an enormous screen behind the podium. Over the howl of the storm came the melancholy voice of Edward G. Robinson reading letters the shipwrecked sailors had sent to the king of Spain, begging for help and signing themselves "your loyal subjects."

Among the haul was a trunk of gold coins. These were offered for sale to children only, the auctioneer scrupulously addressing each peewee collector as "sir" or "madam," while behind him a large scarlet macaw named Julius, purchased by Dad especially for the occasion, screeched, "Pieces of eight! Get your pieces of eight!"

"So, what about this bad boy?" a stagehand shouted as the sale was dismantled later that night.

"The parrot?" my father said. "Oh, I'll take him. My wife was born amongst the wild things. She adores all creatures, great and small."

My mother quickly identified the macaw as an emissary of Satan.

"Lift up your skirt, lift up your skirt," Julius lisped the first time he encountered her.

"So, he's a little gauche around women," my father conceded. He had bought a state-of-the-art perch and was filling its seed cup with salted macadamia nuts.

"But personally, I find him most companionable."

Indeed, whenever my father was at home, the bird's manner was as unctuous as that of Mr. Collins from *Pride and Prejudice*. Bowing deferentially, Julius would squawk, "You OK, Captain? At your service, at your service." Soon as Dad left for the office, though, he would decamp from his perch and take flight, beating his wings against lampshades, displacing pictures, and depositing exquisitely sculpted blobs of pistachio-vanilla whippy-shit in difficult-to-clean places. The geography of our apartment was unusual, consisting of a series of rooms connected by an isthmus of a corridor. This strip of land Julius commandeered as his personal runway. Blasting off from the dining room, he managed to work up quite some momentum before reaching the sitting room, where in lieu of braking, he'd crash-land on the tops of the curtains, apply a little reverse thrust, then rake his claws down the fabric, shredding the chintz as he went and ignoring my mother's attempts to level him with a broom.

These avian capers went on until the moment my father's key rattled in the lock, at which signal Julius would calmly take up position on his perch, tilt his head coquettishly, and trill, somewhat camply, "Welcome home, Captain! Make a sale, make a sale?" After which he'd burp, a sound I believe my father mistook for a kiss.

"He's got to go," Mum said.

"We're his only family," my father countered. "What kind of message would that send to the children?"

"A farewell one," came the acid reply.

For a while, Julius had the upper hand, so to speak, but my mother was no slouch in the revenge department. She patched the curtains and bided her time.

"Take care of Julius, won't you?" my father entreated, before he left on one of his last-minute peregrinations to Chile.

"Oh, you can bet on it," my mother said sweetly and promptly sold the macaw to an unlicensed pet dealer in an obscure corner of Queens.

In retaliation, on his next trip my father brought home Papagoya, a South American caique.

Papagoya was dazzling. A compact, Liquorice Allsort sweetie of a bird with a black crown, plump orange cheeks, emerald wings, and a bright yellow chest.

My father had successfully smuggled him back on the plane, or so he claimed, by sedating him with vodka and hiding him inside his shirt. When at first light Papagoya woke up and began emitting hungover bird noises, the passenger in 10C said nothing, possibly assuming that Dad was suffering from a debilitating stomach ulcer. A couple of generous Bloody Marys saw all three of them through customs and immigration. But there can be no yin of the pusher without the yang of an addict. From the day he came to live with us on Ninety-Second Street, Papagoya was a feverish alcoholic.

My father took his vodka neat without enhancers—no ice, lemon, or Schweppes. Papagoya matched him shot for shot. When not blotto, he was everything you could want in a pet. A lively little parrot, full of personality, he slept against my father's chest, making wet rasping noises. When awake, he'd roost for hours on Dad's shoulder, chewing devotedly on his ear lobes while Dad read the newspaper. And if his snuggling took on a new urgency at cocktail hour, it has to be said that the entire family willingly enabled him. Sunday lunch, traditionally a festive occasion, soon became even jollier. While the family tore into roast chicken, Papagoya guzzled booze from my father's glass until, on more than one occasion, he toppled unconscious to the floor.

Numerous after-lunch games were hastily invented for the little caique's amusement. Voyage Around the World saw Dad swinging him round on his finger at high speed while Papagoya held on for dear life. Spin the Parrot on the Lazy Susan produced even louder squeals of delighted terror. Another of my parents' Sunday rituals was to force my sister and me to walk around the table with books balanced on our heads to improve our deportment. Onto a stack of Ed McBain's 87th Precinct series, my father would now drop the little bird, who would shuffle from foot to foot like a dizzy windup toy. How we laughed at his endearingly cross-eyed expression! How we giggled at the eighty-proof hiccups erupting from his mouth.

After washing up, my father would slip Papagoya into his pocket and the family would head for Central Park, where a baseball diamond would be constructed out of sweaters and the bird pitched from backstop to infielder in the manner of a feather softball. For

Papagoya, it was a far cry from his Amazonian origins, but his naturally obliging nature combined with a high blood-alcohol ratio made him happy to go along with almost anything. What a cutie! Not even a new baby, not even a fat little biblical angel—and heaven knows, they're pretty adorable—would have been as welcome an addition to the family.

There was only one problem.

Papagoya was not only a drunk but a card-carrying white supremacist.

Was this perceived? Inherent? Cause-and-effect conditioning? Surely racism requires complex thinking and bias that birds do not possess. Nevertheless, the minute he heard Lenor's tentative tread outside the kitchen, Papagoya puffed out his chest and began goose-stepping up and down his cage, muttering slurs under his breath. Poor Lenor tried everything. She cooed at him, sang to him, but Papagoya regarded her with absolute disdain. When I look back now, I wonder how we could have missed the burnt-rubber fumes of hatred filling our own house. I mean, we knew Papagoya didn't like Lenor; we just didn't understand that he disliked her because she was black. In retrospect, it was no wonder she put off cage cleaning by taking up the art of laundry origami. There's nothing quite like the joy you get from transforming a simple white shirt into a flower!

Lenor never ratted, she never complained. I only noticed that from the day Papagoya arrived, instead of leaving before we got home from school, she began mysteriously meeting Susie and me at the elevator. In the hallway she'd silently hold out her hand for my Afro, sweeping every protest aside. "Coils," was all she'd say, hanging the wig on a hook. "They need to rest from time to time." Then she'd put on her blue coat and press a finger to the down button. Gone were the glory days of Afro

Sheen and grooming tips. Regarding my ambition to be black, Lenor's commandeering of my wig felt like a giant backwards step.

One afternoon the elevator opened to an empty hallway. Inside the apartment, Lenor's blue coat still hung on its hook. I thought little of it. With no wig check to delay me, I boogied on down the corridor with nothing more pressing on my mind than a bowl of après-school junket. I barely registered the sound of Papagoya's screaming. That was the deal with winos—they often woke up screaming.

I pushed open the swing doors to the kitchen and stopped. Papagoya was jabbing at Lenor's radial artery with his beak as she attempted to extract the gooey newspaper lining his cage. Momentarily distracted, he rotated his head in my direction. An electric-eyed monster, he blinked in disbelief at my Afro and then, fastening me with a look of outrage, launched.

"For the love of God, duck!" yelled Lenor. But I remember only a blizzard of colour, then the Afro being wrenched from my head, and the sight of it, lifeless, in Papagoya's beak, as he flew it straight out the open window. Considering that his wings were clipped—considering that we lived on the ninth floor, this was quite the political protest, and finally I understood: Lenor's later departure time, meeting me in the hall, the wig on the hook—selfless protection, all of it.

She grabbed my hand and we jammed ourselves into the elevator and hurtled down to the lobby. Out in the street, Lenor retrieved the Afro from the top of a fire hydrant but of Papagoya there was no sign. No parrot patty on the road, not even a single kaleidoscopic feather spiralling down on the currents of the evening's heat haze.

Later that evening, after a short but respectable period of mourning, my father hit the drinks trolley. As he tore the lid off a bottle of Smirnoff, there was a sharp rap at the window. Papagoya—edging his claws gingerly along the ledge and tapping his beak against the glass with all the impatient self-righteousness of an ex-pat deprived of his sundowner.

Cold turkey was a painful but necessary process. If we excused the bird, it was on the grounds that alcohol turns the finest of men mean. The newly sober Papagoya still cuddled and snuggled, but we were never able to look at him in quite the same way again. *Once you know, you know, right?*

Lenor forgave both Papagoya and us, her generosity of spirit never in question, but there was no more living under the rock of white naivety. Maybe this wasn't the first time I'd witnessed intolerance, but it was the first time I really *saw* it, and it delivered a stunning jolt to my sensibilities. If a parrot could mimic human behaviour, then what was to stop a human from acting with animal aggression?

After that things changed. Maybe I would never know what it was like to walk around in somebody else's skin or hair, but I tried hard to look at the world through new eyes.

My Afro, stained and shamed by its part in inciting racial hatred, I relegated to the dressing-up box. Maybe one day my grandchildren will rediscover Pam Grier. Sprinkled with talc, she'll be just the thing for their searing reenactment of Phil Spector's murder trial, but my own ambitions to be black were over.

As for an identity, I kept on looking, and it took me the longest time to land on a career. Eventually, I peeled back all the skins I'd tried on in childhood, until there was only the soft, translucent one of writer. I still have the greatest trouble when it comes to polite conversation, but that's OK, because writers live mute, locked into the mirrored chamber of narcissism, in a state of mind close to sociopathy. There is one question, however, that still makes my ears spontaneously bleed.

When I hear it I don't try to be funny or facetious anymore. I don't tell people that I want to spray-paint Pluto or wrestle the ink from the silvery sac of the giant squid. When some nosy, insensitive small-talker asks me what I do, I take a deep breath and muster as much dignity as possible before replying.

"I do my best."

HIERARCHY OF RULES

Night hours pass slowly for the exhibitionist. It's a bleak moment when the storybooks are shut and the spotlight of parental attention fades. To combat the loneliness, to ward off the bad dreams that often come, new entertainments must be improvised, with my faithful companion—a threadbare cat with marble eyes and knitted cardigan—positioned affectionately by my side to admire them.

One such night, I was lying in bed, blowing the most glorious Bazooka bubbles ever seen, when my mother came back into the room to reclaim the brooch she'd left on our chest of drawers. My mother was hardly the crazed disciplinarian, but she was strict about sweets, or candy, as the other girls at school would say. This was not a healthy-eating issue. Back in the early 1970s, everyone was too busy scoring birth control to worry about counting out chia seeds or squeezing the *légume* for its juice. Marching for women's rights was the number-one exercise of the day, and chain-smoking widely accepted as a top tip for breaking the ice at social occasions. America was a kingdom still under the lenient reign of fatty foods, and it was to be a good few decades before the Hyphen War unleashed its crusading heroes of trans-fat, gluten-free, and high-fiber upon our unsuspecting guts. When I was growing up, nobody cared what food contained so long as it tasted good. A blueberry donut was just the thing after a pizza supper, and both were best washed down with a bottle of Coke, a delicious beverage advertised by wholesome-looking kids who sang nice.

Sweets, though? Well, sweets were different. My mother claimed to have soft teeth and was fearful we'd inherited the same.

In those days our family dentist operated out of a Lexington Avenue basement that my siblings and I would eventually dub the Cave of Torment. He was a thickset man with a gruff manner and such a profusion of hair on the backs of his hands that we imagined him commuting after work to the deepest recesses of Central Park, where moonstruck he would forage for berries, decomposing pigeons, and the occasional small child foolish enough to leave their bed after lights-out.

During summer, when the pavements burned with heat and a shorter-sleeved model of the dentist's coat was called for, it was apparent that this hair problem, which Susie, Marcus, and I had assumed to be localized to his hands, was in fact full-body hypertrichosis. Sprouting from his finger knuckles, it ran like black industrial cabling up his arms and across his shoulders, meeting, we could only presume, in a ruff down the centre of his back. It probably didn't help that his name was Dr. Wolff. *Planet of the Apes* had recently been playing in cinemas, and we were smart enough to figure out that if the US government was overrun by monkeys, it was equally plausible that the annals of Manhattan dentistry might be dominated by werewolves.

"Rinse, please," Dr. Wolff would growl, indicating a flimsy cup of mouthwash with his amber nails. Instead of making an effort to disguise his hybrid form, he was more than willing to put his supernatural abilities to good use. Enhanced sight meant there was no necessity to burden our parents with costly X-rays. Anaesthetics, too, could be done away with as, according to werewolf mythology, cattle and children could be paralysed with a single, focused glare. Even tools were superfluous. The moment the slightest wobble was detected in one of our milk teeth, in went the paw. Seconds later, a poor bloodied canine would clatter into the porcelain bowl kept on hand for such occasions. The first time this happened to me, I merely blinked in astonishment, too stunned to scream.

At the end of every session, impervious to our piteous tear-stained faces, Dr. Wolff would deliver a hoarse sermon on the perils of a sugary diet, before loping across the room to his supply cabinet and inviting Susie, Marcus, and me to choose a flavour from his assortment of lollipops, reserved for children who had been "especially brave and good." Even at our tender ages, we recognised this as a trick. Obviously, we wanted the lollipop. We'd earned the lollipop, but accepting the lollipop in the face of the no-sugar diktat would surely result in more time spent in the dentist's chair—or perhaps even being bitten and bringing the curse of lycanthropy upon ourselves. And then the concept of being rewarded for being "especially brave and good" made us doubly suspicious. Mum's bedtime story of choice was Saki's "The Story-Teller." The heroine of this tale was ghastly little Bertha, a girl generously decorated with medals, whose reward for obeying rules and being *horribly brave and good* was to be devoured by, well, none other than a wolf.

In the end, greed trounced caution. The lollipops were the old-fashioned kind—flat, bright coins wrapped in cellophane—and after a moment's hesitation, during which Dr. Wolff idly picked at the hard, long bristles underneath his tongue, we'd snatch a handful of the things and make a dash for the waiting room, where Mum would be patiently flicking through her copy of *Life* magazine. Dentistry was an occasion when the family candy rules were relaxed. My mother was a thoroughly fair person, happy to allow us lollipops after any kind of major ordeal, but in general, sweets were rationed. And at the top of the sweets embargo was bubblegum.

Not only did bubblegum ruin your teeth, but the chewing of it was *loutish* and *un-English* and meant *eating with your mouth open*—a crime ranked on the Charter of Manners above *slouching*, the heinous *putting of elbows on the table*, and my own personal weakness, *showing off in front of grown-ups*.

As English children, we already talked odd so it went without saying that fitting in was a matter of life and death. My mother was happy for us to embrace most things American—peanut butter with jelly, ice hockey, *I Dream of Jeannie*—but gum, spearmint, bubble, or any other kind, was forbidden.

The black market for candy was school. Every morning, shuddering down in the walnut box of our elevator, I'd snap open my Dick Dastardly lunch box and check for suitable currency.

The stock value of fruit was low, but any snack bearing the Hostess logo, be it a Ding Dong, Sno Ball, or Twinkie, was a cinch to move. The day's trading opened at milk break. At the bell, there'd be a rush to the playground. For the next fifteen minutes, it was all the mayhem of the New York Stock Exchange as seasoned traders cleaned up, rookies were shafted, and the rest got their hair pulled. Combine a cheating nature and plain greed with the lucky draw of being an auctioneer's daughter, and it was no surprise that I nailed this vocation.

On days I scored Bazooka, I would take it home and hide it under my pillow. After lights-out—*No talking! No roughhousing!*—I'd slide out the small, neat, rectangular brick, with its pleasing hospital corners, and peel it slowly, revelling in the waxy feel of the packaging, the seductive whiff of artificial fruit, and those heady first chews when the gum was soft and grainy with sugar. After the initial high had worn off, I'd lie dreamily on my back, one arm bent under my head, and send vast quivering planets up into the dark universe of my bedroom. "Bravo!" cried my threadbare Kitty Cat. And it was right then, as my mother returned for her brooch, that my bubble, quite literally, burst.

A parent coming back into the bedroom after lights-out was my cue to manipulate whichever one it was into staying as long as possible. *Tell me the story of me! Tell me about being born in England! About you*

and Dad landing in New York when I was a baby and being asked to sign
a government waiver promising I wouldn't start a revolution! This time,
however, I turned my face to the wall, scraped the gluey dregs off my
mouth, and, for reasons that still escape me, pressed the resulting mess
into the crotch of my pajama bottoms.

Viyella is an absorbent fabric, and the gum lost no time sinking into
the crossroads of interlocking stitching, where it flattened and spread
its tentacles like a malevolent, pink cuttlefish.

I glanced at Kitty Cat. As a little girl I was wont to channel my
naughty self through this stuffed toy, and it had got me out of trouble
for a mixed bag of wrongdoings. But now that I'd hit double figures,
my parents were finding "The cat did it!" less and less charming as a
defence strategy. I toyed with removing my pajamas and dropping
them out the window, figuring a single gust of wind could have floated
the evidence to the river. But what if Susie woke and squealed? What
if two cops knocked at the door—one holding out my waterlogged
pajamas on a stick, the other directing my mother's gaze to Nanny's
punctiliously sewn name tape on their waistband? *The throwing out of
perfectly good clothes before they'd been outgrown* was another rule, one
that came under the subheading of *Waste*—and that led unavoidably to
the *Poor Starving Children of Africa*. Like most kids, Susie, Marky, and
I were prepared to suspend disbelief for Father Christmas and Happy
Ever After, so you'd think the poor starving children of Africa would
slip by unchallenged, but there was no getting away from the absurd
contradiction it posed—namely that eating everything on our plates
left nothing for starving kids, whereas leaving a little something at least
gave them a fighting chance. Still, even had the tossing of *perfectly good*
pajamas not come under the by-laws of *Waste*, it would undoubtedly
have been categorized as *Littering*, an offence, according to my mother,
right up there with not voting and tax avoidance.

I shut my eyes and tried to ignore the grotesque muck in my crotch, but remorse and disgust escalated until the idea of confession began to seem like a relief.

I crept through the apartment, holding the pajama's waistband stretched as far away from my tummy as the elastic would allow. I found my parents in the study, staring at the TV, on which a man with a roughly creased face and a sweating upper lip was addressing the nation.

"Creep!" My father shook his fist at the screen.

"Weasel!" my mother yelled.

I waved my gummy pants under their noses, sighed and stamped my foot, but my parents couldn't have been less interested. Nixon's attempted cover-up trumped my own.

For a child hard-wired to feel short-changed on the quantity and quality of attention, I'd long ago identified news as the enemy. The stuff was everywhere—flashing on the television, spilling out of the radio, and strewn over the kitchen table in a riddle of print. I don't suppose my parents were more distracted than anybody else's; nevertheless, every headline seemed specifically worded to shift focus away from me.

When my father was interested in something, he had a habit of taking off his glasses and pinching the bridge of his nose between his thumb and forefinger. Likewise, my mother would catch a strand of her hair and twiddle its ends. That night, as I took in my father's nose pinch and my mother's hair twiddle, I had an epiphany. News was not the enemy. Rather, it might become my salvation.

The pajama pants went into the wash the following morning. The bubblegum melted in the heat of the machine and became an integral part of the garment, like a shiny gusset on a new swimsuit. I was fine with that. I'd moved on. By then sibling rivalry was a childhood habit as second nature to the three of us as breathing. Let Susie win a tricolour rosette for French spelling. Let Marcus draw a cute picture of a hamster with a Brussels sprout head. From now on these pedestrian achievements would be eclipsed. My bulletins would be hard-hitting. They would sway opinion. Here finally was a career path that could be rewarding and meaningful. News happened every day. All I had to do to get a jump on the others was wait for the opportune moment to report it.

"Guess what," I said to my mother after school. "On the way home, I passed a lady on the street pushing triplets!"

"How lovely, darling," she said, swiftly returning to the headline *Landmark Roe v. Wade Decision* in her *New York Times*. I was put out. Whatever *Roe v. Wade* may have been, surely my story appealed to a broader female readership?

I tried again a few weeks later.

"Guess what," I said to my father. "A yellow cab ran into the balloon cart on Lexington, and all the balloons floated way up to the—"

"Not now, Froggins." Dad held up his hand. Walter Cronkite was on the news. "NASA launches the *Explorer 49* into lunar orbit."

Scooped again, I thought sourly. The business of reporting was not as simple as I'd imagined. What did I have to do to get that nose pinch and hair fiddle? I collected everything I knew about Watergate. Facts were not enough. A story needed a hero or a villain. It needed excitement and danger, and if these could be rooted in perjury, corruption, and criminality, so much the better.

It was the year my sister turned twelve. In preparation for teenagedom she was granted a number of privileges related to the themes of *independence* and *enhanced responsibility*. Independence translated into a hike in pocket money and permission to walk unsupervised to certain preordained locations. The corner shop had been allowed at age eight, the local library at eleven, and now Central Park was added to the Map of Free Movement. This was no minor upgrade. The park was a jungle. An ungovernable snarl of caves, lanes, and tunnels. It was, or so I briefed Kitty Cat, a gift of ice slicks, mossy lakes, and prehistoric trees, the spreading canopies of which happened to be the kingdom of the Oolie Oolies, sturdy troll-like creatures whose feckless monarch, queen of the Oolie Oolies, wore a magnificent headdress sewn from discarded Good Humor wrappers. Central Park was a blast, the place in the world I most liked to explore. But Susie's new privilege came with an unacceptable line of small print: *Look after your younger sister and never let her out of your sight.*

One day, after we'd been in the park barely an hour, my sister announced it was time to go home. I was far from ready to leave, so I kicked her. She argued her authority with the patience of a high-court judge. I kicked her again.

"Find your own way home," she said, storming off.

I watched her go, considering whether to treat her to a neck punch or a dead arm on her return. To my surprise, she didn't return. Five minutes passed. Ten. My lip began to wobble. Central Park was where the bogeyman lived. It was the hunting ground of opportunist werewolf-dentists with X-ray eyes and yellow tongues. It was where little unattended girls were hauled through tunnels by their white ankle socklets and expertly fish-filleted.

"I'll tell on you," I sniffed. But even as I said it, I wondered: *Would the telling be quite enough?*

My mother had instilled in the three of us a special set of rules pertaining to the subject of *Lost*. These rules were sacred and had to be memorised along with our home telephone number and zip code.

I stopped sniveling as an idea formed in my head. If I couldn't simply *relate* it, I'd have to *become* the news instead.

Rule number one of *Lost* was: *Stay where you are!* This I understood. It had something to do with ebb and flow, with mathematical probability. Once you went searching for missing persons, gaps widened, crowds multiplied. Without this rule, children didn't just get lost, they got lost forever.

And suddenly that didn't seem like such a bad thing. I felt the anarchic thrill of freedom. Performing a happy heel click, I skipped off, fetching up, in due course, on the far west side of the park where I contemplated rule number two.

Ask for Help had a drop-down menu of elaborate subheadings. We were to ask for help but only from authorised people in a formalised order. Top of the list was a *person in uniform*. Cops were the guardians of law and order. Firemen, though rarely seen in the park, were self-sacrificing and brave. Sailors—well, sailors were considered unsuitable. A sailor might be drunk or have the clap or break into an embarrassing dance routine, though I dare say had I returned to Ninety-Second Street high kicking between Gene Kelly and Frank Sinatra my mother would have forgiven me. If no one in the appropriate uniform was available, we were instructed to wait for a *nice family* to wander by. Failing the complete assemblage, a *nice mother and child* were acceptable. At a pinch, a *nice young couple* would do, but only if they looked as if they *liked* children or might even want to have children of their own as soon as they committed to down payments on a bigger apartment.

The *nice* thing was confusingly subjective. My mother had once observed that my science teacher Mrs. Bloemeke had a *nice* face, but my father countered that the layout of her teeth suggested she was directly descended from the genus *Crocodylus*. Nevertheless, we grasped the spirit of the thing. To those candidates who qualified, we were instructed to explain our predicament in a clear, high voice—*no panic, no sentiment!*—before politely requesting delivery to the nearest police precinct.

And that was it.

Strangely, old people didn't feature on the list at all. I do remember that my mother had recently read *Rosemary's Baby*, and though she fell short of telling us that an elderly couple might drug us and force us to copulate with the Devil, I imagine that for a while she may have been thinking it. Out of the question too (exempting those covered by the uniform law) were single men. Even a single man with a flock of doves at his heels; even a single man accompanied by an angel with gossamer wings. Forget it. In the event that a single man was to offer us anything—*Candy! A lift in his car! An invitation to see his collection of shrunken Peruvian heads!*—we were to scream as loudly as possible, bite his hand, then run like crazy things in the opposite direction.

On this ambrosial New York afternoon, with Central Park crammed with families of every size and permutation, with cops galore queuing up for cones of lemon sherbet, with heroic ash-smeared firemen resting their smouldering backs against the trunks of trees and reading Boris Pasternak, it was harder than you might think to track down a single man, especially one who looked uncannily like the *Rosemary's* evil traditionalist, Roman Castevet. Finally, I settled on a sinister creature lurking at the water fountain. With dark, intricately woven eyebrows offset by unnaturally white hair, he was reassuringly ancient and dressed in a coat, bow tie, and hat, the mode of which hinted at broken wicker furniture, a whiskey habit, and satanic paraphernalia. Once I'd checked there were no mitigative dogs or female relatives in tow, I threw myself across his path and duly started bawling. Startled, he looked up. Water ran in rivulets from his mouth to the point of his beard and dripped onto his waistcoat. "Dear me," he said, dabbing at the patterned silk with a natty handkerchief. "Whatever's the matter?"

"My sister left me here," I whispered pitifully. "She left me *all alone.*"

"*All alone?*" he repeated.

"Yes. *Toute seule.*"

"Oh, dear." He looked round sympathetically. "Right here?"

"Yes."

"In this very spot?"

"Yes, yes," I said impatiently. "I haven't moved a step. *Pas une petite étape.*" I don't know why I'd starting speaking in French, to be honest. I just felt like it. And then—didn't all abandoned little girls in storybooks speak French?

"Good girl," he said. "First rule of being lost. But are you sure your sister is not coming back?"

"Positive. After all, I've waited here for such a very long time."

"What about your parents?"

"My parents?" I lowered my eyes. "Yes. I miss them so much."

"And you don't have a nanny or someone else taking care of you?"

"I've never had a nanny."

The old man looked at me thoughtfully. "You do seem awfully young to be in the park without a grown-up."

"Indeed I am very young, *monsieur.* I am only ten." I had an inexplicable urge to perform a series of pirouettes for him in my brand new, *Madeline* school shoes.

"I see. Well, well, what a predicament. Have you told anyone?"

"You mean like a policeman?"

"Yes. Or a fireman, perhaps?"

"What about a sailor?"

"A sailor?" He hesitated.

"Nobody knows I'm here. Nobody *dans toute le monde entier!*" In French lessons I'd been classed as a troublemaker, but now I felt my teachers would be proud.

"That settles it. How about we go and find a policeman together? Would you like that?"

Actually, no. Not one bit. To be brought home by a policeman would be far too easy and might cast the suspicion that it was I, not Susie, who had done something wrong. This story was about courage and resourcefulness in the face of criminal neglect. It was a story that would have more personal resonance than anything printed in a boring newspaper, plus it would have the added bonus of getting my sister into serious trouble.

There was nothing for it but to hurl myself against the damp silk of the old gentleman's waistcoat and marshal fresh tears.

"Don't you understand? A policeman can't help me. No one can help me!"

Even at ten I suspected I was laying it on with a trowel, but the old gentleman merely patted me on the head.

"In that case, would you like me to take you home myself?"

I peeped up at him through sparkling eyelashes. This reporter-as-part-of-the-story thing? Easy once you knew how. "*Tiens, monsieur,*" I said. "I surely would."

Down the path, under the bridge, then, a thought: Where was Susie now? Home? Searching for me? Harnessing the assistance of her own suspect old benefactor? The risk of running into her was slight but could not be discounted.

"Must we really walk?" I whispered. "I'm so very tired and my legs so very short."

"I have a car," the old gentleman said, smiling. "But first, why don't we get something to pep you up?" He stopped at a food kiosk. "Tell me, what's your favourite candy?"

For a moment I considered him. For Susie to be in the greatest possible trouble, I had to be in the direst peril. But what did that mean exactly? My parents had never felt it necessary to expose their children to the scratchy underbelly of reality. Consequently, the villains of my imagination still hailed from storybooks. This was just an old man. And how dangerous could an old man really be?

When encountering an adult, politely ask questions, Mum liked to tell us. *It's important to have an inquiring mind.*

"What do you do?" I asked.

"Oh, bless you for your interest," he said. "I'm a collector of rare South American artifacts."

"Ah . . ." I looked at the dark, wet stain on the front of his waistcoat and tried to imagine it as blood. But truly? It looked more like water from the drinking fountain.

"Bubblegum," I said.

"I beg your pardon?"

"Bazooka is my favourite candy."

Within minutes I was sitting in the front seat of his Buick, blowing the most ravishing pink bubbles you've ever seen.

He glanced over. "You're very good at that."

"Thank you. I practise a lot."

My assailant's car was sleek, his steering wheel a Hula-Hoop of burnished oak. If this was kidnapping, it wasn't half bad. We'd rub along fine together, the old gentleman and me. I pictured a classic brownstone, interior walls lined with first editions, and on his desk a set of quills next to an antique globe, perhaps a shrunken Peruvian head or two. My own living quarters might be cramped and to the rear of the house, but surely he would give me an eiderdown and a Batman night light? Even if he elected to keep me outside in a rickety shed covered in chicken wire, I'd find a cockroach or a desiccated rat dropping with endearingly human features to befriend. The point was I'd be OK; I'd make it work.

At home, though? My sister? A different story.

In our family, minor infractions were dealt with by Nanny; punishments included being sent to our rooms, a smack on the bottom, or a ban on her famed cheese, potato, and onion pie. More serious transgressions were referred to our mother, who would further threaten, should the crime merit it, an audience with our father. For Susie, this would be only the beginning. When my image on the back of milk cartons yielded nothing, after the last candle had been blown out at my funeral-in-absentia, she would become increasingly reviled, an untouchable for the rest of her days. For my parents too, this story would be front-page news for—well, forever.

Except . . .

We were out of the park now and cruising up Madison Avenue, past the ice-cream vans, past Joe's Pizza Parlor, approaching a traffic light only a block from home. I stared at the light, knowing that the colours would soon change and aware suddenly of the crossroads they presented.

Straight on meant chicken wire and cockroach friends. A right turn equaled warm bed and cheese and onion pie. The line between calm and chaos was thinner than a whisker, and as the light merged from yellow to red, *Madeline, bravest and most outgoing of little girls, began to feel a tad quivery.*

Another thought. What if the old gentleman didn't live in Manhattan? Or even in New York. What if I was forced to leave my beloved city for somewhere new and unfamiliar?

For the first time in my life I thought about home and what it meant: the Sunday-morning pillow fights and picnics in the park. Being dangled on the end of Dad's arm and swung up into the tallest tree. Mum's spiky brooch that she unpinned from her cocktail dress before kissing us good night. The smell of my father's old tweed coat. What would mornings be like without the Wall Street banker who roller-skated down Park Avenue every day wearing a cherry-decked hat? Or the friendly cop we'd once passed in the subway who shouted, "Hey, watch out for the man covered in Jell-O"? Home was yellow snow and potbellied Santas and the panorama of water tanks and fire escapes. Home was home, and what if it was gone forever?

Red gave way to green, and my eyes went to the old gentleman's hands on the wheel as he rolled the Buick straight through the intersection.

"I think this is the wrong way," I said, in a very small voice.

"Don't worry." His frown relaxed as he took the next corner. "I was only trying to avoid the traffic."

In the hallway, my mother sounded grateful. The old gentleman called her madam and tipped his hat. I said my prettiest *merci* and waved as he stepped back into the elevator, one gloved hand raised. As Mum closed the door, I opened my mouth to explain further, but here came Nanny to fetch me for supper. Susie was already at the table, calmly picking the onions out of her potatoes. Had she not thought this through? Even if I was in for a telling off for the kicking I'd given her, I'd learned the hard way about the relative value of news—and there could be no doubt, Susie's crime eclipsed mine.

A key turned in the lock—my father, arriving home. I smiled in anticipation as he and my mother disappeared into the study. It was only a matter of time. In my head I rehearsed my story in a high, clear voice, *no exaggeration, no emotion.* Then it would be Susie's turn in the dock. My parents operated a hugely effective good cop, bad cop routine, my father cutting, powerful, my mother gently reproachful, disappointed. I saw my sister, a mess of torn hair and hot salty tears, being led to the dungeons of Château d'If. Oh joy . . .

I took my plate to the sink, where Susie was already rinsing hers. We exchanged sneers.

"Stop that nonsense," Nanny said. "And now you've finished, go and see your parents, both of you."

In the study, on the linen jacquard sofa, against the intellectually abstract wallpaper so very much of its time, Susie and I were arranged side by side, our parents, in two single armchairs, facing us.

"Can I go first?" I piped up.

"Wait a minute, darling," Mum said.

The door opened again, and Nanny ushered in my brother. He zigzagged over to the sofa and mashed himself between us.

This was not right. Not right at all.

I studied my parents. My father had removed his glasses; my mother's face was taut as she reached for a twirl of hair. Then it hit me. Of course! I'd been trumped. A bigger story had broken. Wade had reversed Roe! NASA had accidentally exploded the sun!

I wanted to cry in frustration, but instead I sat quietly. We all did. *No fidgeting, no pinching.* Three little piggies to the slaughter.

"Darlings," my mother said. "Your father and I have come to an important decision." She looked quickly at Dad, then away again. "Your father is moving out."

Three little mouths popped open in surprise.

"You see, your father works very hard and must therefore live somewhere closer to the office."

Three little snouts turned to their father.

Dad nodded, as if to confirm that, yes, the distance between home and the office was something of a deal breaker.

I waited for more. Nothing came.

"You understand, don't you, darlings?" Mum said.

Sure, I understood. It made perfect sense. Sotheby Parke-Bernet was a good ten, fifteen-minute walk away. Of course Dad must find somewhere closer. All of us hated walking.

"Good." Mum pulled us into a hug. "Well, that's all right then."

A strange atmosphere had filled the room. I'd never felt more confused. That was it? The so-called big news? The headliner that had knocked mine off the front page?

Mum scooped up Marcus and left, followed by Susie.

Flummoxed, I stayed. I needed Dad to explain. Had this been a hopelessly misjudged editorial decision by them, or had my theory of relativity been way off the mark?

I turned to Dad, but he remained immobile, staring through me. Miserable, I went back to studying my knees.

"*Pssst.*"

I glanced up. Susie was standing in the doorway. I forced myself to meet her eyes. I'd always been a poor loser, and despite my machinations she'd triumphed. She wasn't looking smug, though; she was looking sad.

"Come on." She stretched out her hand and beckoned. "Bedtime."

I hesitated. Susie had never before put me to bed. As yet, there was no legislation regarding bedtime, but it sort of felt OK. The earth had shifted on its axis, if such a thing were possible.

Leaving Dad behind, I went slowly to her. When I put my hand in hers she gave it a little squeeze.

"We'll go to bed at the same time tonight," she said kindly, "and, if you like, you can tell me one of your stupid stories." I shrugged and together we walked back along the hall.

I couldn't put my finger on why exactly, but at that moment, I could have really done with a lollipop.

Mum stayed behind to sort stuff out.

But why do we have to go?

Turns out that our Dad moving closer to work meant our parents were separating.

My parents said it would be okay, we would have
two homes. I didn't see how that would work.

If a home was split in two, wouldn't
I be stuck in the in-between?

On day two we hit a hurricane.

Everyone was sea sick.

Everyone, except for us...
Now, it was an adventure.

The storm blew us all the way to London.

And that's when the real fun and games began...
Kidhood
Mum & Dad DIVORCE Grow up 3 spaces
PERIOD STARTS
STOP! Don't move

LONDON

GODFATHER?

Part 1

I was fourteen when, as a dare, I swiped a random hardback from a London bookstore. Bad luck it happened to be a memoir, but once I'd read it I couldn't get enough of the genre. The lives that excited me most were those set against a backdrop of danger and tagged "freighted by history." Exile from Cambodia worked well, as did China's Cultural Revolution. Whatever the geography, these stories ran to a pattern. If their authors had not been part of some country's bloody coup as toddlers, by the time they reached adolescence you could count on their family's having fled an oppressive regime and relocated to the more bohemian *arrondissements* of Paris or Jerusalem to spend languid summers thereafter under a canopy of orange trees, tersely debating the political issues of the day with a group of thinkers and activists, all of whom looked exactly like Arthur Miller—particularly the women.

The most compelling of these exiles would be appointed the author's godfather. He would teach her at thirteen to receive a compliment without simpering. On her sixteenth birthday, he would take her to a damp underground place where glasnost was understood to be a policy rather than an unattractive noise you made while sneezing. At the end of this evening, the young author's enlightenment would continue in his apartment, on a bed dusted with yesterday's philosophy, where she would be initiated into the symbiotic worlds of sex and self-loathing. And it would be her fractured, displaced past, alongside this mentor

relationship—never fully understood, forever tinged with sorrow—
that would one day propel her to write a memoir lauded by critics as
vivid and haunting.

OK, so I understood there was suffering involved, but to me these
lives contained the poetry of every grand emotion I couldn't wait to
feel. My own life, by comparison, seemed prosaic. London was full of
dead buildings and depressed pigeons. Who were we there but misfits,
hybrids, belonging to neither one country nor the other? New York
had always been my city, and shut off from its corridors of light and
mirror, I felt like an outsider, face pressed to the window of an achro-
matic world. A world where I no longer woke up happy and I no longer
woke up curious.

The only oppressive regime my parents had fled was marriage,
and though the grace with which they handled their separation was
matched by the diplomacy of their subsequent divorce, a bloodless
coup is still a coup, and we three children had been exiled to English
boarding schools.

Summers were spent as they always had been, in feral isolation
on a tiny Hebridean island off the coast of Scotland. Once the nub
of jolly family holidays, it was now a place where my mother went on
long windblown walks along the cliffs, and my father drifted in and out
of our lives like the shiny treasure of a beachcomber. By then our kid
ranks had swelled to seven, my mother having inherited three nieces
and a nephew on the death of her sister. We were all a little lost in the
years that followed, but somehow my mother re-grounded us in the
remoteness of those islands.

I had a godfather. Who didn't? But neither he nor his wife looked
remotely like Arthur Miller, and for my sixteenth birthday, instead of
lessons in the art of seduction, I was presented with a five-pound book
token from WHSmith, valid only in Glasgow.

*   *   *

My introduction to sex came via a godfather of a different kind. Our house on the island had a library of well-thumbed paperbacks, a selection of which invariably found its way to the loo during the course of the summer. When I spotted a copy of Mario Puzo's crime masterpiece hidden between toilet bowl and flue, I was intrigued. The broken spine flopped open onto a torrid paragraph, which had Sonny, pants wrinkled around his ankles, pressing slutty maid of honour Lucy Mancini to the bedroom wall at his sister Connie's wedding.

And, cheeks burning, I read it, over and over and again.

But if *The Godfather* was my portal to sex, I was already well versed in the ways of the Mafia. Our New York City apartment had been located in a predominantly Italian neighbourhood with a smattering of eclectic shops: the Old Brewery on Lexington, a place on Madison where you could buy delicate hand-painted kites, and right next door the narrowest space ever leased, in which an old Russian called Chernoff sold warm piroshki and cheap caviar. Children cannot live on kites and piroshki alone, so for everyday items there was always the corner store, a blessing for my siblings and me had it not been for the foul-mouthed owner, Mrs. Picardi, whose loathing of children put the Child Catcher to shame.

"Might I please have a Twinkie?" my brother would ask prettily.

"*Jack of the harpsichord!*" Mrs. Picardi muttered, slamming one on the counter.

"And some Cheez Doodles for me?" my sister might add.

"*Mah! How even the lice cough loudly! Don't you filthy donkeys have somewhere better to be?*"

We hated and feared this she-devil, but every Thursday she would be cowed by a man in hat and overcoat, who entered the store and stood wordlessly at the till while Mrs. Picardi placed a brown envelope into his hand.

"Why does she act so scared?" I asked my father. "Who is he?"

"Mafia, I expect. She's probably paying protection money."

"What's that?"

"He'll hurt her if she doesn't pay up."

"Hurt like a smack?"

"No, no, more like toss her into the Hudson. Pull out her tongue perhaps."

As a child I was troubled by nightmares. "Think happy thoughts," was my mother's sage advice, and the image that consistently worked for me was that of Mrs. Picardi roped to the shop's countertop, wriggling helplessly while the man in the overcoat went to work in her mouth with a pair of pliers.

I can't say for sure whether appreciation of organised crime was responsible for my marrying an Italian, but it surely helped. I was twenty-one by the time I met Giacomo, old enough to know better, too young to have a clue, and somehow running a small fashion company that I'd cobbled together with bits and pieces of borrowed know-how. Giacomo was an art dealer and a horse gambler, who'd been chased out of Italy by some bookies to whom he owed a frightening sum of money. He arrived in London, HANDLE WITH CARE stamped all over him, and soon, the pale, tender bones of young girls were being spat out of his lair.

"Stay away," warned those who thought they knew me, and after that it was only a question of time.

Giacomo burned intensity as though it were fuel. But if his smile was animal, his glower might have been developed in Sing Sing. He was the beautiful maths equation I couldn't solve and the first boy who made me feel as though my romantic future was not to be an exercise in painting by numbers.

As a gambler he was not interested in the moneyed graveyard of the roulette table. I was proud that he backed spirit and courage and heart. My professional world was full of colour and texture, enticing scraps to touch and shape. The world he roamed was dirtier, edgier, and I found it exhilarating. With each new experience we shared, my own heart, formerly a neat contained thing, began to unfurl like a plant in the heat, and I dropped feverishly into love.

On a weekend visit home, my mother diagnosed the vomiting that accompanied this fever as morning sickness. A wedding was hastily pulled together. One setback, though: Giacomo was Catholic, raised Jewish, engaged to a knocked-up Protestant who was toying with atheism.

"Given your religious backgrounds," the local priest advised, "the Catholic Church will require lengthy preparations before your union can be considered."

"What you mean 'lengthy'?" Giacomo challenged. There was no doubt that his delivery tended a little towards the aggressive.

"At least a year."

I looked down at my burgeoning stomach and giggled.

"You!" Giacomo stabbed his finger at the priest. "Fuck off and quickly," although naturally he said this in Italian. "We find another way."

"There is only one other way." The priest flatlined his mouth into a condescending smile. "Permission from the Pope himself."

Giacomo rose slowly. "The Pope, you say?" His eyes drilled into the oily sheen of the man's head. "In that case, my father will speak with him this afternoon."

This much I knew about my prospective father-in-law. Gilberto Algranti was shaved near to bald and drove a duck-egg-blue Rolls-Royce. As a boy, having already lost his parents to the camps, he'd been dragged out of hiding and put on a train with fifty other children bound for

Dachau. In a pre-arranged sting, an Italian guard unhooked their carriage and re-attached it to the rear of another train heading back into
Rome, where the children were rescued and sheltered by volunteers
all over the city. For the duration of the war, Gilberto was hidden deep
in the basement of the Plaza Hotel, the very hotel in which we were
now anxiously waiting to meet him.

The minute he swept through the lobby in his cashmere coat, I
felt it—a magnetic charge so strong I could have sworn the chandelier
crystals tinkled uneasily. Had I imagined it? No! Everything about
Gilberto radiated power. As he approached, the now-ancient bellboy
and bartender, formerly his protectors, began weeping openly. Gilberto
embraced them, before finally turning to me.

"*Eccola*," he rasped, sounding like an emphysemic prescribed a
thousand cigarettes as a cure for laryngitis. He kissed me twice. "*Ma
che bella figura*."

I shifted from foot to foot like a pelican.

"No." Gilberto pinched my cheek, a mark of affection that was to
become a painful and oft-repeated habit. "The compliment is something every woman must learn to accept."

Oh, how I wanted to be accepted by my father-in-law. It was as though
every story I'd ever read had been in preparation for this relationship. I
resolved to be the daughter he had never had, conveniently forgetting
he already had three. I would be his *consigliera*, his trusted *tenente*. I
alone understood the horrors he'd been subjected to—the murder of
his parents, the destruction of his faith, the transcendental draft into
the Israeli secret service. If anybody had struggled to find humanity
in a godless world, it was Gilberto. As he released my cheek, his eyes
dropped to my T-shirt.

"Nice titties," he said, giving my right breast a generous squeeze.

Being felt up by their prospective father-in-law might make some girls a little tight-jawed, but I accepted that, as his son's *fidanzata*, by extension I belonged to him too. In the same way he felt compelled to interrogate a chef as to the cut and quality of his veal chop, the size and firmness of my breasts was the gauge of how good a wife I'd make his son. In retrospect, a little feminist grit might have served me better, but I had developed a thing about belonging. The yo-yo geography of my early years had invoked feelings of confusion and displacement not entirely dispelled by my parents' recent remarriage—back to each other. Who cared what world Gilberto belonged to as long as I could be part of it too? *Cosa Nostra and all that.*

"My father is not Catholic, he's Jew," Giacomo said later as we dressed for dinner.

"A Jew with a hotline to the Vatican?"

"That's his thing."

"But isn't that what *Cosa Nostra* means?" I had taken to leafing through an Italian-English dictionary for just these kinds of prenuptial spats.

"Why you say *stupido* things?" He scowled.

Giacomo was my love, my *amore*, but over the year we'd been together, I'd noticed anger flaring in him like bright red ribbons. So, soon after that, I stopped saying stupid things and only thought them instead.

My parents issued an invitation to Gilberto on stiff Smythson writing paper: "Come and stay before the wedding!"

I paled to think of the proposed itinerary. The brisk country walks, Bloody Marys, and a dinner of *pie of the cottage,* as Giacomo called it, after which would begin, I supposed, a protracted negotiation about my dowry or maybe my breasts, now arguably one and the same thing. Thank *Dio*, then, that from Gilberto there was no reply.

*   *   *

Two hours before the wedding, a limousine with blackened windows swooshed up over the gravel.

"Christ, what now!" muttered my father, suffering a rare lapse in humour. On this special day, with his up-the-duff daughter marrying a foreigner—and a horse gambler whom he'd once taken for the local garage mechanic—he needed no further surprises.

"Your new father-in-law looks Middle Eastern," my mother said, peering out the window. "And is that an Uzi he's holding?"

"Why your mother say stupid things?" grumbled Giacomo. "That's the chauffeur from Claridge's hotel."

The Claridge's chauffeur opened the door of the limousine and out streamed Gilberto's six other children like so many purple butterflies in their chiffon and frills. Out spilled Rosanna, Gilberto's second wife, fragrant in lavender. Finally Gilberto himself emerged, hunched into his overcoat despite an energetic June sun. Again I felt the electro pulse in the air. The turtledoves hiccupped and the petals of the rose bush threw themselves one by one from their thorny stems.

As the two families faced off across the sitting room, even the air felt awkward. The Algranti brood, aged thirty down to five, stepped up in turn to receive glasses of Robinsons Barley Water while Gilberto coiled around my mother like a python, squeezing compliments into her ear. It was soon apparent that he had timed his arrival for an imagined pre-wedding feast. He kept surreptitiously glancing out to the hall as though expecting to see great dishes of *gamberoni* and marinated hearts of *carciofi* being carried by in the arms of comely peasant women.

"Do stay for lunch," my mother offered gamely. "We're having beans on toast."

Gilberto clicked his fingers. The family rose as one. Out on the drive, the chauffeur sparked the engine.

Chipping Campden is one of those dozy Cotswold towns built from nostalgia, thatch and honey, in whose quaint dwellings, or so tourists are inclined to believe, hobbits still live, eating soup from a cauldron suspended over an open fire. A wedding is a big deal in the shires, and a couple of hours later the streets to the church were dotted with well-wishers. Of Gilberto there was no sign. Mindful of a hot and restless congregation, my mother urged the organist to play another round of Bach's "Sheep May Safely Graze," though looking back I find it hard to imagine that sheep would ever again feel safe to graze, traumatised as they must have been by the limo streaking through their country lanes, the poor chauffeur feverishly scanning the horizon for a church spire, while Gilberto harangued him from the back. "*Sock filled with the dung of a rat! Are you stupid?*"

"*Cara,*" Gilberto purred, late by a full hour. "I am honoured you will marry my son." He nuzzled his shoe-brush moustache against my neck and poked at my cleavage.

"So big and swollen," he murmured. "*Brava, bellissima.* And may my firstborn grandson be both a male and masculine one."

Part 2

Like his father, Giacomo was an art dealer by trade. Vermeer's dimpled milkmaid or the humdrum life of a city vividly realised by Canaletto was not for the Algrantis. Their tastes ran bloodier—a nice Cruci-fixion, or John the Baptist's dripping head in the triumphant grip of Salome. After the wedding, we moved into Giacomo's tiny London flat in Mayfair, which doubled as his gallery. Every morning as I prepared to stumble off to my office, my biblical morning sickness came face to face with Romanelli's *Massacre of the Innocents*. In the background a curly-mopped infant, head hanging by a sinew; in the foreground the sweetest of babes, intestines spewing onto marble. I begged Giacomo to turn it to the wall, like a portrait of an ex-girlfriend, but God knows we needed the sale. My fashion business looked good on paper, but it was not the sort of paper that bore the queen's head and a pound sign. Giacomo was cavalier about money. When his horse romped home first, he'd turn up for supper with an expensive gem from a Bond Street jeweller. When he lost, we lived on dust.

It was kind of cool.

The first few summers after the baby was born were spent in Gilberto's house in a tangled scrub of hills off the west coast of Italy. It was a low, whitewashed 1970s building with tall windows, guarded by sentinels of poplar and surrounded by juniper and prickly pear. Outside, a terra-cotta pool overlooked the sea. Inside, heated by a ferocious sun, the house was always oven-ready and had something of the feel of a compound, not helped by a large number of guard dogs, chained, thank God, whose psychotic chorus of snarling and slavering woke us every dawn without fail.

In the mornings there was a beach outing, Gilberto parting the crowds in elegantly patterned Speedos. Lunch was produced back home by a local woman, Paola, who wore a perpetually bewildered expression, which, after a number of days, I found myself unwittingly adopting.

Dressed in a string vest, clumps of wiry chest hair tufting through its holes, ending one phone conversation with "*Ciao!*" while simultaneously embarking on another with "*Dimmi!*" ("tell me"), Gilberto sat at the table moodily forking up spaghetti. Food for the rest of the family arrived strictly à la carte from a menu that didn't exist. Gnocchi for one of Gilberto's small sons, ossobuco for his eldest daughter, a feminine slither or two of bresaola for Rosanna, my stepmother-in-law, slave to her *dieta*.

There was no conversation. Entertainment was either *Chew!* (physical theatre created from the everyday noises made by the eating and banging of cutlery) or *Grumble!* (an unstructured free-for-all, during which all family members would loudly empty themselves of a medley of grievances). When the volume became overpowering, Gilberto, or *Nonno* (grandfather), as I was now required to call him, would lean forwards and deliver a powerful slap to whichever of his children happened to be nearest. Chiccy chac, he called it. Chiccy chac was a counterproductive discipline setting off an even noisier chain reaction. Rosanna screeched. The abused child wailed. Giacomo swore. Paola the cook rattled her pans in disapproval. And finally Jesse, or rather Jesse *Gilberto*—for that was what we had cunningly named our firstborn male and masculine son—would start weeping.

Rosanna was a thoroughly decent human being. A doctor before retiring to marry Gilberto, she'd suffered an aneurysm during the birth of their youngest son and had fallen into a prolonged coma, during which she claimed to have struck up a friendship with God, eventually settling on a deal with him. If he permitted her to live, she would adopt a "retarded" child. When Rosanna awoke to find herself semi-paralysed, instead of negotiating with God for a rain check, as any lesser person might have done, she adopted a seven-year-old, whom, unsurprisingly, the entire family addressed as *Il Stupido*.

Jesse's puckered-up mouth was the prompt for Rosanna's latent doctoring skills to kick in. Her own chiccy chacced child might be suffering a brainstem bleed from Nonno's left hook, but it would be little Jesse who she'd evaluate with shrewd professional eyes.

"*Ah, poverino.* He is sick?"

"I think he's just scared."

"*No, è malato!* I am sure of it!" She'd hunt down a thermometer from somewhere and mime sticking it up his butt. I'd mime back that it should go under his armpit, as in every other civilized country, but nothing short of up the butt would do.

Belonging to this world, even part-time, was harder than I'd imagined. Instead of thriving on the energy and tumult, I felt jolted by each cultural variance, as though it charged an electrical wire running through my body. I figured this would pass. My Italian had not yet progressed beyond the names of market produce, plus I was exhausted— from a bottleneck of work, from the heat, from the red-eye feeds of the baby, during which I'd invariably bump into my father-in-law, a raging insomniac prowling the house in his underpants, one phone in each hand, hoarsely shouting his *ciao*s and *dimmi*s over the rabid barking of the mastiffs.

"Why the dogs?" I asked Giacomo. "Are they for protection?"

"Protection? What use would protection be?" Giacomo retorted. "Why you say stupid things? The only people who want to kill my father are already in this house."

And thus the days passed.

Every afternoon, siesta time for the rest of the family, Nonno would hold court behind closed doors, granting audience to a stream of cigar-smoking petitioners. During these protracted visits, the sitting room was declared a no-entry zone, until quite suddenly Nonno would loom in its doorway, cloaked in a fog bank of smoke and yelling for his son.

"*Ball-breaking old Jew, go and fetch mice!*" Giacomo muttered, rolling off me. It was never easy finding time for spontaneous lovemaking, with a new baby, an autumn/winter collection to design, Giacomo's six half-siblings, four dogs, two roosters, and one father-in-law bursting randomly into our bedroom—no knocking deemed necessary.

"*Ciao, carissima.*" Nonno stroked my ankle under the sheet before turning to his son.

"You!" he thundered. "Go speak with Signore Federico."

"*Mah, sei pazzo!* Why I must talk to this Signore Federico?"

"*Why? Why*, you ask? Because I tell him you catch a fifty-kilo barracuda, and now he want to know which rod you use."

No one in the world has ever caught a fifty-kilo barracuda. Giacomo did not fish. His hand-eye coordination was such that he was incapable of removing a guppy from its bowl, even with the aid of a net. His thumb and forefinger would meet to form a circle, a sign that, before I'd witnessed it being thrust up another person's nostrils, I'd taken to mean "everything's OK."

"Why you tell him that?" Giacomo snarled. "Are you stupid?"

"Me stupid?! Are *you* stupid?"

And they'd be off.

I once saw two crocodiles getting pretty snappy with each other at the Central Park Zoo. This was nothing compared to Algranti father and son. They shared a skill for pulling a grievance out of the ether, spinning it into a rage, and flinging it in any direction they chose. But if Nonno was egotistical, Giacomo was unpredictable. Even on our honeymoon—after a disagreement about the rules of backgammon—he'd packed his bags and left for the airport, the pink flower I'd given him still tucked incongruously behind one ear. Grand passions were all I'd ever wanted; nevertheless, I'd cried most of that night, clutching

the hard swell of my stomach and working through every literary heroine trying to recall one for whom being pregnant and abandoned had
turned out well. When Giacomo reappeared in time for breakfast, he
dropped his suitcase on the floor and, grinning, presented me with a
sprig of honeysuckle, as though he'd stepped out only minutes earlier
to cut it.

I told myself that rage was mostly theatre, but I had no frame of refer-
ence for mild irritation delivered as a metaphorical sock to the jaw.
Giacomo's anger was chemical, irrational and it scared me. Even the
lightest of skirmishes was presented as an epic confrontation. I come
from a long line of sulkers. Our anger burns like dry ice, feels like cold
war. We like to hover for months with our finger over the red button.
We don't want to destroy the world—just make it a dark and miserable
place for everyone else to inhabit.

The Algrantis were all about detonation, a blast impossible to con-
tain in time or space. Even when it was not directed at me, there was
fallout—a cloud of poison, absorbed like secondary smoke, that seeped
into the hollow spaces of my bones and remained there, generating a
crop of soft, slow-growing tumours.

I tried not to blame Giacomo. To be sucked into lies, to be torn
between protecting himself or his father was not what he wanted. But
Nonno commanded obedience. There was always an enemy to be pun-
ished or a business contact to be impressed.

"*Mah*, don't you see?" Giacomo would round on me should I risk
taking his side against Nonno. His father's entire power structure might
crumble should this conversation about barracuda fishing not take
place.

And so, in the end, dutiful son enters the room where Signore
Federico sits, perspiring in his ill-fitting clothes, his cigar a smouldering

thumb of ash on the table beside him. A weary smile is raised. A hand beckons. "*Eccolo! Venga, figlio.* Your father has told me! What a fish! What a fisherman!" And poor Giacomo, once again written into the small print of his family's invisible contract, broods and fumes and broods some more.

"See why my father is not Mafioso?" he'd shout, pacing the bedroom at midnight. "If he were Mafioso, he would be *dead* by now with all his tricks and lies!"

Nonno's driver was called Fabio the Ox. Outside a car he was a leaden draught animal, all hoofs and square head—a man born for pushing boulders up hills. Inside the car he was grace itself. His wheels never screamed, he had no need of a horn, he rarely touched the brakes. Occasionally, aware of doleful milky eyes watching me through the rearview mirror, I'd attempt to engage him in conversation. I fell back on English staples. Wasn't the *tempo bello*? What were his thoughts about a little rain later that afternoon? There was never an answer, only the soft tap-tapping of perforated leather gloves on walnut, as though he were driving by Braille. The silence made me self-conscious. With my sneakers and careless ponytail, had he taken me for a poor example of a woman, compared with my Italian counterparts? Was I not good enough for the firstborn son of Nonno, the Godfather Grandfather?

"Nonno," I asked one day. "Why won't Fabio speak to me?"

"Ah, Fabio . . ." Of late Nonno's voice had become so deep, it was as though he'd accidentally swallowed the ashes of his own fireplace. "Fabio has no tongue."

"I'm sorry," I whispered. "Repeat, please?"

"No tongue." Nonno made a slicing motion across his mouth.

I felt something inside me disintegrate. "Why? Why in God's name, Nonno, do you have a driver with no tongue?"

Nonno twisted my cheek with great affection. "He very loyal, *cara*, very loyal."

Later I mulled over the no-tongue thing. Was Fabio loyal because the state of tonguelessness afforded less opportunity for betrayal? Had Nonno specifically advertised for a driver with no tongue—as in, say, "no computer skills necessary"?

As these were *stupido* thoughts, I did not share them with Giacomo, but it was hard not to dwell. What did I really know of Nonno, Godfather Grandfather? Who was he outside the family circle? What complex system of chiccy chac did he employ to keep people quiet, to keep himself out of jail? So what if Nonno was Jewish and not Catholic? *Kosher Nostra*. That's still the way it rolls.

Close-up, stripped of the warm tones of the cinematographer's palette, without Nino Rota's haunting music to distract from the moral ambiguities, this Godfather thing wasn't quite like the movies. I thought of Mrs. Picardi, inert on the counter while the man in the homburg hat went to work with his pliers. I thought of the woman's severed tongue, gasping on the floor like a dying fish. Poor Mrs. Picardi, poor Fabio, and poor Luca Brasi, who literally sleeps with the fishes.

Of course there was something of the big fish about Nonno himself. Who knew which of his stories were true, his paintings stolen, his children legitimate? All the murkiness, so toxic and intoxicating at the same time. What did it say about my own warped values that I was able to spin gold out of such grubby straw? But this was not a question I dared answer. It was not a question I wanted to answer. I loved Nonno and you could have pliered out my own tongue, and every one of my teeth too, before I lost faith in him.

It wasn't just the Algranti men I'd fallen for—it was all of Italy. Rome, that citadel of crumbling ochre and verdigris—an entire city

of ravishing decay. All the hand kissing and burbling and wolf whistling and finger stabbing. How I loved the morning smell of coffee
and bread, the winking medallions around the necks of Praetorian
youths. I loved the tousled fawns on scooters, cheeks resting against
their boyfriends' warm backs. I even loved the teak-coloured old men
leering and preening on street corners, enjoying their gelato in a way
they must have once enjoyed women.

It seemed to me that Rome was a giant Shakespearean playground,
as though the Montagues and Capulets had decided that Verona was
too small a stage for their reconciled families and had stormed the
capital instead.

Under Nonno's protection we were all honorary Romans. Cue the
soundtrack, observe the scene! as he breezes through the city, dispensing
his ubiquitous *munificence*. Witness him inviting every barista, newspaper
vendor and carabiniere to admire his family. *See my son, my successor!
Brave slayer of the monstrous barracuda*, his proud expression demanded.
*Behold my daughter-in-law with the nice titties, mother of the firstborn male,
masculine grandson*. In Nonno's chosen restaurant, it is genuine charm he
bestows upon the proprietor. How are the man's ailing parents? And his
brother, "Hemorrhoids" Pornello, currently residing in Turin? Waiters
dance attendance. Chef hurries from the kitchen. Washer-uppers nudge
each other at the sink. Signore Algranti is here. No matter that there
are other customers—well-heeled patrons all of them, waiting on their
branzino with capers—for Signore Algranti, all work stops.

Nonno absorbed the crowd's adulation with a shrug—but you see, *la
storia* was not about him, he'd say, whisking out little Jesse Gilberto as
though unveiling a hitherto undiscovered Tintoretto before an assem-
bly of museum curators. And because *bambino* equals miracle—no
matter that thousands are born every second—because *bambino* is the

center of Italian life, faces would crease into smiles. *È un tesoro! Che bello, che intelligente!* A sly litany of compliments aimed at the grandfather directed through the conduit of the grandson.

I loved those lunches too, but sometimes, walking by the tables of magistrates and bankers, with their drifting smoke and dragon breath, I felt it—ruthlessness. Alongside the smell of garlic and rosemary was the whiff of corruption, of *Tangentopoli*. There were times though—no use pretending there weren't—when a black car would glide to a stop outside the entrance, and ever-watchful Fabio, driver with no tongue, would tense, his hand moving to his pocket for the dense, comforting weight he knew to be there. And I wondered—were I to snatch up little Jesse, dive for the *gabinetto*, would I return to find Fabio garroted and Nonno face down in his *spaghetti alle vongole*? I prayed not. I prayed like crazy for the long life of my Nonno, my Jewish-Italian, Mafioso, Mossad, Kosher Nostra papà-in-law, because his circle had finally closed around me, and in it I wanted to stay.

Part 3

Until I didn't.

In London the rest of the year, away from the opposing force of his father, the needle of Giacomo's rage increasingly shifted my way. I tried to deflect it but lacked the skill. We had another baby now, Samuel Peregrino, and the stakes of marriage had grown higher. I worked late hours in a world that held no intrinsic or cultural interest for Giacomo. He took no pride in the things I created. My black-market love, once so prohibited and desirable, was now too bitter to be sweet. It was my managing director, Gerry, who held my hair when I threw up with nerves before shows; Gerry who zipped up my dress before award ceremonies, at which I looked at Giacomo's empty seat beside me and wondered what transgression would be most likely to set him off on my return home. I no longer felt centred in the spotlight of love. I felt like a prison escapee, trapped in the warden's searchlight. Move in any direction and risk a bullet.

Stick your foot into the snare of bad-boy love, and it's going to hurt pulling it out, but the pain of my failing marriage wasn't bloody and raw in the way I might have imagined. After three years, it was the gradual dulling of every nerve ending. After five, it was the agony of numb.

Sometimes, when I was sad, I'd watch all three Godfather films back to back, hoping to find the thread of whatever I'd lost. Through the thick glass of the television, I'd try to extract the smell of juniper from the air. If I could only reconstruct my reality out of the doomed romance of the Corleone saga. But there's little romance in wrong choices. I was immersed in this story the way I'd always wanted to be, except it was a different story. My body was not in danger but my heart was in dire trouble. I'd always heard it took two to dump a relationship at sea, but what did it matter who was to blame? I was an English scruff who had no idea how to be a wife, married to a man who needed to destroy the things he loved.

One evening I escaped to the movies with my dad.

"Tell me something, Froggins," said the father who never asked personal questions to the daughter who never invited them. "Are you having any fun in this marriage of yours?"

Whatever it cost him to pry, it cost what was left of my pride to say no.

Dad took my hand. "Then get out," he said gently, "right now."

Giacomo was not happy I wanted out. And because he was unhappy, he said *stupido* things. "I will call my father to come," he said, and Nonno would take his first- and second-born male, masculine grandchildren back to Italy, where they would be hidden in the hills. "And you will never find them and you will never see them again."

"But I thought your father wasn't Mafia," I wept.

"Of course my father is Mafia!" Then he made the sign of the fingers close to my nose.

Things got bad. Within the confines of our marriage we took to pacing separate enclosures, spitting and snarling. One of us needed to be shot with a tranquilizer dart and relocated somewhere far away, but who knew how that kind of thing worked? Some nights I heard him talking to his father on the telephone.

"Papà, I need your help," he said. He spoke in thick, fast-flowing Italian. It no longer sounded exotic, merely lonely and foreign. "My father is coming for you," he'd say each time he hung up. *Soon . . . in a month . . . sometime next week . . . any day now*. Nonno was coming to get me and I would be sorry.

I was already sorry. *Mio Nonno, beloved papà of my ex-amore!* I knew Gilberto loved me, but I had lost my right to belong, and in his world there were no second chances. So I was both sorry and scared, but I was no longer *stupida*. I alerted the police and customs, hid my children's passports in a place I wasn't revealing, and made sure the au pair knew how to dial 999. By day, the air between Giacomo and me grew dense with the spores of fresh grievance. At night I held my *bambini* under the covers and inhaled their damp, comforting smell. But as time ran on I forgot to eat and I forgot to breathe.

One morning I woke up trembling in the aftermath of a violent power surge. It was as if the earth had sneezed and the trees were shuddering inside their hoary barks. Outside, on London's blackened sills, the pigeons ceased their grumbling and shitting. A shadow was approaching our front door, and even distorted through the etched-glass panel he was recognizable. Behind me in the hallway, I heard footsteps.

"It is my father," Giacomo said. "He has come."

Upstairs the children were sleeping. I had a flash of the au pair throttled and the children carried off, one under each of Nonno's arms, like two paper parcels stamped "Fragile." But if one side of me was cold war, the other was claws and sabre teeth. I would kill before I let them be taken.

"Open the door," Giacomo ordered.

People say everything happens quickly in situations like these, and people are right. Nonno came straight at me. There was the softest brush of wool against my cheek as he passed. I steadied myself. Turned in a daze. Behind me in the narrow corridor he had his son pinned against the wall with his forearm. Their faces locked.

"You!" Nonno snarled, and I saw the flecks of spit in his breath. "You pack your bag and get out." Then he stepped towards me, eyes black as onyx. "And you . . ." He raised a gloved hand and I resolved not to wince. "You, *cara*," he stroked my cheek with his finger, "you come with me."

In the street, a car was purring. I wondered about rapping on the driver's window, but the angle of parking was fractionally off so I knew it could never be Fabio.

"Where are we going, Nonno?"

I looked back at the window of the boys' room. Nonno was ferocious but never callous. I knew that the children would be safe, that they would not be taken from me—and yet I shivered. It was a cold winter that year, and unhappiness made it colder still. In a gesture that felt achingly familiar, Nonno took my hand and placed it into the warm pocket of his coat.

"It's OK, *cara*," he said.

I understood something in that moment—that the father was some kind of metaphor for the son. I understood too that the romance of their world worked only within the context of its own mythology. In the here and now was another matter. I might belong to Nonno from afar, but I could never live with his son up close.

We ate lunch in Scott's Restaurant in Mayfair, where everything is expensive, especially the fish. Nonno ordered two Dover soles, but I had to cut mine with a fork, because he still had hold of my hand.

I cried then, just a little.

"It's OK, *cara*."

"I'm so sorry."

"Why you sorry? I love my son very much, but I always know."

I blew my nose on the starched napkin. "Know what?"

"It was impossible."

"Why are you here, Nonno?" I asked after a while. "I mean, why are you here with *me*?"

"You?" he said softly. "With you?" And I think by then he was crying a little bit too. "Because you tried, *cara*, you tried."

Time passed. Just when Giacomo and I thought we'd been clever enough to avoid litigation, Nonno offered me an Old Master painting for my share of the London house which turned out to be mortgaged to one of his businesses. The firm I went to for advice demanded the provenance of the painting.

"Show me the paperwork," the lawyer said.

"Listen to me, *carissima*." Maybe Nonno's throat was especially sore, maybe the line was bad from Italy. "This paperwork . . . is question of trust. You are still family, and there must be trust and honour within families. *Capito*? I come to London. I see this lawyer, and we will sign everything together, yes?"

"Yes," I said. Because the code for our relationship had always been written around trust and honour.

"Don't even think about taking the painting without papers," my lawyer snorted. "And don't meet with him either. The old man could get nasty. Put the screws on you."

Here's the lesson about trust and honour I was to learn. Later, when Giacomo had stopped spitting and snarling, he too found himself in a legal office. "Great news," his lawyer told him. "Stroke of luck. Your wife's legal team has screwed up. Forgot to file some form. Know what that means?"

"No," Giacomo said.

"Means you are not legally bound to come up with a penny. Not for her, not for the mortgage, not even for the kids!"

Even now when I tell this story, I like to picture my ex-*amore* rising slowly, making the reverse OK sign with his fingers, and sticking it up the lawyer's nostrils.

"*Anchovy brain! Are you stupido?* How you *dare* say I cheat my wife? How you *dare* say I don't look after my children! Now fuck off and quickly!"

I, too, should have told my lawyer to fuck off and quickly. Instead, I shut my eyes and wondered where on earth my babies would sleep inside an Old Master painting.

"Protect your interests," said my lawyer. "Go. Leave now before he arrives."

I went, but I felt my heart, the heart I'd once been so proud of, wither to the size of a dried seed in my chest. As I scuttled through the glass and chrome maze to the exit, I caught a glimpse of Nonno, motionless in his dark glasses and camel coat, rising on the escalator, staring straight ahead.

It was to be seven years before I saw Nonno again. He refused to take my calls. Never answered my letters. I got it, I supposed. We all destroy the things we love, and after all, where he was concerned, I'd been the one to pull the trigger first.

One fall afternoon, with the London sky mellow and lamplit, I was walking down New Bond Street when behind me I heard the guttural sound of "*Ciao!*" followed swiftly by "*Dimmi!*" I spun around. Coming towards me in a wondrously soft overcoat was Nonno—talking on two mobiles at once, flanked by an entourage of *guardie del corpo*, a new wife on his arm.

"*Cara.*" His face broke into a smile, while I nearly wept to hear that familiar, if now barely audible, cheese-grater voice. He was once again living in the Plaza Hotel in Rome, he told me, but this time in the penthouse suite. Italy was going to the dogs, but business was good. He embraced me, though made no move on either of my breasts. *This relationship with Nonno, never fully understood, forever tinged with sorrow.*

"Enjoy life," he rasped. "Is the only thing that matters." Then he pinched my cheek and was gone. It was the last time I ever saw him.

Years later, long after I'd had a daughter of my own and Giacomo had become her adored godfather, Nonno died. I hadn't been sure whether I'd be welcome, but Jesse and Sam attended the funeral. In a vast, marble-columned church somewhere outside Rome, in an unholy and unusual alliance, they watched their grandfather's body washed and prepared by the rabbis before being handed over to the priests. The flesh had belonged to the Jews, but his soul to the Catholics.

In the cemetery, a tight circle of people stood around the coffin, discreetly chain-smoking, as it was lowered into the earth. Nonno's four wives, ranked from oldest down to youngest, stood in the forefront holding hands and passing a single damp tissue backwards and forwards between them. At least twenty of the mourners, men in glossy dark suits, were unknown to them or indeed anyone else in the family.

Nonno had been eighty and active to the last. He died intestate. No one knew where his money or assets were kept. There was nothing to pass on, nothing to inherit, and thus in some ways the madness died with him.

Noting the look on Sam's face as concrete was poured into the open grave instead of soil, one of Nonno's nine children put a hand on his shoulder and, half tearful, half laughing, said, "Sammy, come on. You remember what my father was like alive? Imagine how he would be as the undead! The cement is to make sure he never comes back."

But, oh how I wished Nonno *would* come back, just as I wished to still belong inside his magic circle. Nevertheless, I liked to think of his soul leaving his body, those watchful eyes hidden behind shades, his stocky frame encased in his camel coat, and a phone to each ear, growling "*Ciao*" as he hung up on one life and "*Dimmi!*" as he embraced the next.

DRY CLEANING

In London, in the spirit of single parenting, I decided to save on the electrician's fee and mend my own leaky washer-dryer. Maybe my mind wasn't on the task, maybe I was far from being safely grounded during that period; either way, the shock of the current passing through my fingertips short-circuited what was left of my snap, crackle, and pop. After that, I took the family washing to the launderette, where the thump of the machines beat in sync with the refrain in my head: *goddamnit, goddamnit, goddamnit.* At first schlepping clothes around the corner felt like a chore, but I began to look forward to the nothingness of those coin-operated hours. The launderette became a refuge of sorts, an egalitarian hideout where there was no need to wear a face for anyone.

Zoned out on the slatted bench, high on the perchloroethylene fumes, lulled by the slap of cotton against glass, I was struck by the thought that I had made a living out of these oddities known as clothes for well over a decade now. I'd pieced together my company during the Thatcher era. Boom time for women. I was a confused feminist, the kind who secretly loved being whistled at by men on building sites. But even as a surly teenager I'd understood the transforming power of fashion—how it could make you feel brave. And here was something I could do for the cause. Empower the fellow shy; dress them up to take down inequality. That idea alone had been enough to make my accidental career feel like it had purpose, and I'd been good at it, too. But now my marriage was gone, my company was being crushed between the hydraulic hands of big business, and my beloved managing director, Gerry, was dead.

Gerry hadn't been just my managing director; he'd been my managing everything. I tried to cry for him on those laundry evenings, but it was as though I'd lost the skill. I'd always been an excellent crier—at least when no one was looking. I cried after Giacomo told me he wanted me to have his baby. I cried too the first time he lost his temper—turned away from him and, leaning out the window of his Curzon Street office, watched my tears drip onto the turbaned head of the doorman at the entrance to the Persian restaurant below.

But I was exposed, on a street corner, the time our two neighbourhood Puerto Rican prostitutes cruised by in their car, tossing their perms and calling out to me as they passed. "Hey girl, how is your *chico malo*? Your bad boy? Hey, *preciosa*, I hear you have a new *bebé*! You need help with anything you let us know!"

And they'd grinned and waved, oblivious to how close I was to taking them up on their offer. *Please tell me, oh dazzling putas with neon teeth and steel-wool hair, how should I move through life when my chico malo is so angry all the time, because sometimes I feel like even the air might sting me.*

Now as the wash cycle cycled and the spin dryer spun, my thoughts ricocheted between these two men that I'd loved. One so solid and protective, the other, who'd gambled with everything, even his family. I suddenly remembered the inaugural board meeting with the executives who'd bought my company. A secretary was moving along the table, laying out pads and pencils.

"Shall we begin?" our new chief executive officer suggested, and Gerry caught my eye. A month earlier Giacomo had put all the money we'd had on the roulette table and bought a horse with the winnings.

"*Stupida.*" He kissed me when I complained. "The horse will win."

The horse had been a beauty, with a buffed conker hide and a single white sock. It romped home last in its first race and failed to make it out of the starting gate in its second.

The day of the board meeting, it had been slated to run in its third race. The prize money was huge, as was the risk—the losers eligible to be sold for next to nothing at auction afterwards. Nevertheless, I'd promised to put down a bet, and now it was too late. Caught between being labelled a bad time manager or a shitty wife, I stared unseeingly at the lined paper in front of me as the CEO began to spout projections and goals.

"Wait!" Gerry said, holding up his hand and embarking on some shamelessly revisionist version of my quandary. "So our first order of business," he concluded, "should be to bet on this horse. Think of it as an act of faith, a good luck omen for our future."

The CEO looked incredulous, then laughed and led the seven of us—most mismatched group of punters ever—down Oxford Circus to the nearest betting shop, directing us back into our boardroom chairs just in time to catch the horse streaking first past the post on the big wall screen. That was the day I thought all our money troubles were over, and they would have been, too, had the poor horse not gone lame twenty-four hours later.

Not only did Gerry have my back; he was a proxy father to a diaspora of painters, dancers, and singers. Lost boys, all of them, turned out by hostile families into a society increasingly hysterical about AIDS. The time would come when we would watch Gerry's boyfriend die, a malevolent wreck of his former self. Gerry made me swear that if he ever got sick, I would not let him go as horribly.

"I mean it," Gerry said, as his boyfriend railed at the nurses, at Gerry, at God. "Pills, poison, stake through the heart. Promise me you won't let me lose my humanity. Promise me."

I promised. The idea of my despotic commander-in-chief being anything but in control was so preposterous that I agreed as carelessly as if he were asking me to lend him a tenner. Besides, he'd been tested, he assured me. He was fine.

Shortly afterwards, our CEO, wielding his controlling interest like an axe, fired half my employees and merged our business into his company's French subsidiary—rivals of ours. While Gerry stayed in London to sweep up our splintered remains, I began a long year of commuting to Paris.

A standard issue bedbugsit, my rented apartment was balanced on top of a rickety external staircase deep in the red-light district of Rue Saint-Denis. Dotting the pavement below, hookers in fur coats and red stilettos roamed the streets like cartoon foxes, sniffing out custom and blowing smoke rings into the night air. I was miserable without my team. I missed the brilliant collaborative insanity that was fashion. All those late nights, pale faces, and terrible jokes. *It was business, not personal*, the CEO had assured Gerry and me, with his trademark concerned indifference. But alone in Paris, I felt as though I'd pricked my finger on the spindle of corporate nastiness and fallen into a hundred-year sleep.

After Gerry finally broke down and confessed he'd been HIV positive all along, our mutual if baseless guilt—his for lying, mine for not being there for him—made us both furious. His sickness devastated me, first because I knew his lies had been meant to protect me and second because I knew the size of the boulders that lay on the road ahead of him. Lesions, blindness, madness. So many beautiful boys dying on so many hospital wards.

A year later he was confined to bed, attached to pipes and valves, unable to speak. He was a bony head on a stick, no longer able to embrace life but a dry shell into which life was being dripped bag by bag. No one knew whether he had days or weeks left, but by then we were nursing him in shifts. I was alone in the room when I noticed he was signaling with his eyes. For a while I'd been feeling pinned under the weight of my promise. It's not like you can watch someone die slowly without going crazy yourself, and in warped solidarity I'd developed all his symptoms: night sweats, insomnia, weight loss. At night my bones felt hot and flinty, as if they might spontaneously combust and send fire flickering through my joints. I ticked burial choices in my will and wrote my children long letters, which I hid in a drawer.

That day in the hospital, I looked down to find I'd picked up a cushion off the chair. I stood at the foot of his bed, stunned by the enormity of what I was considering. Gerry's eyes were fastened on mine, beseeching. I squeezed the cushion between my hands, squeezed and released, not knowing whether he was giving me the go-ahead or pleading for more time. Where were the rules for this? I had never needed anyone in that moment as much as I needed my mother. *Tell me what to do, Mum, just tell me what to do.*

Humans are breathtakingly adaptable. Illness shrinks our world down to improper fractions, yet still we manage to find happiness. Quality of life is a complex arithmetic, and a braver person than me might have done the sums for him, but I dropped the cushion back onto the chair. Marriage, my company, Gerry. I hadn't been able to fix any of them, and failure of that magnitude leaves a person stripped naked.

After Gerry died, the flesh-and-bone me went about its business as normal, but my spirit hit the streets, drinking liquor out of a brown paper bag while a violin screeched out self-pity in the background. Breaking down is a dangerous thing to do in public. I was raised on superhero pop culture and everyone knows you don't risk dropping a bomb on a crowded city—you fly it out over the bay and detonate it somewhere safe.

And finally I figured out where that one safe place might be.

East to the West Coast of America. It's the iconic road trip. Three thousand miles of car fever, candy wrappers, and Corn Belt USA set to the rose tint of nostalgia. At least that's what the songs tell you it's going to be. But the only thing playing on the radio that month was Billy Ray Cyrus's "Achy Breaky Heart," a good companion piece, I suppose, for the Humpty-Dumpty one I was trying to put back together again.

I'd been looking forward to the trip, but from the start there were tensions. One of my travelling companions, AK, who I thought I knew well, turned out to be an avid yo-yo dieter. The other, her friend KC, who I'd met for the first time at the airport, introduced herself as a devotee of the macrobiotic religion. *Slimcea* and *Evangelista*, I nicknamed them privately. I had my own issues to deal with, no use pretending otherwise, but as far as eating was concerned, this was America, and I intended to barricade myself into every rib shack we passed and lay siege to its specials.

Mum had taken the boys for three weeks of brisk country walks, *pie of the cottage*, and bedtime readings of *Orlando, the Marmalade Cat*. I was twenty-nine, newly single, and coming home—back to the eleven-year-old who had stood on the deck of an ocean liner while a hurricane turned her world upside down. Somewhere in my head was the thought that I could reverse that voyage. Sail back to the girl from the woman I'd become. Shed a skin that suddenly felt too old and emerge with new wings, soft and folded tight against my body.

* * *

In his will Gerry left me a postcard. "The best thing for being sad," he'd written, quoting Merlin in *The Once and Future King*, "is to learn something. That's the only thing that never fails. Learn why the world wags and what wags it." On that journey I was learning that you don't pass along the road—the road passes through you, and its rumblings stir up all those feelings you've tried to bury deep. It was my internal landscape, not the view from the car window, that was desolate, full of torn billboards and freight trains going nowhere.

Still, ever since my mother told me she'd done it herself in the late 1950s on a dollar-a-day Greyhound bus, driving across America has been synonymous in my mind with freedom and new beginnings. Whenever we spotted that familiar dog logo parked up on the freeway, I imagined her, shoulders freckled in a cotton dress, stretching her legs by the side of the road—my mother, already so much wiser at twenty than I would ever be. *Tell me what to do*, I longed to ask her again, *tell me how to steer through this*. But how could she possibly have heard me, ghost of her future? Back then she'd had her own journey to go on, her own questions to ask. I knew that and so we kept driving.

In the smoky haze of Virginia's Blue Ridge Mountains we overtook a patrol car, hooting and catcalling into the wind. It wasn't our fault. At the speed we were going, no one could have seen those flashing lights until it was too late. The sheriff drove behind our rental for a while, toying with us like a prize marlin before throwing on his siren and reeling us in. We watched him climb out of his manly four by four and perform a little authority shuffle: Twist the hat! Snap the shades! Hitch up the gun belt! As if these law-and-order clichés were government protocol designed to enchant the tourists. After he'd finished, he stiff-legged on over, expression on his face suggesting he planned on sending us straight to Riker's Island. The truth is he never stood a chance. We were three English girls in a pink Cadillac, all of us pretty.

"Y'all were goin' mighty fast back there," he drawled, but then his eyes passed over KC's legs, sweetly anaemic in her shorts. "But since I've been behind you," he amended, "you done real good." We thanked him and admired his royal blue campaign hat. "Best-dressed law enforcement in North America," he agreed, returning our compliment with a pack of Wrigley's and an unconvincing lecture about civil obedience. It was the first of many lectures from bashful sheriffs. We could have broken the sound barrier that spring and not got a ticket.

Somewhere in the Carolinas we came across a diver, serious-minded and intense, who described how he searched for sharks' teeth in the silt and murk of the Atlantic. When he climbed off his bar stool, I saw that his legs were so short compared with his upper body that they would only make sense elongated by flippers. I pictured him down in the abyssal depths, lonely and disoriented, fumbling blindly for something he might never find, and I thought that as a metaphor for life, there wasn't a person to whom this image didn't apply. But then I guess when you're hungry enough for answers you can find them just about anywhere.

"What does the Bible say about divorce?" an old Baptist minister was shouting in a church we wandered into in Mississippi. He was black and fierce, with a rubbery face and eyes as blue as bird shells. He placed his hands flat on the pulpit and leaned forwards. "Let me tell you what *I* say, brothers, sisters. You gotta git off that Juicy Fruit train! You can't just chew all the flavour out of marriage then spit it out!"

And I thought, *Holy fuck, is that what I did?*

Later in a bar we flirted with boys whose pickup skills amounted to dropping their lighters on the floor so they could gawp up our skirts.

These were exactly the kind of boys the Baptist minister had warned against: "Daughters, don't show him your package, lest there'll be nothing else for him to buy!" But what did he know? Since Giacomo, since Gerry, I'd used boys and men as prescription meds—sleeping pills, antidepressants—effective for eight hours with few lasting side effects.

AK had inherited money and was generous with it, so every third night we slept in style, but KC and I were each on a penny-pinching budget that took us to motels with cot beds that smelled of toes and mildew. There were times when I'd lie awake, listening to our synchronised breathing, sideswiped by longing for my two babes back at home.

In New Orleans I dreamt that Jesse was a roast chicken and Sam a cricket trapped in a lidless jam jar. My task was to carry them across the sandy waves of the Sahara, the one hot and slippery with grease, the other scrambling up the glass sides, bent on escape. I woke, feverish with anxiety, and scooping the girls' washing off the motel floor, took it to the nearest Laundromat. Somewhere during the spin-dry cycle, I began to think how easy it had been to pin everything bad on Giacomo's temper. But what if a darker truth lurked beneath the surface? *Blame it on the cat* had been my childhood refrain. What if I was the one with creature blood running through my veins? I'd had plenty of funny, nice boyfriends before getting married, but I tended to hurt men who made life too easy for me. Perhaps Giacomo had been exactly what I needed—a boy with enough wild in him to keep my own in check.

I stood up, restless. It was time to get out of the city. *Keep going,* my mother would say whenever I hurt myself—which, being a clumsy child, was often. *Keep going and everything will be OK.*

I'd long held a secret objective for this trip. Drive to Monument Valley and cry. If there was a way to feel normal again, that was it. Go to a place where the days stretched long and wide, and let the heat and the wind sandblast you to nothing. Those great monoliths in Monument Valley had been scorched by lava, flooded, crushed and ice-aged. They were survivors. I figured they could take a few litres of tears, and once they'd finally washed out of me, a multicoloured piñata would float into the sky, burst overhead, and release happiness, along with tens of thousands of Hershey Kisses.

At least that had been the plan.

We'd been on the road nearly three weeks by the time we got to Utah, and the atmosphere in the car had turned glutinous and nasty. It felt as if the girls were playing two's company and I'd been cast as the crowd. Earlier that morning, when I'd asked KC to turn up the volume on my favourite Simon and Garfunkel song, she'd changed the radio station to '80s disco hits. Later, AK spat a sunflower husk out of the window, and announced that I wasn't to go near her ex-boyfriend back in London.

"You wouldn't guess it to meet him, but he's dark—really fucking complicated, you know." I knew her ex-boyfriend from a distance. He'd always struck me as sweet and funny. It had never occurred to me to venture closer.

"Although the pair of you are such emotional flatliners," she'd added, "chances are you'd get along fine."

I'd been stunned. There was so much pent-up emotion in me I was as stable as plutonium. But then, how could she have known? I was the only one living inside my skin.

"I'm starving," KC said, as we pulled into the motel. "After we check in, let's head into town and hit the supermarket."

"You should stay behind and rest, BP," AK said to me. Through the rear-view mirror her eyes, refrigerator cool, slid across mine. "KC and me are sharing a room anyway."

"We'd thought you'd be happier on your own," KC added insincerely.

Maybe I should have told them why I had really come to America, but I was new to the concept of friends. Back then my family doubled as my friends. The people who worked for me had been my family, and men were the wolves I slept with.

In the motel room, *Field of Dreams* was playing on the television. Kevin Costner standing under a stormy Iowa sky. *Build it, and he will come.* I perched on the bed and watched, feeling the counterpane jump with static under my hand. The motel walls were cheap and thin. As soon as AK turned on the shower and KC slammed the door, shouting something about an ice dispenser, I crept into their room, snatched up the Caddie keys, and was gone.

Through the car window, the sun heated the hairs on my arm to burnt threads. The sky was turquoise. Dust motes hung in the air. Nothing moving in that vast land except my Tonka toy car. The desert was a glaze of cinnamon dotted with sage and pale green brush. Clumps of tiny white flowers lining the verge blurred into streamers as I passed by. In the distance, the monuments shimmered, coppery and jellylike in the heat, drawing me closer as though exerting a beckoning spell. Emotional flatliner my ass. *Behold the tangle of rose and snapdragon that will one day grow on this arid square of desert soon to be irrigated by my English tears.* Bitches. I couldn't have been happier to leave them behind. Too bad if they were stranded in a cronky motel with only a swamp cooler for company.

I leaned on the gas, scarcely aware of the miles passing or the sweat sticking my T-shirt to the leather seat. A signpost. A left turn. Dead ahead now, the monuments rose out of the sand, craggy and imposing as a war cabinet of old generals. I felt exhilarated. I was here. The place I most needed to be. Except . . .

Oh!

OPENING HOURS: 8 A.M.–5 P.M.

What?

I stared at the notice and then checked the clock on the dashboard: *5:12 p.m.*

Monument Valley was closed? I shunted forwards as though ground gained could be subtracted from minutes lost. An old Indian with long faded hair and a turquoise belt materialised from the side of his truck, draining a can of soda and waving his arms. *Closed, sister. Scram.*

I badly wanted to run him down. How could a valley be shut? This was the West, untamed and untameable. It did not bow to the pedestrian whims of park employees or bourgeois timetables. I stood my ground and crossed my arms. *Put that in your pipe and smoke it, mister.*

The Indian spiraled his finger in a "turn around" gesture.

I smiled grimly. *Forget it.*

He started shouting.

Cocksucker. I U-turned, followed the last of the camper vans back along the track, out the entrance, and left towards the motel, disappointment firing to anger, anger launching like a missile straight at the girls. If KC hadn't done her flirty thing at reception. If AK hadn't made that extra gas-station stop. Stupid, of course. It was nobody's fault but my own; still if I was going to fuck this up too, I badly needed someone else to blame.

In my rear-view mirror the road behind unfurled like grey smoke. I slowed down until a hoot forced me off to the side. A pickup grumbled by, a sheepdog quivering in a flatbed full of hay, eyes slit to the breeze. I climbed out of the car and leaned against a metal gate. Presently a piebald trotted up and stuck his head over the top. He was so skinny he looked as if he'd swallowed his own carcass. I fetched him one of AK's furring apples. He nickered, and I pressed my head against the bony plateau of his nose, nearly missing the Greyhound bus as it rattled by. Out of the back window, a little girl was waving. She had pale freckled arms and a floral bow in her hair. *Keep going and it will be all right.* To hell with it. Only Mum had the answers that made sense. I lifted my arm slowly and waved back.

At the entrance to the valley, the Indian was gone. A thick metal chain now hung between two free-standing posts. For a moment I balked, but the West *is* untamed and untameable. Cordoning off a hundred thousand acres of desert with ten feet of chain was as hopeful as restraining Gargantua and Pantagruel with paper handcuffs. Nosing the car down the slope, I drove right around it.

To begin with, I kept to the official track, heading methodically from one monument to the next like a grand cattlewoman checking her fences. As each approached it opened out into a complex architectural structure—one a Gaudí basilica of pinnacles, another shaped like a ruined amphitheatre—each more surreal than the last, yet every one familiar from their starring roles in virile John Wayne westerns. After a while, following the tire treads of other cars didn't satisfy my need for solitude and I freewheeled aimlessly until I lost myself in open space-time dreaming, only subliminally aware of the pull and drift of the suspension and the hiss of sand, but with every spin of the wheel feeling a giddying sense of freedom, as though an unseen hand was twirling me out of lengths of mummifying bandage.

Finally I drew up to a towering stalagmite, a hundred feet high and skirted by a mound of fine red earth. Climbing out of the car, I turned my face to the sun, feeling an almost crystalline focus. This was it. *Valley of Dreams. Find it and they will come.*

The light tiger-striped from yellow to orange. The soil darkened and the shadow of my legs stretched long and thin—*the shadow of a new me,* I thought, lighting a cigarette and drawing the cool burn into my throat. *Cry, girl, cry.*

I waited a bit more. Lit a second cigarette off the dying tip of the first. Nothing.

On the CD player I fast-forwarded Michelle Shocked to her bleakest ode, then lay on the Caddie's hood absorbing the heat of the metal, deliberately thinking the saddest thoughts imaginable. The sun hung low in the sky, soft as an egg yolk. Still I waited, patient. The egg sun broke and poured its yolk along the line of the horizon.

Still nothing.

In the fading light a hawk powered by, wings slicing the air. A jackrabbit skittered across the sand, twitching curious satellite ears. I lit another cigarette. As the match flared, daylight drained and in an instant darkness fell. In desperation, I worked steadily through the Caddie's supply of beer and cigarettes, my throat increasingly raw, but it was no use. I must have got the rules wrong. What if you couldn't make the decision to be done with sadness? What if *it* was supposed to relinquish its pit-bull hold on you?

That thought in itself was enough to prompt a tear; I squeezed but none came. An insect flew into my eyeball and promptly dried to death.

I didn't get it. I have a stream of schmaltz so wide no amount of cynicism can bridge it. I weep easily in movies, in the hospital wards of strangers, whenever I spot a Chelsea pensioner labouring down the street. Had something inside me calcified?

Then I remembered. It had been a conscious decision. One day, shut inside the bathroom after a row, I'd picked up a pair of nail scissors, a revelation coming to me: the only way not to hurt was not to care. A metaphorical snip through the emotional nerves. Maybe AK and KC were right about me being a flatliner, but it was only ever supposed to have been a temporary solution.

I peeled myself off the car's hood. Head back to the motel, and the girls might yet make it into town, but which way was the motel? I checked the line of the horizon. The darkness was complete, and remembering the treachery of the soft washes and sharp drops from earlier, I felt the stir of unease.

I've always had a shaky grasp on the earth's compass points. The technician in charge of my design fatally short-changed me on spatial intelligence. It's not a coordination thing. I can park on a dime, pitch an orange over a tall building and then pretty much catch it on the other side, but my inability to generate cognitive maps is so profound it further suggests a baby-dropped-on-head incident to which my parents never confessed. I climbed into the Caddie. Fuck the untamed West. Surely a few helpful road reflectors wouldn't be amiss?

I fired up the ignition. The monuments sat patiently, chess pieces waiting for my next move. I crawled forwards carefully, determined not to make a bad play, but after only five hundred yards the wheels began to sink. Instinctively I hit the accelerator. The engine roared in protest, then coughed asthmatically, choked, and died.

Night collected around me. Small furtive things whispered in my ear. I stabbed uselessly at the power button as a bat swooped through the open roof. I tried to picture walking the twenty-odd miles back to the motel, padding through the desert, moving sure-footed across the sand, but that braver, more feral self belonged to my future. For now, I curled up into a tight urban ball. Addendum to my mother's rules of Lost: *Stay put and remember not to drink the battery acid.*

*   *   *

I woke to the pain of a full bladder. Peeing out a foamy stream of beer, I admired the dancing pinpricks of fireflies in the distance, but as they enlarged into torch beams, I yanked up my jeans in alarm.

I had been raped once. Well, at the time I hadn't *felt* raped, at least not the way I imagined you were supposed to feel. Consequently, I'd tried not to think about it afterwards, but I thought about it then, with night stretching out and voices and torches closing in.

I'd been twenty when it happened. A letter had landed on my desk from a leather and suede manufacturer based in Germany. He liked my work and wanted me to consult on his range. I was flattered—not just by the generous fee and business-class ticket he was offering but because the professional compliment made me feel grown-up. Someone would pick me up at the airport, his office wrote. *Someone would look after me.* The manufacturer himself came, in a classic sports car. He had swashbuckler's hair and the sort of brooding looks that might have been attractive on somebody less Lilliputian. There are plenty of jokes about small men and fast cars, and certainly this one drove as if his death wish was big enough for both of us. When we arrived at his *Schloss*, as he called it, I remember thinking, *Wow, he has an actual castle.* I was surprised, too, when he told me his staff was off for the weekend. Nevertheless, he was businesslike, formal. He suggested we go straight to his factory, where rows of cow skins hung over washing lines bleeding different-coloured dyes onto a concrete floor. We spent the afternoon sketching and discussing the relative merits of leather versus suede, after which he proposed a drink. Glasses were raised to the start of a lucrative collaboration. My next conscious thought came in the basement of the castle, where we were having sex. If, from then on, the bigger picture was blank, smaller details always float back to me with clarity: the dark satiny sheets, the knobby mole on his chest. I remember being repulsed, yet the me who was repulsed was hovering above the bed, gazing down on a different me, one who appeared strangely acquiescent. The remainder of that weekend, when played back, still feels like an old movie from which key reels have been damaged in storage. I remember the basement having a steam room. I remember the manufacturer lying naked on a marble slab. I remember thinking that if I drank the water he kept supplying, my head might clear.

Later, I woke in a bedroom that appeared to be mine. My clothes were hanging in the cupboard, and my shoulder bag lay on a chaise longue. I could hear Mozart being played on a piano that sounded far away. Whoever was playing was very accomplished. Hungry, I tried to leave the room, but there was no handle on the door. The phone by the side of the bed worked. I called England.

"I think I'm in trouble," I told my sister.

"What kind of trouble!" Susie said, alarmed.

"Remember *Story of O*?" I asked, but too bleary to articulate further I hung up in confusion. I drank the bottle of water by my bed. My memory began again around lunchtime on Sunday. The manufacturer and I were sitting in a local *Biergarten* eating bloodless sausages at a trestle table. Next to us, other Germans were laughing and drinking, but talk was stilted between the manufacturer and me. I had no feelings of outrage or anger. I had no feelings at all. It wasn't until after he put me on the plane home that I realised Saturday had gone missing altogether. I fudged the story with my sister. I never told my parents. I felt young and vulnerable and stupid.

The shadows behind the torches turned into two Indians. I clenched my fists, but they were boys, not men, no more than nineteen or twenty, with sweet faces and smooth buttery muscles. Winston, the shyer of the two, was exquisitely tattooed, with black symbols running across his shoulders and around his chest in the bolero curve of a matador's jacket. Oba, the talkative one, was rangier, wearing basketball shorts and an Aertex singlet.

For a while they tinkered under the Caddie's hood, grunting and smirking. They were Navajo, Oba told me, living in the valley with their parents, and it was their land I was trespassing on. They thought this pretty funny. Not as funny, obviously, as my having no idea where to locate the catch on the car's hood. Then again, what did I know? Not which direction I was facing in the world. Not how to unthaw my tears in ninety-degree heat. Not how to recognise who my friends were.

I would not find out until later that AK and KC had misinterpreted the note I'd left—*Something important to do, something I must do on my own*—and called the local sheriff.

"We should never have left her alone," AK fretted. "It's not the first time she's disappeared. Once we saw her in the launderette, head in hands, just staring at the washing going round. We nicknamed her Depressionata, though not to her face of course."

"All that junk food she was eating!" KC said. "The wrist-slitty stuff she listened to on the radio. We were just trying to give her some space, you know?"

"I even tried to reverse psychology her into taking an interest in my ex-boyfriend," AK added, "but she didn't take the bait."

Winston slammed down the hood. Oba turned the key in the ignition. My pink Tonka toy hummed into life.

"I never saw a car this colour," Oba said. "You win it at the casino?"

"It's my getaway car."

"You done something wrong?"

"I sold clothes," I told them, and they grunted, unimpressed.

Then and there I decided I was done with fashion. Done with its ephemeral buzz. Done with seesawing on the pendulum of profit and loss. I had never truly fit into that world. I had never really belonged.

They offered to lead me out of the valley, but now I felt like staying.

We lay on the desert floor, two sweet Indian boys and me, smoking and looking up at the sky.

In the distance, lightning whipped across the blackness like a bright, loose wire.

"Hey, you see that?" I said, and as thunder broke and echoed, I held out my hand for rain.

Winston shook his head. "Dry storm. Time of year."

Ha, ha. No rain—an emotional flatliner of a storm.

Another lightning strike, this one as intricate as the veins and capillaries of a leaf.

I suddenly remembered New York, the week before we'd sailed to England. Another dry storm, and my mother hauling the three of us out of bed to watch it break over the city. The lightning had taken out the power grid, and our city, the city that never sleeps, was black and still. As we crowded at the window in our pajamas, my mother had us count: over a hundred strikes, each exploding across the sky with a biblical intensity that left behind a visual echo of its shape. One struck so close it illuminated the windows of the building opposite, and in that second's flash I saw a woman and man holding hands, sitting together at a kitchen table, before they too were swallowed by darkness. The image imprinted as a negative on my mind, like some secret story, its plot hinted at but not fully revealed. I remember thinking that behind every one of those windows, in every apartment, across every city in

America, stories were being formed, even as one was being formed now out of the nothingness of the desert. People like to say the world is small, but how could that possibly be true?

I knew it then. I was done with grieving, too. Sadness is another layer of clothing we pull around ourselves to keep warm. Another skin to be shed and left behind or stripped off and washed clean.

Wind rustled the scrub. Dust was rising, and deep inside me something tensed. I stood up, sensing a change in the air.

The first drop landed on my cheek, a splash of coolness, a single tear. I rubbed my eyes and looked up. Rain was falling in slim hyphens that quickly turned heavier, blunter, drumming against the ground, soaking my face. Thunder ripped through the sky and rolled through my body. Lightning flashed, again and again. I counted the strikes. One for Gerry, one for Giacomo, one for everyone in my company who had worked so hard for me.

"I never seen this." Winston held out his hand, and I knew it would sound silly if I told him the rain was for me.

When it was over I took a final drag of my cigarette and blew smoke into the warm, clear air of tomorrow. Winston and Oba stood up. "Time to go," they said.

My mouth felt smoky and peppery. *I will kiss a man I like with this mouth*, I thought—not today, not next week, but at some point in the future. I will kiss a man and it will feel good.

GHOST OF MY FUTURE

The film was playing at the best kind of theatre—one not so run-down that the decay distracts, but one whose quirks had kept it from falling into the homogenizing grasp of Cineworld or Odeon. This art deco building was a faded star, a Norma Desmond of cinemas. Black stains ran down her pale breeze-block like streaks of a diva's mascara. But if her once-smooth facade was now riven by cracks and flaws, inside she was still a beauty.

There are so few of these independents left in London, idiosyncratic, stubbornly holding on to their old-fashioned formalities. Under the painted dome of the box office, tickets are issued on stiff white paper. The popcorn is hot and spitting, and the minute you step into the darkness of the auditorium an usherette is on hand to look after you—that day, a Hungarian lady, "Goscia," I read on her enamelled badge. She led me down the aisle, the look from her to me confirming what I already knew—that the two of us were in collusion, that she was to be my ally in this temporary escape. Then she noticed my stomach and the way I paused as a spasm broke over it like a hairline fracture across an eggshell.

"You OK?" She caught her lip between strong white teeth. I was in labour, and in her voice there was such kindness that I nearly invoked stranger privilege and confided in her. *I have a new love, a new job, and very soon a new baby. I should be OK. I should be terrific, but I'm not. I'm here because I've done something very peculiar.* Only in this velvet womb, with its soundproof walls and dimmed lights, might it have felt safe to confess such heresy, but how could this nice lady with her red papery jacket and carefully applied lipstick begin to understand what I myself was having trouble rationalizing?

"Here you are." Goscia stopped at a brass plaque nailed to the floor and flicked her torch across the crimson upholstery of row F. Her spotlight found and held on my number. The seat yawned tiredly as I pulled it down. I was early, and the cinema was empty. This is the best way to see a movie, sneakily, in the afternoon, while outside real life marches on, governed by the hours and minutes of the day. Time, though, is not as inflexible as we are led to believe. It moves more slowly down in the dark than it does up in the light. In the space between there is a temporal swag to be had, and where better to spend it than alone in the cinema?

Except that I wasn't alone. As my eyes adjusted I noticed a solitary man, already parked, front row centre. Suddenly he leaned forwards, light catching on a hawkish profile, and before I could stop myself I thought, *Dad! Hey, Dad!* before laughing at my idiocy. Dad, my ass. More likely a pervert, shrugged into his grubby raincoat, too cold and demoralised to roam the streets looking for women to flash. I glared at the back of his head, though God knows I shouldn't have been so ungenerous. To walk out of your own story and into someone else's has got to be the answer to everything life throws at you. The cinema is the first place I go when I can't figure out what to do. I went to see *Teenage Mutant Ninja Turtles II* the day Gerry died, *Mrs. Doubtfire* the day my company closed; and after Mac, AK's ex-boyfriend, proposed, I checked into a late-night showing of *True Lies*. Daytime cinema, especially in theatres as gloomily lit as this, has long been a haven for a certain kind of refugee. Right on cue, front-row man shifted in his seat and stretched out his legs. *Great*, I thought, *here we go*.

Every country has its nationalistic brand of dirty old cinema guy. Once, while working in Paris, I snuck into a matinee of *Betty Blue*. That time too the theatre had appeared deserted, until I heard a soft groan and noticed a Frenchman a couple of rows behind me, slumped low in his chair and vigorously masturbating under a copy of *La République*. For a while it was just the two of us, accompanied by his elevated breathing, until another man edged in and, with well over a hundred and fifty seats to choose from, levered himself into the one directly in front of me. He ripped the staples out of a bag of hot, greasy fries and began noisily troughing on them. Under normal circumstances I might have moved, but the labours of *La République* man had reached feverish levels by then, and some innate Englishness made me feel it would be impolite to do so until he had finished. A few minutes passed before there was a long, heartfelt sigh, then the sound of a chair flipping up as he made his way, somewhat unsteadily, towards the exit. God knows I understand the need for a shadowy place to lose yourself, but I remember being shocked that he hadn't wanted to stay for the rest of the film. After all, *Betty Blue* is a classic.

Cinema saved me that year. Paris was a city gridlocked by strikes. Farmers blocked motorways, air-traffic controllers grounded planes. In Charles de Gaulle Airport, where more than once I found myself sleeping the night, I fell in with an actual refugee, Mehram Nasseri, an Iranian with an epically mournful face and a thick moustache daubed under his nose like a brushstroke of tar. Mehram, whose plight was later re-imagined by Steven Spielberg, was bound to limbo by some Kafkaesque bureaucracy to do with his entry visa and lived a stateless existence in Terminal One. After spotting him in the same corner seat in Burger King for a number of weeks, I finally twigged he was homeless and began buying him food. What with his poor English and my nonexistent Farsi, our relationship never developed much beyond grimacing at each other over flame-grilled Whoppers while he scribbled in his notepad and I kept my eyes trained on the departure board for further flight cancellations. Mute was fine by me. I was consumed by such glittering anger during that period of my life it was safer not to speak to anyone.

I risked another look at front-row guy, but he was up to nothing worse than tackling his popcorn. My stomach twisted, as though a series of internal bolts was being tightened. Labour had come on suddenly while the boys were dive-bombing banana splits in their favourite restaurant. After they were done, I'd taken them home with every intention of packing a hospital bag, but when it came to shutting the case, I saw to my horror that instead of a nursing bra and baby clothes, I'd thrown together boots and jeans and tossed my passport on top. I was so freaked out that I backed into a corner and held on to the windowsill for support. The contractions were regular. I knew I ought to call someone. Mac, for example, the man I was in love with and had recently married under the cedar tree at my parents' house. Mac, who ran baths for me and left small posies of freesias by my bed. Instead, wondering what kind of monster I was, I had kicked the suitcase into the cupboard, taken a cab to the cinema, and bought a ticket to the first movie showing.

I let out my own long, heartfelt sigh. As if responding to a service bell, Goscia appeared, tendering a small cushion, then waited, quivering with maternal righteousness, while I positioned it behind my back. I summoned my cheeriest smile to dismiss her. This was the best place for me to be, and I didn't need anyone telling me otherwise.

I was six when my father bunked off work and took me to my first movie. One afternoon in New York, he came bursting through the door on Ninety-Second Street and ordered my sister and me to put on shoes and coats. "And be quick about it, too," he said. We did what we were told. My father coming home in the afternoon was no ordinary event. Dad was busy. He was taking bids at auction. He was visiting a collector in Santa Barbara or serving time in a Chilean prison for a crime nobody has ever quite got to the bottom of. My father got around a lot, but where he rarely managed to get was home.

Outside on the street dozens of off-duty cabs streamed by. "Run for it!" he shouted. "Head for the park!" He didn't wait for our stumpy legs. No matter, we followed his long tweed coat like two choirboys at the hem of the Pope. Central Park in May and the clusters of cherry blossoms looked like the floral bathing hat Great-Aunt Kay liked to wear in her Long Island pool. Frisbees floated through the air. Students kissed under the shimmering contrails of a jet plane. No one in a hurry except us. We darted across the path of a roller skater, who avoided a collision with a leisurely figure of eight. He mock saluted as my father shouted his British apology. On to Central Park West, where my sister stopped, mutinous and out of breath. Dad grabbed her hand, zigzagged us another few blocks, until finally we were there, outside an art deco building, staring up at the name "Metro" spelled out in cursive neon inside a strip of blinking bulbs.

"*Fantasia*," my father said at the box office. "Three please."

After *Fantasia*, it was *Modern Times*. *The Gold Rush*. Later, Dad and I graduated to *Airport*, *The Towering Inferno*, *The Sting*. Double bills leading to treble. Fred Astaire, Bette Davis, Woody Allen. Entire oeuvres consumed across a single weekend. Together we've been to a thousand movies. It doesn't matter how overblown the acting, how hackneyed the plot or laughable the script. I've walked out of more relationships than I have feature films and, it has to be said, so has my father.

We don't share as much of each other's lives as we'd like. There is never enough overlap, but Dad and I share cinema. Perfect father-daughter date.

The lights dimmed, the screen widened, front-row perv blew his nose. I caught the edge of heavy black-rimmed glasses, and again there was the Dad thought. It happens a lot, these fake glimpses of my father. Sometimes it's his heavy black glasses, sometimes a flash of grey hair through a cab window. *Hey!* I think, before I catch myself. *Dad!*

Life has turned the hair grey on many of London's twelve million inhabitants. A significant number also wear heavy black glasses, but whenever it isn't him, I suffer a jolt. Why do I keep conjuring up my father in total strangers? No doubt there's a syndrome with a Greek name and a pill to cure it, but I'm pretty sure it has to do with death. Regret for time not spent together. We all find ways of keeping the people we love close to us. I'm guessing these sightings are mine.

Except that my father is no ghost. My parents are alive and well and living a hundred miles outside London. If there's anything to say, I can pick up the phone. If I want to see them, I can be at their kitchen table within two hours, pouring us all vodka shots from the greasy Smirnoff bottle they keep on the drinks trolley.

Not that this changes anything. I'll be driving through the city, minding my own business, when I see something—a tweed coat, those damn glasses. *Hey Dad!* Pavlovian to the end. Why so sentimental? So mawkish? And how long before I begin to see my mother, too?

But every once in a while, a comic double take, because this time it will be not Ghost Father but the real one, emerging from a fishmonger or ambling along the street with a paperback copy of some out-of-print detective novel under his arm. In a city of twelve million this has happened more times than seems statistically feasible and I wind down the car window, excited, bemused, and frankly more than a little put out that my father has made the long journey up to the city, *my* city, without making me the absolute focus of his day.

"Dad!" I shout.

He will turn, somewhat quizzically, to find me bearing down on him, waving like a loon. "Oh, hello, Dau," he says casually, as though this was a pre-arranged meeting for which, as usual, I'm the tiniest bit late.

"Dad, for goodness sake!" I will try but fail to keep the pique from my voice. "What are you *doing*?"

"What am I *doing*?" Through his glasses, his eyes are mocking, something pithy lurking in the wings. "What an extraordinarily impertinent question! But since you ask, I'm off to see Angie, my hairdresser." Or it will be his bank in Pall Mall or an appointment with a doctor whose name he can't recall for a test about which he will be maddeningly vague.

No matter. We fall into our established routine.

"Stay," I tell him. "We'll catch a movie."

"Ah." He shakes his head.

"But, Dad, I've not seen you for ages!"

"That's because I'm astonishingly busy and important." This reply despite the fact that my father passes the day as though time is something he never spends but instead assiduously recycles. When I persist, he lays his hand on mine to shut me up. We will then express mutual delight at such a chance encounter, before I drive on slowly, the child in me not understanding. Does he not love me? Want to hang out with me? Enter a new world with me?

Sometimes my mother calls to tell me Dad is coming to town.

"Great!" I'll say and offer to collect him off the train. Dad will refuse. I will insist. He will eventually agree but on condition I wait for him in the car. *I'm not to waste money on a meter. I'm not to waste time when I should be improving my grammar, composing better English.*

"Aren't you supposed to be a writer these days?" he likes to say.

"Your father will meet you on the street next to the taxi rank," my mother confirms. *Sure, Mum, whatever Dad wants.* But I couldn't care less what Dad wants. I park on a meter and then wait at the platform barrier, checking movie listings on my phone. I love train stations as much as I love cinemas. The miracle of lost and found. The word *departure*, and all the mystery and romance it promises. There's nothing lonely about train stations, with their perpetual business of coming and going.

When the train shunts in, passengers stream out under Brunel's wrought iron arches like workers of the Industrial Revolution. So much purpose, everyone to some preordained destination.

Everyone except Dad.

He pauses at the carriage door, an orange-brown stick in a sea of grey steel posts. He looks around, as though preparing for whatever fresh amusement the day might bring, then he steps down and strolls along the platform, his overnight luggage—a plastic bag with a rolled-up copy of the *Telegraph* inside—hooked to one finger. Sometimes I wonder how people view him. What's with the ancient coat? The manky toothbrush sticking out of his breast pocket? Is he a hobo, a museum curator, or a forensic etymologist? Of course no one pays him any attention at all. He doesn't walk through their dreams, only mine.

After he's passed through the ticket barrier and into the main hub of the station, I scoot back to the car and drive to our appointed rendezvous, where he will be waiting, a faintly sardonic smile on his lips. "Late again," he will say.

I can't tell you how much he hates it when I'm on time.

*   *   *

Ads were running on the screen. The budget all-you-can-eat graphics of the local tandoori restaurant gave way to forthcoming attractions. A sugar-sprinkled *American Pie* into which Jason Biggs was inserting his penis led synergistically to *American Beauty* and Kevin Spacey beating off in the shower. And still the theatre was deserted except for front-row perv and me. But even as I was looking forward to calling Dad later, expressly to tell him I had mistaken him for a flasher, I was thinking how very familiar the shape of the man's head was. Something to do with the way that grey hair sat over his coat collar, and then— suddenly illuminated in the terrestrial glare of the newest Star Wars trailer—there was the coat itself. Orange-brown herringbone. That oh-so-particular 1940s raglan sleeve. My grandfather's coat that Dad has worn for as long as I can remember. His way, I guess, of keeping his own father close to him.

"Well, good Lord," he said, with the grace to look mildly surprised as I joined him. But he soon recovered and raised both fists in a sign of triumph, as though this rendezvous had been his idea all along. As though Fate had been sweating over the calendar for chance encounters in order to accommodate him and him alone.

"So." He flipped down the seat next to him. "What's up?"

"Oh, not much." I matched my tone to his. "I mean, since you ask . . . I'm in labour."

"In labour!" He dragged his eyes from the screen. "In labour—are you really?" He stared at the general area of my stomach as though the fact that I was nine months pregnant with his third grandchild had come as an enormous surprise. "Well, good for you!"

"Um, thanks, Dad."

He watched as I manoeuvered the vast pod of my stomach and eased into the seat, then he gripped my shoulder and peered closely into my face. "You OK?" he asked.

Under his scrutiny I nearly lost it. Here's the thing. The half of me whose heart was vested in roots and relationships *was* OK. I knew that what I was carrying inside me—the fusion of atoms and stardust soon to become a tiny person—would change my life irrevocably. *I will take you as you are. To have and to hold, from this day forward till death us do part.* A vow that can only have been written for our children and no one else. But my other half, my restless self, the one on standby, ready to hoover up even the smallest crumbs of adventure? Well, she was cutting up rough. When the boys were babies I made a deal with myself. Be smart, be patient. Give up whatever you have to, because your time will come. But at nine and six years old, my boys were babies no longer. Love is hard. Giving your life to just one person is hard. Make someone happy, make a whole family happy—these were the woods I'd just stumbled out of, and if I was dragging my feet about going back in, it's because I got so lost first time round. Then I could never shake the feeling that there was a shadow of something moving ahead of me that I needed to catch and sew myself into before I would find out who I was. Going backwards, starting over, was to open up a greater distance between me and whatever it was I was looking for, and I was scared.

Dad took my hand in his.

I looked down at our long pianist's fingers, intertwined.

There is an inheritance of behaviour, a genetic disorder that marks you out as distinctively as a crooked pinky or a rogue fleck in the eye. I watched how my Dad went through life and I always knew. Like him, I was predetermined to drift. I'd seen the pain this caused and so, consciously or not, I tethered myself to responsibility: work, babies, marriage to the trickiest of men. But the tighter the ropes, the greater the struggle to break free. How could I admit this to Mac, who had given me so much of his heart? Mac, who was funny and clever and a little bit fucked himself. To have a baby with someone you love is the most powerful statement of hope there is, and I wasn't about to let my fear of the past dim the bright picture he had of our future.

Here, though, in the liminal dark of the cinema, there didn't have to be a future or a past. Here, even if only until I caught my breath, I could exist in the gap between the two where time didn't move at all.

Besides, *The Man in the Iron Mask* was playing and musketeer movies have always been Dad's first love. And mine.

On-screen Leonardo DiCaprio battled with his villain twin while I struggled with my own. It's all very well keeping your other self secret and imprisoned, but one day she will out.

But not now, I begged her. *Please, not now.*

A flutter, like the whir of helicopter blades pushing against my skin, and then my stomach contracted again. In my mind I touched the tip of my finger to the palm of my unborn baby. They say trouble makes you stronger, but even I know it's love that makes you grow.

Breathe, I thought, *breathe.*

"Froggins?" Dad was still waiting.

"I'm good," I said airily. "Why do you ask?"

"Just checking," he replied. But he, too, looked down at our long pianist's fingers.

And he smiled.

It occurred to me then that if we were one and the same, kindred spirits divided by a generation, he was my canary down the mine. Dad also took a corner too fast on his career. He also had two sets of children, ducked out of family life, packed that airport bag. In the end he was smart enough to recognise that my mother equaled home, and he always came back. Doesn't matter how much he loves us, though, he still needs to run away from time to time. A part of him will always crave flight, and that means a part of me will as well. It's no accident that we are sometimes accidentally in the same place at the same time.

The contractions were stronger now. I squeezed his hand. He squeezed back. He didn't ask why I wasn't in hospital.

He knew.

For the same reason he had driven a hundred miles to London, parked his car on an overpriced meter, and paid to see a movie instead of watching a video at home: To lose himself in the dark. To steal time.

Dad . . . hey, Dad.

This is why I keep conjuring up my father in strangers. So he can ask me if I am OK. Because only he understands why sometimes I'm not.

As my hand relaxed, he offered up his red-striped paper bag.

"Popcorn?"

"Don't mind if I do," I said.

See? Perfect father-daughter date.

Mac told me the story of him
He showed me all the things
that made him happy.

He showed me what he loved
and what he wanted his
life to look like.

I said, consider it done.
I can be part **of** your story.

Let me show you how brilliantly
I can fit in.

And he said, my perfect wife.

My beautiful girl

My dreamboat

My inspiration

Now what about you? Show me what you love.
Tell me what you want your story to be.

I said, I don't know for sure.

but I think this is what it might look like.

And I said, my mountain man.

My saviour

My hero

My rock

I thought –
it's going to be wonderful.

Now all we had to do was write the story of us.
What could be more simple?

THE WEST

2% MUM

Some nights their faces swam in front of me like a photo line-up of the NSPCC's most wanted. Anya, who hid Beefeater gin in the back of the pram; Sticky Lisbette having sex in my bed; Munchausen Sal squeezing blood from her own thumb into baby's nappy so she could raise the alarm of internal bleeding—and this was only a sneak preview of the au pair saga. Had these girls always been psychotic or had they turned into child-loathing, passive-aggressive sociopaths after a month or so embedded in my family? Too many hands had rocked my cradles, but with four babies now, what were my options?

I would live and die for these small beings I had brought into the world, but if they were to make it through park outings without being molested by the royal swans or a trip to the department store without being dragged through the teeth of the escalator, they were always going to need a more attentive eye than mine. Out here in the San Juan Mountains, though, things would be different.

Here, nine thousand feet high, at the end of a twenty-mile dirt road, in a rolling meadow of wildflowers, Mac and I had found a place like nowhere else. When a snip of homesteading land cropped up for sale one day, we bought it over the telephone. Two years, a thousand scribbled drawings, a posse of locals, and a lake of Budweiser later, Mac decapitated the last of the monster thistles from around the doorway and carried me over the threshold of the home we'd built together—a big barn made of reclaimed pinkish wood with a view onto a million acres of wilderness.

*   *   *

After the nervy tightness of London, the vastness of the West was like a cool liquid running through my head. Here was a place we could lose ourselves without getting lost. A place where itchy feet didn't feel mutually exclusive with raising a family. A place to focus on creating something new, even if that something was made out of words and sentences instead of colour and thread. And truth be told, it was time to get on with it.

Sudden withdrawal from any drug comes with side effects. A month after our CEO closed down my business, my body shut down. In the weeks that followed, plank-like, except for a comic limb twitch or two, I was wheeled off by Mac to a succession of doctors who tweaked and cracked their way to a diagnosis. It was idiopathic, psychosomatic. It was dilemmatic, melodramatic. Either way, the episode trapped something in the base of my spine that I still felt from time to time. Pain, sharp as a cattle prod, a reminder of something lost, something integral to my sense of self.

But I had it all worked out. Up at the barn, Mac would run his business remotely and shoot pack rats. I would write at the table in front of the big window while keeping a benign eye on the kids, as they skipped through the Indian paintbrush and charmed grass snakes with flutes carved from the branches of a fallen aspen tree. I had little difficulty picturing myself stuffing hay into pillows and trimming our winter coats with marmot fur, while the children churned butter out of dandelions and perfected their needlepoint. Forget Thai take-out, foraging would become our new byword. We'd live off the land. Tickle trout onto our dinner plates and garnish them with chanterelles harvested out of the still, quiet forests of the Rockies.

Alas, the marmots were ridden with fleas, the trout laughed in our faces, and the only grass snake in the valley died of cardiac arrest at its first human encounter. Isolation meant no playdates for the kids, and after a few days they turned gloomy and began draping themselves over the furniture like pressed flowers, demanding microwaved dinners and mourning the lack of Gymboree. I myself was disappointed to find that a move to the wilderness was no cure for my feeble housekeeping skills. Laundry piled high and dust patterned the floors in crop circles, while the big glass window quickly became ticked by battalions of kamikaze insects. If weaving up and down the mountain for supplies took, well, six hours, bulk buying resulted in the autopsy drip of rotting salad and bowls of penicillin-sprouting lemons.

They say that on retirement former powerhouses of multitasking quickly deteriorate to the point where they can barely manage a chore a day. Looking back, I marvelled at how much I got done while in the business of fashion. I hacked up cloth, wrangled with lawyers, got hammered with factory workers, smarmed up to buyers, hauled Freddie the dyspeptic tailor out of his bed in North London twice a week, and still had time for a vibrant second career as agony aunt to all fifteen of my employees. Post-fashion I managed one thing only—fractional movements of a mouse over a pad. I used to have a range of excuses for devoting too little attention to my kids, not least of which was the geographic location of my office, but the day I went to work in my head was the day my mothering skills really died on the vine. Oh, I soothed and patted and hugged and praised, but there were robotics involved and my children were not fooled.

My pioneering spirit lasted a week before I caved in and posted a sign in our local Walmart:

HELP REQUIRED: MUST LOVE KIDS. EXCELLENT DRIVER. NONSMOKER ESSENTIAL.

Enter Pamela.

She blew in one stormy day sporting an orange sun visor—which, it would transpire, she wore all year round, indoors and out, irrespective of the weather.

"Keeps the goddamn flies from biting, ya know?" she said, shaking off her wet plastic poncho to reveal an interview outfit of spangly boob tube over a pair of velour leggings that bagged fatally around the ass whilst obscurely managing to give her a camel toe at the same time.

Pamela was a lanky woman, with dye-stained hair, intelligent eyes, and the slight look of a codfish around the mouth. Originally from Texas, she had a drawl that bent every phonic rule in the book and she delivered it in startling monotone, uninterrupted by a single *um* or any other speech disfluency. Right from the start she made it clear that helping with kids was out of the question.

"They're a little rich for my taste," she stated, as though I'd offered her a sugared plum along with her cup of coffee. "And don't go expectin' me to give these up"—she pulled out a crumpled pack of Pall Malls— "because a true addict never quits." She struck a match and drew on her cigarette with relish. "Now listen up, because this shit you only get to hear once."

Over the next hour, Pamela laid claim to a tough life, and there was no question that it showed in her slate-coloured teeth and mottled gums. I swear this woman had wrinkles in places I'd never seen before. She alluded cheerfully to halfway houses, a daughter long since given up for adoption, and an old flame living in a Detroit penitentiary whom she liked to visit from time to time. "So you get why I don't come cheap," she concluded, stretching out her sandals and admiring a farrow of toes playfully crawling one over the other like unruly piglets. "But I'm fast and I won't slam you on the hours."

Everything about Pamela should have been heartbreaking, but nothing was. I looked at the flimsy wad of my manuscript and couldn't think of a single reason not to hire her.

Pamela was soon working for us three times a week. She arrived mid-morning in an ancient Dodge stippled with rust. She drove like a *Pulp Fiction* character: insanely fast, Sonic Burger in hand, fag jammed between her lips. It's a long and deeply rutted road from town up to our barn, and the Dodge didn't always make it intact. It was not unusual to see her freewheeling the final hundred yards down to the deck holding her burning exhaust pipe out the window and hollering at the children to fetch duct tape.

The interior of her car was an artwork that might have been short-listed for the Turner Prize under the title *Everything I Have Ever Consumed*. The upholstery was yellowed by nicotine, the seats dotted by cigarette burns and tacky with Gatorade. If the clutch was sometimes difficult to depress it would be due to the pile-up of browning banana skins wedged beneath it. The floor was littered with spent cartons of red wine, and every time Pamela opened the driver's door, she triggered an avalanche of crumbling Styrofoam.

This might not have been the greatest CV for home help, but it turned out she was a fiend with the broom and had an Olympian skill for folding laundry, even if everything she washed came out of the machine the same colour.

When I suggested the dividing of loads into whites and colours, she declared: "That's a myth. I don't buy into any of that holistic, organic crap." Before long the whole family was dressed à la Pamela in outfits of fatally bagging greige, but who cared? I was back working. As far as achieving something, we are all given a finite amount of time. The more of it I spent in the real world, the less accessible my imaginary one became. I still didn't understand how this trade-off worked, but I knew that each time I went through the magic wardrobe, I was leaving lost children behind me. Pamela might not be the obvious choice to bring balance to our lives, but help, as the saying goes, comes in unexpected ways.

Cleaning was far from Pamela's only skill. She had a degree in evolutionary psychology, "plus," she informed us, "I cook real good, too." I never dared take her up on the offer, but occasionally, standing at the stove, I'd hear the familiar slap of flip-flops behind me. "Scoot!" she'd order, hip-bumping me out of the way. "Cookin' relaxes me." And I'd watch, helpless, as she stirred into my black bean soup ash from the tip of her cigarette along with the cache of flies off her sun visor, many of which weren't actually dead but had been resting against the orange plastic as if kicking back against the windshield of a yacht and enjoying the view.

Pamela may not have liked children, but they were very taken with her. Within days Jesse and Sam began scripting a sitcom based on her imagined home life with an idler of a husband who lounged around in soiled Carhartts while Pamela served up retaliatory cat-food dinners and beer full of spit. In no time at all, the whole family was talking in Pamela's vernacular, but this was safe to do only once she was done with work and careening down the mountain again. Not only did Pamela's knowledge span an eclectic variety of subjects, she was also blessed with supernatural hearing.

Yes, Pamela could hear a watch tick in space. She could hear water bubbling in the earth's shallow crust. She was everywhere and nowhere. Say the discussion turned—as discussions sometimes do—to Meat Loaf's real name. Pamela would switch off the vacuum cleaner and from the other side of the room drawl, "Oh, that'll be Michael Lee Aday." No matter how obscure the question, no matter how far she was from its point of origin, Pamela had the answer. "That'll be Kissinger!" she'd say, emerging from the charred intestines of the grill.

"Sweet Jesus, will ya check in the Book of Genesis?" she'd shout up from the hinterland of the basement.

The only time Pamela had trouble hearing was when it came to actual cleaning instructions.

"You want me to dust the *what*?" she said, tapping dustpan and brush against her crepey leggings.

"The baseboards?"

"Why, in God's name?"

"They're dirty."

"Nobody looks down there!"

"The tops of the pictures too, if you wouldn't mind."

"Say again?"

"The tops of the pictures?"

"Goddamnit, I'm tall as a stork and I never had the urge to look that high. Don't waste my time."

Right again. As long as the bears weren't snuffling through the garbage, as long as our pillowcases weren't infested with earwigs, what did it matter? Sometimes you need someone to come along and teach you how to prioritize.

Whenever Pam's workload became too heavy she conscripted the children to active duty. They became adept at keeping the animal traps baited, and her habit of heckling them, whilst necking beer from the bottle, only drove them to try harder as they struggled in and out of biting storms, arms piled high with firewood. Honestly, things seemed to be coming good for all of us.

At some point during her assemblage of careers, Pamela had been a counsellor of sorts, and she'd certainly developed a refreshing way of dealing with self-aggrandizement.

"You any good at that?" she'd demand, each time I settled in front of the computer.

"OK, I guess."

"Got anything to say that ain't bin said already?"

"Uh . . . well, I'm trying . . ."

"Those words gonna mean something to anybody apart from you?"

I'd scuff my heels and stare at my sentences, helplessly trying to squeeze some divine truth from them.

This cut no ice with Pamela. "Well, it ain't no rhetorical question. Will they or won't they?"

"Probably not."

"No wonder you got pain in your back, slumped all day at that thing. Shut it down and help me fold this goddamn sheet."

I did as she said. Moreover, on top of every page of text I took to scribbling Pamela's initials, along with Voice! Point! Universal truth! Just as a reminder that pretty much everything else could be incinerated.

After she'd been with us awhile, Pamela began to bring items up to the house that she figured we might be interested in buying. The first time she delved into her knotted black garbage bag we feared the worst, but out came a first edition of an Ansel Adams book, for which she asked five dollars. "And don't you dare smoke me on the price!" she warned. The following month she arrived with a four-by-six-foot Magnum poster of *The Magnificent Seven*. "I know how y'all like this film crap," she said, hauling it out of the back of the Dodge and staggering up the steps with it on her back.

"Where do you get all this stuff, Pamela?" I wondered.

"Folks who don't need it no longer," was all she'd say.

The print was in wonderful condition and signed. The framing alone was worth two hundred dollars.

"Yours for twenty," Pamela said.

Despite her modest prices on these finds, Pamela had indeed begun slamming us on the hours. "Yeah, I don't really work that way," she said, brushing aside the time sheet I eventually produced. "So what if I'm a little off here or there. God help me, I'm worth the extra, and it's not like you're gonna do it, right?"

She had a point.

"You wouldn't have a prayer without me," Pamela liked to remind me every now and again. "My time is a gift, and don't you forget it."

One morning, eating cereal, I noticed that the milk didn't taste right. Its texture was so watery it barely constituted nutrition. I checked the carton in the fridge. I AM THE 2% the slogan proclaimed. I placed the carton back in the door shelf, feeling the thermo-chill in the air. Was that me as a mother? Diluted? If time was a gift and I was giving 98% of it to writing, then Pamela, even with her egregious clock punching, was heaven-sent. So I suppressed my doubts, hoping that, as with the colour of our Pamela-laundered clothing, the money would all wash out even in the end.

From time to time Pamela complained of loneliness. "Oh, it's not the sex," she'd remark to four-year-old Mabel, who she'd taken to treating as a confidante. "Sex I can get anywhere. It's the companionship, know what I mean?"

The children proposed a match with Rabbit Charlie, who lived in the woods in a classic silver Airstream, which he shared with a hundred floppy-eared rabbits. Rabbit Charlie had pellucid blue eyes and immaculately combed white hair. It was rumoured that he'd once been a Mr. Chips–style philosophy professor undone by the death of his wife, though an equally reliable source claimed he'd never so much as kissed a woman. The only thing that convinced me the relationship was ill-starred was an image of Pamela skinning his beloved rabbit family, one after the other, asserting, "Hey, a girl's gotta eat, don't she?" Turned out, though, Pamela had her own recipe for romance.

The first time she brought Sean to meet us, he walked into the barn with the jerky motions of a man who'd exchanged his daily shot of home brew for a snort of Clorox. Whatever his tipple, it wasn't doing much for his health. He was so skinny he could have hired himself out as a draft stopper, and in the harsh mountain light the whites of his eyes looked as if they'd been poached in saffron.

Pamela was smitten. The boob tubes were traded in for sprigged blouses that, tied girlishly over the leggings, resulted in a fashion statement dangerously close to Laura Ingalls Wilder let loose on PCP.

On discovering we were avid fans of "collectibles," Sean, who had a burgeoning career in This&That, decided to take over sales. "I got some real good shit," he boasted, dragging a sticky burr out of his beard and examining it curiously. Within a week he'd turned up with a set of cotton sheets printed with buttercups that appeared to have been extracted from beneath his dying, incontinent grandmother. "Bargain at a hundred and fifty," he stated.

"Pamela, you sure about this guy?"

She shook her head in disgust. "Ya think you can count on your friends to be happy for you, but in the end, jealousy bites everyone in the ass."

Pamela's billing became increasingly erratic. "I'm charging you double the hours I worked," she announced, openly taking a slug of tequila from the bottle we kept in the cupboard, "because that's how long a regular person would take to get around the place." When I demurred, she asked for a raise. "People like me don't just grow on trees ya know!"

Besides, Sean needed to make bail. Sean needed to make a down payment on his La-Z-Boy. Sean could really use a mini-break in Reno.

"Pamela, this guy is bleeding you dry," I told her.

"Hey," she retorted. "It's a helluva man that lets a girl pay his bills without getting all edgy." Pamela was nothing if not street-smart, but loneliness can get the better of anyone. We knew Sean was to blame for her ripping us off, just as he was to blame for her knavish timekeeping and distillery breath, but after every last drop of alcohol had finally disappeared from the house, we knew something had to be done.

When it came to firing her, I practised in front of the mirror all morning. However, as soon as I heard her car belching up the track to the house, my nerve deserted me and I came over all politically correct.

"Whaddaya mean you're letting me go?" she demanded. "Go where?"

"Um, we need to try something new for the house."

"Like what?" she snorted. "Not cleaning it?"

I mumbled something.

"You know your problem?" she said, and I cowered at what might be coming. "I know what I want, and I ain't afraid to go out and get it, but you—" She pointed a prophetic finger at me like the wicked godmother at a doomed christening. "You will *never* be happy."

Charlene came next. She was a chatterbox, the kind you end up sitting next to on planes when you have a career-making presentation to deliver on landing. Tonya was obese and ate only coleslaw from large rancid vats she kept in the fridge; Meghan, Chinese by way of

California, had bouncy Herbal Essences hair and came with references from a family restaurant in Los Angeles. When the proprietor said to us, "Oh, she's a conscientious one, all right—a real busy bee," we failed to detect the irony in his voice. Meghan lived in for the summer, and by day she was marvellous. As soon as we'd gone to bed, though, she'd emerge from her room to unload the dishwasher and aggressively pass a broom across the floor.

"Hey, Meghan," I said, the first time this happened. "You really don't need to be working so late."

"Is working hard a problem?" she replied, her voice rising dangerously.

Night after night, to the noise of the oven being dismantled or the floorboards re-grouted, Mac and I lay upstairs blinking wretchedly into the darkness of our bedroom—the ugly employers trying to get their beauty sleep while poor Cinders toiled below. It felt so churlish to complain. Two weeks into her contract, Meghan was gone, hitching a lift back to California with the FedEx guy, who must have been moved by her tales of domestic slavery.

Just when I was ready to concede that there wasn't a single Mary Poppins left in the world, Tom showed up. One moment the old black camper van in which he kept his life was parked outside the barn, and the next there he was, on the deck, explaining the intricacies of bow stringing to the children. They made their first kill within minutes, and even though their target was a ratty cork deer with three legs and a singed ear, they were hooked.

Tom had thick black hair hanging in waves down to a pronounced hunch on his back. He was, as he was fond of reminding us, 25% Cherokee, though he was more reticent about the remaining 75%. His nose was aquiline and his features so pointed that even when not in profile he reminded me of the Flatiron Building in New York. He'd been a boxer in his younger days, but there wasn't much muscle left on him, only a sinewy cabling threaded under his skin that did a barely adequate job of connecting limbs to torso. His movements were so out of concert with one another it looked as if invisible hands were working his arms and legs with strings and a paddle. When I asked him what happened to his boxer's frame, he looked sad and said, "I lost it"—as though it were a bottle of duty-free bourbon he'd carelessly left on a flight.

As soon as the kids became proficient with their bows, Tom asked permission to take them to the woods, in which sacred environment he intended to impart hunting methods gleaned from his Indian ancestors. I thought this was an outstanding idea, and it certainly beat their regular entertainment—committing multiple homicides on Grand Theft Auto whilst listening to Slim Shady endorsing lesbian rape on the CD player.

For weeks they returned forlorn and empty-handed, until one evening Tom slapped a baby grouse—wretchedly premature and out of season besides—onto the kitchen table with such pride and gusto anyone would have thought he'd felled the mighty bison.

"Oh, Great Spirit, whose voice I hear in the wind," he intoned, "hear my thanks for the harvest of one of your creations." He plucked an arrow from the soft leather quiver slung around his neck and ostentatiously began cleaning it. "May your hand be always steady and this arrow tip forever straight."

This last was too much for Sam, who leaned forwards and whispered, "Mum, just so you know, he caught it with a butterfly net."

Tom liked to take local schoolchildren on what he called "wilderness adventures," a program billed as "an invigorating way for the earth's

sons and daughters to better get to know themselves in a safe environment." If the first part of this statement was true, the latter definitively
was not. Tom was the kind of man who alerted you to the presence of
a banana skin only once you'd slipped on it and shattered your pelvis.
There was also something dodgy about his eyesight—dodgy in a way
that might have benefited from a white stick and a dog.

We grew very fond of Tom, but you sent your children outward
bound with him if not at your own risk then certainly at theirs. Students could look forward to an instructive week of camping in the
desert—inadvertently shacked up with a nest of rattlesnakes that he'd
mistaken for old coils of ranching rope. Others had to be winched
up from the bottom of a slot canyon whose narrow opening Tom
had admired as a sliver of shade in the hot desert sun. If these exciting overnight packages were too free-range for some parents, they
suited our family well. Tom was the embodiment of the children's
wilderness-survival fantasy, even if, in terms of survival, he was also
their greatest threat.

When the boys grew tired of whittling arrows, Tom pulled two
pairs of old red leather boxing gloves out of the bottomless carpetbag
of his van.

"I had these from way back," he told us, "and I never let 'em out of
my sight."

Boxing is all about technique, and though Tom's instructional
punches were about as intimidating as puppy ears, his inspirational
cries of "I could make you a champ!" were taken by the kids as an open
invitation to pull on the gloves and beat him to a pulp.

The Cherokee were a horse and warrior people, too busy migrating
and organising war societies to cultivate trays of wheatgrass. Nevertheless, according to Tom the ancient code of his tribe decreed that a
vegetable smoothie was the antidote to all of life's ailments. Whatever

the diagnosis, irrespective of the colour-code of emergency, the cure could be found in the dregs of Tom's Cuisinart. "*That mean ol' rattler git ya? Arrow through the eye? Crop failure? Heck, I can fix that,*" he'd murmur, handing over a glass of sludge that tasted like puréed Middle Earth. Only with hindsight is it easy to appreciate how ahead of the curve he was.

Another thing Tom was excellent at was fixing backs. He was a certified practitioner of a physical therapy known as the Trager Approach. As explained, this treatment had something to do with "mentastics." In practice, it translated as a vigorous all-over body shaking. *Broken neck? Tax bill? Pancreatitis?* Tom would probe deep inside you and then toss the offending body part from one bony hand to the other. I like a good shaking as much as the next person, but there was a downside to spending an hour having my back fixed by Tom. It's dangerous to make assumptions, particularly in the landmine area of another man's politics, but the mud cocktails, the Cherokee wisdom, and the peripatetic lifestyle all pointed to Democratic sensibilities. Tom, however, was a fully indoctrinated Tea Party bigot, the kind mandated by Rush Limbaugh, and his massage table was the place where he most liked to expound his extremist views.

"George Bush?" he'd say, grasping my head and dribbling it from hand to hand as though practicing a fingertip drill. "Oh, sure, he's a great guy. He's doing a wonderful job killing all them 9/11 people. Then he's gonna blow up that whole country."

"You don't mean that, Tom. What about the women and kids?"

"Oh, the kids'll throw anthrax in your face," he'd say, in his melodious voice. "Sooner we get rid of them the better."

If your neck hadn't been the problem before, it would now be locked in a vicious spasm. "Rumsfeld?" Tom would continue, pulling on my earlobes as if they were Play-Doh. "Just the sorta guy you'd want your daughter to bring home to meet the folks. Cheney's a sweetheart too."

There were choices. Toss him off the property or accept the principle of the First Amendment and engage in the argument. But if you imagine it's easy to hold a coherent debate while your head is being mentasticked from side to side, think again. It's all I could do to keep my tongue in my mouth, let alone use it for political protest. If I had a stronger moral backbone, I would have refused treatment and taken a Tylenol. Of course, if I'd had a stronger moral backbone, I wouldn't have needed Tom in the first place. And the fact was,—phantom back pain, unfinished manuscript, bored kids—Tom fixed them all.

This was the post-9/11 world, though, and not much could fix that. Even the famously clean air of southwestern Colorado was polluted by suspicion. Neighbours of twenty years viewed each other warily over the fence, and in spite of the pride Tom took in his Cherokee bloodline, there was nothing he mistrusted more than a hint of colour in another man's face, especially should that face happen to surface in our local town. Hunting down newborn grouse was all very well, but Tom's dream was to personally prove himself to President Bush by ripping out the heart of a fully matured terrorist cell.

"By the breath of the Great Buffalo," he said, knocking back a shot of cabbage juice. "Just once before my time's up."

It was during these difficult times that we saw less and less of Tom, and once again progress on the writing slowed, the nerves in my back flared, and the kids turned snitty. As in the post-Pamela era, I realised how much I'd banked on those quiet hours when the children were roaming the forest living on mildly poisonous berries and Cherokee lore. In terms of word count, Tom's patriotism was costing me dearly.

What drove him, I wondered? If I hadn't been so preoccupied by my own back, I might have pondered the strange configuration of Tom's. Had past disappointments formed that hunch of his?

"See, I was never a champion boxer," he told me one day. "And only an adequate healer. All I ever wanted was to succeed."

I empathised on so many levels. I was never a champion designer either. I'd stumbled into fashion with no training, and it was luck I lasted as long as I did. I started my company when I was nineteen, and for a while I was ahead of the game, but I'd been no match for the deadening mindset of corporate strategy. My friends had graduated from university to take over the world, while I'd been left behind, woozy and bloodied against the ropes. Starting over can be tough. I knew all about the desire for a comeback.

But if my work had stalled, Tom's perseverance was about to pay off. One day, in the town's hardware store, he came across a man of "dubious" colour, browsing the industrial-adhesive aisle. Given that our local town is peopled by an even ratio of Navajo, Mexican, and white ranching families—the last of whom are unfamiliar with the concept of sunblock—it's disconcerting to work out how Tom came to the "dubious" part of his diagnosis. I'm guessing a definitive black person would have been fine, but those troubling tones in between?

"Uh-oh," Tom said, "I can fix that," and lost no time alerting the FBI. Agents of that august bureau reacted swiftly to this potential terrorist threat. They subpoenaed the till receipts from the hardware store by e-mail, then rang up the individual in question and left a message on his answering machine, the transcript of which went something like this:

> Hey, sir! How are you today? It's come to our attention that you are a dubious individual! We can't say how we came by this information

because, you know, it's classified. But if you are one—uh, that is to say, an individual who is dubious—could you please call the FBI at your earliest convenience on our 1-800 help line. Thank you, and have a good one!

The recipient of this message was Japanese. There are no secrets in small towns. Ridicule can kill ambition faster than anything. Tom quickly lost his zest for the business of terrorist hunting and disappeared out of our lives, leaving a note on top of a stack of zucchini. *Oh, Great Spirit, when a man outlives his usefulness, let him sing his song and surrender like a hero going home.*

One day in Walmart, while cruising the pain-relief aisle, I bumped into Pamela. She was sheathed in a Denver Broncos tank top tucked into a pair of perforated nylon shorts. She had a new green sun visor on her head, price tag still swinging off the back.

"Well, look what the coyote's spat up!" She gave me the once-over. "You look like shit."

I muttered something about my back being sore.

"Ha! All that picking up after yourself I suppose."

I mumbled something else.

"You were a fool to forsake me."

I managed a third non-committal grunt, but Pamela was on a roll. "House still standing?" she demanded, legs quivering with schadenfreude.

"Sean still around?" My tongue—thank God—there it was.

"That book you was writing done yet?"

"I'm working on it."

"Oh yeah? How those kids growing up?"

"Time will tell." I plucked a box of Tylenol Extra Strength off the shelf and snapped five capsules into my mouth.

"You was always crap at identifying what really matters. I was the best thing that coulda happened to you."

"Maybe you were, maybe you weren't." I checked Pamela's basket: Gatorade, bananas, and Pall Malls. This was the old Pamela, the pre-Sean Pamela. Her hands had made it to her hips now. My God, she was magnificent. Skinny, stringy-haired, straight-backed. The most gorgeous, hideous Wonder Woman I'd ever seen.

Pamela pursed her codfish lips. She'd always had a sharp eye for weakness. "You know ya want me back, so you might as well come clean and admit it."

I shrugged.

"Whatever, but let's get one thing clear, lady. I'm gonna have to put up my rate."

Two days later she arrived at the barn with a green recycling bag slung over one shoulder.

"Here ya go." She unknotted the top and tipped four pairs of boxing gloves onto the long table.

Something small flipped in my heart.

"Where did you get these, Pamela?"

"I told ya. Folks who don't need 'em no more."

I picked up the gloves and held the worn red leather to my cheek. What price Tom's ambitions? The stakes are high and failure leads to dark places. Maybe he'd made the mistake of punching above his weight. I knew all about that one, too, but what of it? Give up dreaming your dreams and your dreams begin haunting you.

"So, you want 'em or not?" Pamela demanded.

"Sure," I said. "How much?"

WITH APOLOGIES TO SAM SHEPARD

The night before we left London to spend the summer out West one year, Mac and I were invited to a play by some acquaintances. If the date was something of a mutual butt-sniffing exercise, their suggestion of the theatre was hardly auspicious. I don't like the theatre. It's not the lack of popcorn, or even those seats that encourage deep-vein thrombosis in anyone with legs longer than a terrapin's; I don't enjoy the theatre because I'm not seduced by the medium of the play. The coy subtlety of the metaphor, those sneaky idioms, *soliloquies* of all things, when you least expect one. I've never considered myself a person with literalist sensibilities, but I have only to see a wooden stage and a safety curtain for suspension of disbelief to fail me. All that flying spittle and hot breath pluming under the lights like genie smoke. Onstage it's only too obvious that actors are, well, *acting.*

These days I never agree to a theatre expedition without checking whether it's possible instead to watch the box set of the TV series derived from the hit movie loosely based on—or better yet, vaguely inspired by—the original play in question.

Thankfully, I married a man cut from the same philistine cloth. I'd go as far as saying that the lack of appreciation Mac and I share for this art form is part of the glue that keeps our odd-shaped marriage together. But this play, our would-be friends assured us, oh, yes, this play, *ne paniquez-pas*, was different.

Written by Sam Shepard, about whom I've had lurid sexual fantasies ever since his turn as wry veterinarian in the romantic comedy

Baby Boom, if *Buried Child* was not quite what I'd first hoped—i.e., the heartbreaking sequel to *Baby Boom*—it had, according to the program, scored a Pulitzer Prize.

"Marvellous," I said. "What's it about?"

"Really fucked-up people," Mac whispered, slipping a box of sweeties into my pocket.

Our friend leaned over. "I hope you won't find yourself too unsettled by the author's deconstruction of the grand narrative."

I nodded sagely.

"And then the material encompasses so many postmodern elements . . ."

Uh-huh, uh-uh. I slammed a fruit pastille into my mouth wishing Mac had invested in the jumbo-size box. I looked around. If our fellow theatregoers belonged to a cultured, bon vivant London that we had once vaguely recognized, perhaps our lean towards the West had now fatally blunted our critical aesthetic. But then the play's tag line jumped out at me: *The breakdown of the American dream in a context of violence, disillusionment, and disappointment.* I perked up. Violence, disillusionment, and disappointment had recently become my three preferred landscapes. "Disappointment, you know," I boasted to our new friends, "is the actual name of a valley not far from our barn in America."

"Oh, that's right," the husband said. "You sort of live out there these days, don't you?"

"Well, not really live—"

"Ah, a holiday home," he said dismissively. "Of course, Shepard's work covers less, er . . . shall we say 'bourgeois' territory."

"Of course," I said, chastened.

"Shepard is a master of the visceral as a metaphor for family discourse." The wife slid a hand onto her husband's knee. "But if you two don't have the stomach for it, we can always leave."

"Yes, we don't mind at all," her husband agreed affably. "We've seen eight productions of *Buried Child* already—three of them," he added, as a hush descended on the room, "Steppenwolf."

Under the cover of darkness, Mac rolled his eyes.

Clump, clump, boots onstage. Curtain up. Lights down. The play began.

I can't find a thing wrong with Shepard's work. I hope more than ever that we will one day meet and become lovers. *Buried Child* is very brilliant without a doubt, and I feel certain that it must be very postmodern too, but after twenty minutes I exchanged perplexed glances with Mac. The so-called visceral material? There was nothing to it really—a bit of murder, a dab of incest. And as for the dreadful secret at the play's end—well, you could say the title was something of a spoiler.

As the final curtain fell and the actors were clapped back onstage, I decided I was, after all, shocked by *Buried Child*. Shocked that Sam Shepard appeared so intimately acquainted with the domestic landscape of our own southwestern terrain. Shocked, too, that having decided to write a play about it, he'd chosen such a mundane incident as its subject matter.

"Only one measly buried child," I muttered, still rankled by the holiday home dig, "*and am I right in thinking it was barely even mutilated?*"

When we'd told our friends that we'd built a house in Colorado, I guess they were thinking après-ski boots and chunky knits patterned with snowflake intarsia. It's possible they were picturing some crazy stone mansion filled with bald eagle sculptures and freshly ironed real-estate magazines, and perhaps up in the north, in Vail or Aspen, that's the way it rolls. OK, so maybe we are ghastly holiday homers, but we're still a long way from *that* kind of life.

*   *   *

Fly with the crow through mountain passes dotted with the bones of settlers, wade down rivers flowing with the sweat of long-forgotten miners, scramble along rocky overhangs still owned by coyote and mountain lion, and you will eventually drop down into a valley of golden forests where the wilderness blows right through you. Here, in places, is the residue of an older era, one trading in a different currency, speaking another language, and upholding its own moral code. Insular, self-governing, and survivalist. Its combination of wide-open space and suffocating isolation breeds an alternative kind of horror to inner-city deprivation. For all the West's spectacular scenery, there's something damaged about this part of the country. There are no metaphors out here, no subtexts. This *is* the breakdown of the American dream, and you can pick pieces of it off the ground and carry them around in your pocket.

And my theatre friends were wrong: I couldn't have more of a stomach for it.

At the foot of our mountain lies the high desert and in the high desert lives John, a Welshman who has become a gateway to this, our West. A maverick with an intellect sharp as a tungsten blade and a babyish sense of humour to rival that of my five-year-old, instead of shaking my hand the first time we met, he picked me up and threw me into the back of his truck. When I giggled, he said, "You'll do, girl," and I've been half in love with him ever since. Stocky, with a barrel chest and a cleft hacked deep into his chin, John too is a figure from an earlier era. A man whose Evelyn Waugh mannerisms and pristine use of the Queen's English form an entirely accurate representation of who he is while at the same time masking something wholly other.

John may not be representative of the *American dream in a context of violence, disillusionment, and disappointment*, but down in the desert he's surrounded by it.

Up at the barn we have the best of neighbours—homesteaders and oddbods who, say our property is being overrun by varmints, waste no time rushing to our assistance with a friendly smirk and a wide selection of weaponry. Our neighbours dance with us, drink with us, and willingly haul us out of ditches, day or night. These are the kind of people who don't care where you come from or who you are. They either like you or don't. Their friendship burns slow, but once you have it, it's yours for good.

Nature, though, is engaged in a continual war of opposites, and between our mountain and John's canyon lives a different kind of neighbour, the kind tucked into gulches, hidden dents, and depressions, where the sign for Lee's Spare Parts Shop leads to the tinkle of wind chimes hung from a trailer saturated in the piss of thirty cats; the kind who lives beyond the mailbox that receives no mail, the mailbox whose address—9 THE WOODS—is daubed on its side in some smeary red ooze that could be paint but almost certainly is not.

Duck under the rope strung between trees. Creep past the bullet-ridden sign marked PRIVATE. Ignore the hairs on your arm, raised and trembling, and follow the whispering leaves along a track rutted with wildflowers and jagged with mining debris. Down you go, down to the bitter end, where the very air feels disturbed and nature's sanctity plundered. Here, in a clearing of weeds, semi-circled by neat monuments of animal bones, sits a solitary cabin, adorned with hummingbirds, their jeweled wings stretched obscenely wide and nailed to the wall above a half-hinged door it would be a mistake to open. These are not the kind of people from whom you borrow a cup of sugar.

In London "don't diss your neighbours" means don't let your dog poop on their front step or don't wake them early on a Sunday morning with an ear-splitting rendering of "Boogie Wonderland" from the shower. Common-sense rules based on the urban proximity of matchbox living—because in a city of matchboxes, nobody should be thinking about lighting a fire. John's tip for our West? Diss no one. When some stranger in a pickup overtakes you on a perilous bend, remember one thing: You're not flipping off an individual. You're flipping off an entire clan.

Behind one of these half-hinged doors live the McKinneys, four siblings known by everyone, seen by few. The eldest brother, Garrett, bedded his sister as well as his middle brother's thirteen-year-old daughter. A year or two later Gideon, the youngest, tried to kill Garrett, throttling him to unconsciousness, then floating his body down the creek. As it happened, this scuffle was not about the incest but a niggardly piece of land amid the brothers' various properties. When details of the sexual molestation and attempted murder finally surfaced, there was a distinct lack of outrage in the community. The brothers come from a revered, if crazy, clan, and there's the sense that a little fingering can go on within any family, especially one as isolated and deliberately old-fashioned as theirs.

Abe, their father, lives further down the same road and brews crystal meth, which he bootlegs to the Navajo on the rez. The first time John told me Abe had two bodies buried in his backyard, I did a quick ghoulish drive-by, looking for signs of displaced earth or a little sun-dried pinky budding up through the wild onions. Then I discovered that "having a body in your backyard" was a euphemism for having killed a man without serving jail time.

Abe's first victim was his wife's lover, whom, in the time-honoured fashion, he found in the sack with his wife. Execution was clearly called for. Mrs. Abe knew the risk involved—as did her lover—and Abe knew no other response. After all, a man has to satisfy not only himself but also the expectations of his peers. The few days he ended up in custody for this first murder were essentially to give the sheriff enough time to file the paperwork. Abe spared his wife because men like Abe like to believe that a woman's infidelity is about weakness not wickedness. The second body in Abe's backyard belonged to a Navajo boy who had come looking for him for some perceived slight or other. They fired at each other simultaneously. Shame for the boy that he was holding a little .22 while Abe was in possession of a .357 Magnum. The boy died. Abe didn't even go to the doctor, and this time the sheriff couldn't be bothered with the paperwork.

The first time I met Ulysses, one of John's neighbours down the canyon, he was standing by John's pickup truck wearing a butcher's coat smeared with dried blood. He looked like a human splatter painting. When he said he'd been trying to pull a breached lamb from its mother's womb, I saw a flash of something in his eye, as though he were enjoying a private joke. Later John's wife, Emily, the local ob-gyn, told me that Ulysses had got so impatient with the birthing process, he'd truncated it by chopping sheep and lamb to death.

John shares this American stage with these characters. He drinks with them, rides with them, and understands the ethics that govern them. They, in turn, have got used to his uniquely English brand of genial aggression. "My dear boy," he might say, while wrestling a man into the ditch for calling his Mexican foreman a *beaner*. "Back down, old chap," I've heard him suggest cordially, chest-bumping a machete-wielding rancher who had taken issue with him over water rights. "This is not how we do things, mate," he once remarked to a three-hundred-pound

Ute Indian, before breaking the man's nose over his brutal treatment of a dog. Prior to settling in southwestern Colorado, John was a restaurateur in New York, a professional polo player in Charleston, a buckaroo in Nevada, and a scholar at Reed College in Oregon. If he's anything, though, with his scars and dirty clothes and blackened nails, he's still the British SAS officer he was before. John holds other men to his own standards of fairness, and they in turn, recognise him as their opposite and their equal. If they didn't, he'd be dead by now.

Mac, who loves much about the West, is not so taken with this seamier side. He does not like broken or dirty, whereas I can be careless. He likes organised but I don't mind the tumbleweed of uncertainty. I tend to forget that, like John, I too am split between cultures, while Mac is the most English of Englishmen, and sometimes that makes us more foreign to each other than we care to admit. If Mac hoards his darkness inside, I seek mine out in shadowy places. And thus, almost without noticing, he and I have begun to sketch out lines of divide.

That first day John threw me into the truck, I saw something in his eyes—an irrepressible spark, a smudge of wild as marked as a coloboma of the iris. John intuitively knows what I'm looking for, because he's out there looking for it too—strange people and new ideas and a surrealist's road full of unexpected twists. I like warming my fingers on the edge of danger, and the more I seek it out, the more I tell myself that I too can become its opposite and its equal. As I dusted down my jeans, John put out his hand. "C'mon, girl," he said and I looked back at Mac, because I knew that if I took it, John could pull me down a hole so deep that Mac would find it hard to follow.

It was the summer of *Buried Child* that I took a quick road trip to New Mexico with my father. Our truck was in the garage, so we rented a car from the airport—situated, as it happens, close to Abe's backyard and next to Lee's urine-saturated Spare Parts Shop. At the Venture booth, we negotiated a contract with a perfectly delightful sales agent who, for reasons of personal safety, I've decided to call Peta Thorn. On our returning the car sometime later, it turned out Ms. Thorn was made not of apple pie as billed but of something infinitely sourer. There isn't a driver in the world unfamiliar with the small print of car-rental crookery. Even Mac advised me to shrug off the $160, but turns out I'm petty that way. Besides, Peta Thorn's rip-off smacked of opportunism. Nobody likes to be treated as a gullible tourist when beginning to fancy themselves as a local. When Peta refused to back down, I drove home and fumed through six hours of *Lonesome Dove*, from which I drew the following conclusions: *Institutional rot runs deep. You can't rely on justice, better to take care of things yourself.*

While I appreciate that if everyone took the Hammurabian eye, the world would go blind, who said anything about Peta's eye? A refund on Dad's credit card was all I was after.

Vengeance requires planning. A trajectory. In the weeks that followed, whenever I found myself close to the airport—and hey, no big deal, it was only a ninety-minute drive away—I'd hunker down in my truck and wait for the moment when Ms. Thorn tripped out to the rental bay with keys and a client. As soon as she clack-clacked round the corner I moved with the stealth of a Sioux tracker. *Out of the truck, across the car park. A deft right hook to the swing-door button, and I was in.* Snatch a fistful of business cards from the Venture counter, foolishly left unattended by Peta, and across them I'd scribble:

I AM A CRIMINAL

Or:

I BELONG IN JAIL

Or even this one, of which I was particularly proud:

I WISH I WERE TRUSTWORTHY
BUT I'M NOT!

Sometimes, depending on my mood, I underlined these statements, sometimes not.

At first there was no reaction. The cards were kept in a help-yourself container, and I worried Peta hadn't noticed or, worse, had decided to adopt a hateful Christian cheek-turning approach. After several weeks, though, I was rewarded by the sight of her clients blundering out to their rentals unaccompanied. *Nice try, Peta, but hardly a deterrent!* After all, everyone has to pee sometime, and she was, I'd observed, a big fan of the soda machine. Occasionally, lurking in the ladies' room myself, I'd head off her potential customers at the hand dryer. Tiny though our local airport is, two competing rental companies had managed to squeeze in their booths. *Word in your ear, girlfriend,* I'd whisper, helpfully punching the dryer's on button for some alarmed bank teller from Albuquerque. *Do yourself a favour. Forget Venture. Try Kestrel!* Though surprised by this new British meet-and-greet directive, visitors to the area paid attention. I like to think that business at Venture tanked while Kestrel profits soared, and in the months that followed, I swear Peta must have aged a thousand years. Not since the hounding of *Les Misérables'* Jean Valjean by police inspector Javert has justice been so diligently pursued. It never occurred to me that my retribution far outweighed Peta's original crime—or that her crime might have been carried out unwillingly in the first place. *Don't matter who it is*, head office might have instructed in the gathering gloom of her job interview. *When the customer returns that vehicle, you stick it to 'em, girl!* And poor Peta, hideously aware of the paucity of jobs in the region, had seen her life's abiding principle of honesty bite the dust. No, Peta's guilt was never in doubt, and with the power of my pen, I thought, gleefully defacing another dozen cards, *I would bring her down.*

"Attribute it to what you like," John once told me. "The West lends itself beautifully to the genre of revenge."

Every time I flew back to my comfy West London life, it seemed flat. How to pass those leaden months until my return? Silver lining? Back in Colorado, Peta never knew when I was coming. Lying in my oversize bed, head cradled by goose-down pillows, I'd fall asleep imagining the crank and twist of her intestines every time a flight touched down. Though mental maths isn't my thing, it wasn't hard to work out three planes a day, times eighteen passengers apiece. I seriously doubted her adrenal gland would cope for much longer.

One July, after this vendetta had been rolling along nicely for a while, my Great Lakes flight dropped onto the runway with its usual fanfare of emergency brakes and passenger prayers. Through the greasy laminate of the window, I could just make out Peta's skirted backside hoofing it to the toilets. Once inside the airport, though jet-lagged and travel-cranky, I still found the time to personalize a few more of her cards:

THERE IS NO PLACE IN HEAVEN
FOR SINNERS LIKE ME.

Done. I headed outside to reclaim my luggage. *Clack clack clack.* I turned. To my surprise, there was Peta, looking, well, simply *awful.*

"Whoa," I said.

Once Peta had been a pleasant-looking woman with a waist and hips soft enough to be squeezed into curves by tight clothes. She'd lost pounds. Her eyes looked itchy and red, as though she'd swiped their lids with paprika, and from the way she was hunched sideways, something was definitely up with her sciatica.

"What happened to you?" I actually don't know why I said this as meanly as I did, but to her credit, Peta let it go.

"I've been wantin' to speak to you." Her tiny child-size teeth were nibbling at the Crayola orange of her lipstick. "Look," she stammered. "What I did was wrong. I know that."

"Uh-uh." I hadn't been consciously trying to intimidate but self-righteousness is dangerously habit forming.

"Please," Peta said. "This has gotta stop. 'Fore someone gets hurt."

"Hurt how?" I scoffed. John had recently alerted me to the where-abouts of the vagus nerve and how to deliver a downwards windmilling blow to it.

"It was a bad time for me," Peta mumbled. "You know . . . back then." Tears gathered in her eyes, her expression that of a pawnshop kitten watching a burlap sack being prepared. "What I'm trying to say is . . ."

Oh cut to the chase, lady. Where's my money?

" . . . I've been havin' a few problems at home."

I softened. God help me, there isn't a woman in the world who can't empathise with "problems at home."

"Anyway, I'm real sorry," she finished.

"Sure," I heard myself saying. "An apology was all I ever wanted." But inside my chest, my heart shivered. What kind of revenge fantasy ends with an apology? This wasn't opposite and equal, this wasn't post-modern or deconstructed. It was a total washout.

"Clean slate?" She stuck out a little paw with a wedding band welded to it.

"Clean slate," I agreed, grudgingly. When we shook hands, hers was tentative—as though she was expecting me to be wearing a metal hand buzzer. *Clack, clack, clack.* Off she tripped in her pumps and viscose skirt. As she went, I noticed a run in the back of her stockings and beneath the nylon mesh a poignant little bruise. *Who wears stockings in hundred-degree heat?* I thought.

The more pertinent question, though, was this: *Now that I had won, what to do with the rest of my life?*

I fantasized about becoming pen pals with Sam Shepard and the inspirational letters he would write me.

Dear Bella,
You can't force a thing to grow. You just gotta wait 'til it pops up out of the ground. Tiny little shoot. Tiny little white shoot. All hairy and fragile. Strong enough. Strong enough to break the earth even.
P.S. I wrote this for Buried Child, *but I think we both know now that I wrote it for you.*
Love, Sam

It helped. A little.

Time passed. The winds grew cooler. The deer hunters came and left. The sky acquired a sickly tinge as the aspen leaves began to blow through the valley. And then one day, a small headline, on page five of the local newspaper:

LOCAL WOMAN MISSING

The article didn't reveal much. Only that Peta Thorn was gone, but the reporter's casual inclusion that "the grounds of her property were being searched" implied so much more. I did a little sleuthing:

Investigation search warrant posted to the Thorns' outbuilding indicated officials were looking for items ranging from human remains to firearms. An inventory list included eight guns, ammunition, shell casings, a sword, hammer, hatchet, drug paraphernalia, and the contents of a burn pile.

Was poor Peta *dead*? And what on earth was a *burn pile*?
The following week, the story moved to page two:
NO BODY PARTS FOUND ON PETA THORN'S LAND!

Not on Peta's land, no, but a small paragraph adjacent to the article announced that a suspect bucket of cement had been discovered in a nearby motel.

Our local town doesn't have much in the way of a crime lab. There was nowhere else for the suspect bucket of cement to go for analysis but back to the airport.

The Venture desk is now manned by Myra, a cheerful paranoid schizophrenic convinced her double-wide is being monitored by the FBI.

"They're clever, I'll give 'em that," she can be heard saying, as she marches clients out to their rentals. "They're trained to leave not so much as a thumbprint—hell, no ways you could ever prove they'd been in. Still, I'm telling ya, these damn devices are so small these days they can hide 'em up a flea's ass."

Inside the terminal, Great Lakes flight 006 was preparing to board. Hardworking Adele had just moved from check-in to security when the sheriff pushed through the door and hauled the bucket of hardened cement onto the conveyer.

"Girl, I wouldn't ask you if it wasn't important," he said. "But whenever you're ready . . ."

I have imagined the scene that followed many times, sometimes in slo-mo, sometimes rinsed through with that extraordinary X-Pro II orange light that renders the opening credits of *CSI Miami* so very compelling:

Adele snaps on her security gloves and grasps her wand. Out comes the grey plastic tray. In go the shoes, wash bag, laptop, and one blue bucket containing . . . What the heck? Adele blinks at the screen and turns pale. "Oh, sweet Jesus," she whispers. "Yep, an unlawful item has been slipped into this one, all right."

*   *   *

It was not Peta in that bucket, if that's what you're worried about. It was her husband's head, separated from its body by her son. If you want the details, and believe me, I'm the last person to judge, then tap "filial rape, patricide, multiple stabbings, dismemberment, skinning, flesh fed coyotes," and—this last one is key—"dog motel" into your computer's search engine. You'll find them easily enough.

Problems at home, Peta had said. *Problems at home.*

On my side of the socioeconomic divide that means the boiler has broken down, your husband is having a midlife crisis, or maybe your teenager has been caught shoplifting a bar of Cadbury's Fruit & Nut.

Had I known poor Peta was married to a man rumoured to be connected with the murder of various local children, a man capable of taking his own son up the mountain with the intention of turning him into "his wife," had I known that her poor boy, abused once too often, would finally snap, I might not have been so quick to take issue with her. I might have had the good sense to steer clear. I might have had a little more heart.

I like to tell myself that I don't enjoy the theatre because it relegates me to the role of spectator, and that's not how I like to learn about the world. I get restless in the back row. I want to climb onto the stage and be pulled into the action, but is there really a difference between those who prefer to watch this stuff from the stalls and those who walk towards it? And if the only difference is proximity, then how close is too close?

I'm OK with being the girl who likes be thrown into the back of a truck, cowboy style, and told I'll "do," but am I really the girl who likes to touch the hand of the woman who sleeps next to the serial killer?

Our West is full of stories like this. They're easy to tell, but they're cheap. Safe in my holiday home, warm in my intarsia-knit sweater, I get so caught up in the fiction of the thing, I forget that for some people it's real.

*   *   *

Had I been Peta, ruthlessly stalked and bullied by some ex-customer over a couple of hundred dollars, I might have exacted my own brand of revenge. After all, she had my driver's license and address on file. It's not as if there weren't several members of her immediate family that she could have sent to remonstrate with me. Turns out, Peta Thorn was made of more principled stuff.

Violence is a tar ball. Prod it and it sticks to you.

I could have got Peta fired.

Problems at home, Peta had said, *problems at home*.

I could have got her *killed* for being fired.

Everyone is the hero of their own life until it's clear they're just another disaster tourist, a grubby voyeur, slowing down to gawp at the motorway smash—a spoiled, entitled, holiday home owner who doesn't have to hold down a full-time job requiring the wearing of itchy tights in hundred-degree heat while trying to protect the members of her family from one another.

Seems I'm the one who owes the apology.

I'm sorry, Peta, wherever you are.

I bet Sam Shepard is also curious about worlds that are different from his. Maybe he too is drawn to the raw and macabre. But I wonder how far he got past the mailbox daubed in blood before he stopped walking and started writing instead.

If I ever get to see *Buried Child* again—and I'm still holding out for Sam and me going together—I will not make quips about there being only one dead baby. The next time I'm invited to witness the break-down of the American dream, I will stay in my seat and be thankful for the sweeties in my pocket.

PARABLE OF FIRE

The electrician stayed for a cold beer after finishing up on the generator. He was a wandering stoner with floppy hair and pale eyelashes. I offered him soup, and he told me his name was Hanson and that his no. 1 meal was catfish, which he rolled in egg and crushed cornflakes before dropping into hot Crisco. The word *catfish* conjured up something prehistoric picking off small children in lakes. Nevertheless I once ate a catfish burger in Memphis and remember it as one of the finest meals of my life.

After he left I wondered what it would be like to live a solitary existence, visited occasionally by strong singular men like Hanson, who'd teach me how to wield a spanner and then slow waltz me to bed before returning home in the tender gloom of first light. It could work. I could make it work. There were a number of these shy western boys, who would thicken into men before eventually becoming Tommy Lee Jones. Any one of them would keep me from the edge of loneliness.

I'd been holed up in the barn for days on end, and the novelty of isolation was wearing off. The solo routine that had once felt so liberating now had me talking to the vegetables with the upbeat self-admonishments of a crazy person. "That was stupid," I remarked to the butternut squash after breaking my little toe on the chair leg. But instead of dispersing into the empty morning, my words were held in the cold tang of air before being echoed back by the walls, a reminder that I was once again alone and would continue to be so for some time. I picked up a Post-it note marked "call home" and, standing in the yellow strip of sunlight from the window, stared at it for an unnecessarily long time.

Any dialogue with the outside world threatened to sever all those strands of thought I'd spooled in my head, so I tended to put off telephone duty until the day had drifted by and the seven-hour time difference made it no longer feasible. Mostly I managed to ignore how bad this made me feel. Expert at cutting conversations short, I faked crackly reception or blamed the horns and whistles of nonexistent trains. In Sydney, another place I'd hidden away for a while, I took to answering any call, irrespective of the hour, in a sleepy voice tinged with mild reproach. "Do you know what time it is?" I'd yawn, whilst jogging through the surfers on Bondi Beach or collecting my evening's takeout from the dim sum bar. My feelings on this grotesque level of subterfuge ranged from thinking I was a genius to suspecting that there was something deeply wrong with me. Still, nobody in the world has ever worked out whether Australia is on their today or somebody else's tomorrow and the interruptions soon dried to nothing.

I stole these weeks, a couple here and there, only now that the children were old enough. Jesse and Sam were at boarding school, the younger two in the puppy-love phase of a new au pair. Even Mac's dance card had been fully marked with football fixtures and curry evenings. No one needed me for a bit, not really. At least, it was OK to believe that, wasn't it? Didn't every woman occasionally yearn to step away from the roles of mother, lover, wife and all the billable hours they entailed, to a place where nobody's needs had to be met but her own?

Mac was supportive of the working mother paradox but found it hard to understand the focus it required, perceiving any move towards myself as a move away from him. I got that. It shut him out of a world that he could never truly be part of—and that was scary for a person who dreaded isolation as much as I sometimes craved it. I was beginning to understand that a relationship is made, not necessarily by how much you have in common with another person, but by your flaws being compatible. What we want and what we need are not always the same. Unable or maybe unwilling to articulate our true feelings, Mac and I had begun sketching out our desires through landscape. I was in love with wilderness, while he was flirting with the English countryside. Roses and hedgerows versus precipices and plains.

A few days earlier he had called for phone sex. The emptiest hours of his night were my suppertime, and I'd answered the phone on autopilot. There were things I'd been rehearsing saying to him, but the unexpected connection sent me into a spiral of panic. I could feel the words in my head disappearing as though I'd opened a can of alphabet soup and poured the contents down the sink. Reluctantly, I'd gone along with it, pretending to strip down naked and lie on the bed, all the while chopping celery and then peppers, my heart constricting. When I risked the blender, attempting to muffle the noise by throwing a tea towel over it, I heard him hesitate.

"What are you doing?"

"Vibrator," I lied, mustering my sexiest voice and congratulating myself on a crisis averted. Only now did it occur to me that he hadn't called back since.

It was the unsayable truth, but to maintain the oneness of first love was to bind each other to a series of impossible expectations. Marriage between two strong-willed people was to repeatedly force irregular shaped pieces of yourself into the jigsaw of another; after a while those pieces became bent out of all recognition. Marriage was a puzzle that required patience and skill to complete, but no matter how often I checked the picture on the lid, there were times when I could no longer get a clear idea of what it was supposed to look like. The conflict this caused was all too familiar, and that's the real reason I was relieved to be out West, on the side of a mountain, on the opposite shore from Mac, with little interest in bridging the gap.

"Love you," he'd said. His official sign-off, and I knew how awful it woud be to tell him I wasn't buying it. I believe in the constancy of give and receive. I believe, too, that love should be proved over and over again. But "love you," like "I'm sorry," can quickly become a complacent phrase, ironed flat of all meaning. Love is not so easily come by and every time I was forced to say it as a reciprocal line to a reflex statement, it became further devalued. "I love you" is something to say when you can't help yourself, when love is flooding out of you like a bath overflowing, seeping over the floor, water marking everything it touches. And this wasn't how either of us was feeling right then.

That night, though, after I'd washed my bowl and played hide-and-seek with an onion that had rolled under the counter, I felt curiously unsettled. The shuttered eyes of the windows appeared to be judging me, and there was a sense of reproach in the shadows of the big room.

I put the unease down to my still-throbbing toe and redrew my boundaries tighter. Upstairs I lit a candle and picked up a book of original fairy tales I'd stumbled over in the local thrift shop. It was an out-of-print copy and might have been valuable had its binding threads not been loose. I read for an hour, reflecting on how much easier it was to buy into the rape of Sleeping Beauty and Cinderella's stepsisters mutilating their feet than the notion of the rageaholic Beast being tamed by Beauty's patience. Anger was an armour that people did not remove willingly. I closed the book and tossed it onto the bed, remembering a W. H. Auden quote and quickly finding a pen to scribble it down: "A fairy tale demands of the reader total surrender; so long as he is in its world, there must be for him no other."

I checked my watch, realised it had stopped ticking, and shook it. An old-fashioned clunky thing, it had been found by the children one winter in the same thrift store and presented with delighted pride. *You say you never have time, Momma, so that's what we're giving you.* The thought was so poignant it had made me cry. The watch face was mounted on leather and bolted to a wrist strap made from five elasticised tortoiseshell links. "One for each of the family," Jesse had said. Considering its age, it was amazing it kept such good time, but as I slipped it off my wrist and tried winding it, the mechanism refused to budge in either direction.

An owl hooted outside. A Navajo once told me the owl was an envoy of the supernatural world symbolizing deception and silent observation. Well, wasn't that why I was here? Weren't deception and observation the building blocks of fiction? I stretched for the David Foster Wallace book in which he'd written something about fiction and really deep serious sex being among the few experiences "where loneliness could be both confronted and relieved." My bed was a patchwork of books and research and pages of manuscript strewn haphazardly over the covers. My work is not tidy, and its manifestations drove Mac nuts— the coffee cups, the spreading paper, the obsessive glare at the screen, often heralding a dinner making it to the table late and—it had to be admitted—carcinogenically burnt. But if creativity cannot be tidied, it can be contained, pushed into a smaller and smaller space. Put enough demands on a person and eventually you will force their focus back to you or split their attention in half. I once read a quote from artist Maggi Hambling about having a crying painting in one room and a crying baby in the other. I got that, too. Of course the "us" of marriage needed honouring, but the more rigid a choice Mac presented, the more fluid I found myself becoming until I began to slip through his fingers.

Behind my eyelids the flickering flame was comforting. Still, the barn was made of reclaimed wood, and what if a spark caught? I looked around at the random kitsch of the room. "What to save in the fire" was a car game the whole family used to play. The children's choices had been predictable—Leonard Rossiter the dog, and stuffed toys when they were small, graduating to Leonard Rossiter the dog and computers as they grew older. But when it came to Mac, it was always the same. "You," he would say. "I'd save you."

"No, you don't get it," I'd tell him. "I'm safe. We're all safe. You can save whatever you like."

"I'd still save you," he'd repeat, and I'd grin and roll my eyes at the children in the backseat. It was so like him to break the rules of the game to prove a point.

The next day I found myself wandering through the barn, wistfully picking up objects as though each represented moments of joy that were gone forever. This was nonsense, of course. A fair amount of these things had been collected in periods of stress and anger, but when I carelessly allowed one to drop—an old painted Donald Duck figurine that I'd given Mac as an anniversary present—I wept so hard anyone would think I'd chucked out our marriage along with the splintered pieces.

It turned out the toe episode was only the beginning. Next it was my shin, whacked on the corner of a plate drawer. Later that afternoon I sliced through my finger with a knife stacked lazily in the dishwasher. In the witching hours of early morning it was my cheekbone meeting with the kitchen's wooden beam, "which is weird, you know," I said to the pack of frozen mince I held to my face, "because I've never sleepwalked in my entire life." Awake after that, I amused myself by writing a review for the soon-to-be-finished book. *The world she created was brutal, yet filled with humour and moments of almost transcendental beauty.* Then, aware of the dull throb in my cheek, I turned it into an epigraph: *Her world may have been one of transcendental beauty, but it was filled with slapstick and moments of painful reality.*

By morning I'd understood the problem. It wasn't that I was suffering from cabin fever—it was the cabin that wanted to be rid of me. My vapid self-recriminations were evidently getting on its nerves. The splayed toe, the dented shin, the sliced finger, and now the bruised cheekbone were all a warning message: *Get out of Dodge, girl, before we hurt you for real.*

"Fine," I said to the empty air. "Fuck you too."

Winter had sneaked into the valley and stolen the leaves from the aspens. Their silver trunks lined up on the distant slopes like an installation of huge darning needles. The air was threaded with sulfur, the ground glittering with frost. Odd, I thought, that with all the time spent staring out the window, I hadn't noticed the change of season. I rolled down the road, admiring an elk grazing on the first bend. After twenty miles I reached the junction to the main road and stopped. To the right was the canyon where John and Emily lived. The four of us had become close over the past years. Turning right would mean warm desert air, John's slow-cooked lamb, and Emily's ob-gyn story of the hour. On any given day her patient load might include a 420-pound Navajo in for a hysterectomy, a dwarf for a smear test, or a Mormon girl wanting advice for her wedding night. After dinner John and Emily would sleep hugga-mugga in the world's narrowest bed, and I'd spend the night counting stars through the tall curtainless window of their spare room.

I turned left towards Telluride, a town that, despite its genuine Butch Cassidy credentials, I was apt to pompously denounce as fake. Telluride was full of well-heeled hippies and creative types, but something told me that this was no time to avoid people just like myself. I wound dreamily along the road, giving in to the landscape, passing the tiny mining community of Rico, the hunched muscular shoulders of Sheep Mountain, and the turn-off to Ophir, a scar of a mountain road cut through scree and so steep that the only time Mac and I had braved it we'd burned out the brakes on the truck. Time passed and I soon found myself approaching the electronic speed sign outside Telluride, whose dots and dashes had heralded Dylan's outdoor concert a year earlier with the endearingly insulting WELCOME BOB DILLAN.

The streets and shops were full of Norman Rockwell folk with rosy cheeks and bobbled hats. I matched my smile to theirs, trying to slip back into the world of people, but the strands of human connection take time to reattach, and I felt dejected. It was as though, imprisoned in a cave for years by dark forces, I'd finally escaped only to discover that no one had missed me in the first place. In the bakery I ordered hot chocolate with whipped cream and flirted with a shop assistant, whose exquisitely matted hair smelled of weed. After a few hours, my automatic settings locked back into place. "I am no longer overwound," I said to the parking meter. "Just a clock whose tick was fractionally off." At which point I remembered the broken watch on my wrist. There was no obvious place to get it fixed, and besides, it was time to go home. Being lonely was romantic when not actually lonely.

A few miles out of town, my phone buzzed into life on the bucket seat of the truck. I hesitated. Mac's and my long distance conversations made us feel less connected than if we hadn't spoken at all. Neither of us understood why. The trick was not to bring your sadness to the table. Wasn't that the English way? To hide behind politeness and manners? *Say what you ought, not what you mean, and sign off with "love you" either way.* If we were constructing barriers around hurt, Mac was building his out of formality, while I was building mine out of kilometres and miles. A lump formed in my throat. I grabbed at the phone but it stopped ringing. I placed it carefully back on the seat, noticing that the sky had sprung a leak and the blue was draining fast.

The storm came out of nowhere. Clouds thickened and began to spit snow, which a rough wind quickly stirred into a blizzard. I wondered whether to turn around. Even on a good day the pass was nothing more than a squiggle of tarmac with a thousand-foot drop to reward those who disrespected its curves. *At least she died doing something she loved,* I imagined Mac's dry addendum to my obituary—*i.e., daydreaming.*

I crawled on. Every so often a mass of fog flew at me in the glow of the headlights and I shivered as the truck passed through its spectral body. My gas was down to a quarter. I frowned at the road. My lousy sense of direction was a reliable source of amusement to Mac, who had a compass in his brain and a fondness for an alley short cut.

On the same Australian trip when I'd gone so ruthlessly AWOL, I'd called him in desperation from the core of the Outback. It had been middle-of-night UK time, but I'd been contemplating death from a circling buzzard, and it had been the most comforting thing when he'd picked up and steered me remotely to the nearest town.

On whim I snatched up the phone but the device showed no service. The world was now in white-out, the road hollowing through it like a sound-insulated tunnel. Maybe I was already dead. *Ice on the road, the skid into oblivion . . .* But that didn't answer the question of where I was heading. At a pinch, I supposed, some mid-level tier of purgatory. I was too lousy a wife to be allowed through the red velvet rope to heaven.

Like the storm, the glow of brake lights appeared out of nowhere. I ratcheted up my speed, calmer now that I had a sensible objective. *Follow that car!* I did so assiduously, until it rounded a switchback and vanished as abruptly as it had appeared. I stared through the windshield but the road ahead was empty. My head began to throb. Could it have driven off the cliff? I stopped the truck and, elbowing open the door, sank my feet into the virgin snow. The sky had been a hard blue when I started down the mountain, and I'd not thought to bring anything more robust than sneakers. Gingerly I picked my way to the edge. No skid marks but then there were no tracks at all. It was as though a magician's broom had swept away all proof of existence. I stood stock-still, feeling the bite of the wind against my face. Watching snow fall was as mesmerizing as watching fire burn, and I found I couldn't move. These spells of nothingness happened to me sometimes. Freeze-frame moments that were hard to shatter. I felt like a flake of snow myself, weightless and insignificant.

Suddenly the blizzard parted like curtains, and I spotted, tucked into the overhang of the mountain, a small café, its bright red roof raised on a lumpy foundation as yellow as chicken feet.

Curious. In all the years I'd driven this road, I'd never noticed a café. Like a toadstool, it appeared to have pushed its way up through the soil overnight. I rubbed at my eyes. Smoke wisped from the chimney. Dancing inside the cabin's window, bright neon spelled out THE FAMILY CAFÉ and, written underneath, the equally seductive message COME ON IN!

The café was small, eight tables, set with ketchup and jaunty plaid tablecloths.

"Anyone at home?" I called, unable to summon a more original greeting. A piece of paper fluttered as the door shut behind me. Pinned to the wall was a torn section of newspaper, an article about wolves being reintroduced to the Southwest. I gave it a cursory glance, drawn inside by the sweet fragrance of apple and cinnamon. A pie was cooling on the high melamine bar at the back of the room. Not just any pie but a dome of golden-brown pastry with a viscous moat of juices around its crenellated edge. Steam puffed through a blowhole in the crust. Next to the pie sat a solitary plate and next to the plate, a lone knife.

"Hello?" I called again, but this time for show only. I knew already I would eat this pie. It smelled like happiness or some equally difficult to source ingredient and I was sideswiped by my hunger for it. But even as I stretched out a hand, the swing doors to the kitchen flew open and an old woman in a wheelchair burst forth and swiveled dexterously towards me. She had sharp little eyes and a mouth dipped slackly to one side, the result of a stroke, or Bell's palsy perhaps.

"Whaddaya waitin' for?" she cried, seizing the knife. If her lower body was wasted, her arms were tight with muscle. "You want some or not?" Without waiting for an answer, she broke through the buttery crust with two quick-angled thrusts, then cranked a full quarter of the thing onto the plate. "Go on," she instructed. "Take it to the table. I'll sit with ya."

Close-up, the checked tablecloths were overlaid with the sheen of ancient spills, the cutlery flecked with desiccated food. I thought about wiping the fork but the sleeve of my flannel shirt was arguably dirtier, and besides, it felt offensive.

The woman dodged her wheelchair around a couple of carelessly parked stools before settling opposite. "Call me Mother," she said.

"Is this your place?" There were flecks of salt in the pastry. Greedily, I forked up a second mouthful. "I like the name 'Family Café,'" I mumbled. "It sounds . . . comforting."

"I got eight kids," the old woman replied. "All home births. The first six were good. Two was brain-damaged." She pointed to a framed portrait of a boy in naval uniform above her head. "That there's Cody, the youngest. He's decent."

"He looks nice."

"You ain't from round here, are ya?"

"England." Christ, I'd never eaten pie this good. Never.

"England, you say?" Mother paused as if the significance of this required careful digestion. "You got schooling?"

As it happens, I've always had a chip on my shoulder about not having gone to university. Chasing down heroin and casual sex in a flat in Earl's Court instead of sitting final exams turned out not to be the key to getting admitted anywhere. I'd worked every day of my life since I was eighteen, but whether I'd learned anything was another story. I flirted with a quip. *I come from the school of hard knocks.* But in this department it was obvious I was facing stiff competition.

"Some."

"Melody!" Mother hollered, and instantly the doors of the kitchen swung open. A flaxen-haired girl appeared, pretty as a fawn, with red lips shaped in an O as if the world she encountered was a perpetual surprise.

"This one's from England," Mother said, inclining her head towards me.

"You're shittin' me!" The girl's expression recalibrated to astonishment.

"I just said so, didn't I?" Mother's voice sharpened. "So go ahead. Ask your question."

"You don' mind?" Melody asked.

"Not at all," I said, praying it wouldn't belong in the genres of general knowledge or geography. Mac had once come up with Nagorno Karabakh for *N* during another family car game and I'd accused him of cheating.

"Well, see . . . what I was wondering was this. If I was to steal a couple of kids and take 'em to England, would that be OK?"

"I'm sorry?" If anything, I'd been expecting a question about the royal family. "What do you mean exactly?"

"Oh, uh, like . . . is there some kind of deal with your country and my country? Would they, ya know . . . try to bring me back?"

"Extradite you, you mean?"

Melody nodded.

"Yes, I'm afraid they probably would."

"Well, shit. That's what I thought." Mother pivoted her wheels in the direction of the kitchen. "Brer!" she hollered.

A man in a trucker cap swung through the kitchen doors and approached the table with a syncopated swagger. There was something familiar about him, though I couldn't for the life of me work out what.

"Brer has a bail bondsman after him," Mother said, by way of introduction. Brer threw himself into a chair and kicked out long legs. His T-shirt rode up to reveal a potbelly melting like soft cheese over the rim of his jeans.

"Bad news, son," Mother said heavily. "This one's from England. She says they'll bring Melody back."

Brer thumped the table. The ketchup bottle tipped over and belched out tomato.

"Jolene!" Mother yelled. "Fetch a cloth, would ya?"

This time when the doors opened, two boys and a girl filed out. I now had a vision of an immense pine tree growing in the kitchen, its roots anchored around the cabin's plumbing, its tip breaking through the ceiling, and all its branches laden with children instead of Christmas decorations. The boys were twins, moving in sluggish tandem, hair orange as a bonfire. The girl between them had a dark monk's tonsure—without the central shave—and a squint magnified by owlish glasses.

"Red, Warren, Jolene," Mother counted as they approached. The twins acknowledged me with the hostile eyes of poker players recently stripped of their aces, but dropping her cloth on the ketchup spill, Jolene stretched out a small timid hand. I extended my own, but Jolene's bypassed it and kept on rising until it reached my cheek, where it stayed, quivering against my skin like an affectionate vole.

"Don't mind her, she's funny," Mother said. "So, what you're saying is—England's not an option. The authorities would haul Melody back?"

"Yes, I believe so."

"Ireland and Scotland too?"

"Well, it is sort of illegal to steal children," I said apologetically.

"The kids are mine, ya know." Melody absent-mindedly touched a finger to a small red patch on her mouth. "He took 'em from me in the first place."

I frowned at Brer.

"Oh, not Uncle B," Melody giggled. She whipped off Brer's trucker cap, releasing greasy bangs, then kissed the top of his ear.

I squinted at my plate. *Uncle?*

"Her ex has got 'em," Brer said, catching the girl's wrist and deftly twisting her onto his lap.

Melody settled into him like a kitten. "How was I to know a restraining order meant don't run him off the sidewalk?" she said.

"So, your ex-husband has been given custody?"

"He says I'm unfit."

"I'm sure that's not true." I tried not to stare at Melody's lip, which now looked puckered and raw with sores.

"Tell that to the state," Melody said hotly. "You've any idea how easy it is to lose your kids?"

My hand went unconsciously to the tortoiseshell links of my wristwatch. "You're saying social services took them?"

"Workin' hard don't mean I'm neglectin' 'em!"

"Of course it doesn't!" But suddenly I wasn't sure about this. "I'm sorry, really I am."

"Melody could use some help turnin' things around," Brer said.

"You know any doctors?" Mother fixed me with her small bird eyes.

Only a few days earlier Emily had rung to tell me that a ranching couple had brought in their daughter, who had eaten a dead mouse. "The kid hadn't just eaten it," Emily said. "She'd made it into a sandwich with Miracle Whip!" I considered giving up Emily's number, but I had a feeling she wouldn't thank me for the referral.

"See, meth ain't real good for the new baby," Melody said, pulling Brer's head down to the hilly contour of her belly.

So she was pregnant! Dear Lord, please let "Uncle" be a cute lovers' nickname. "Well, that pie was excellent," I said, "but I really ought to be going."

Mother gripped my wrist. "So can you help her?" Close up the woman's hand operated more like a raptor's talon than a human appendage.

"I'm really sorry, but I don't think I can."

"You're selfish, ya know that?"

I felt a sharp pain in my stomach, as though something important had ruptured.

"Selfish," Jolene parroted softly. Her small pink tongue poked in and out of her mouth.

"Maybe a lawyer?" I stammered.

"Lawyers cost more than doctors," Brer snapped.

"What are you doing here anyways?" Mother asked, a belligerent edge creeping into her voice. "You ain't one of them rich European people living up the valley, are you?"

"*Our* valley, Ma?" the twins singsonged in duet.

It dawned on me then that I must be in the company of the notorious Rubio clan, whose ancestors filled up the forlorn little graveyard close to the barn. Theirs, too, had been the deserted cabin in the woods where passing horses tended to nicker in fear. This latest generation was reputedly responsible for a number of thefts up and down the river. *Keep well clear*, local warnings ran. The Rubio family was drunk and violent, with an extra special interest in kiddie porn. No one had mentioned anything about the exemplary baking.

"Oh, no, I'm just passing through."

Mother wheeled in closer. "No husband with ya?"

"He's waiting for me in town." I spoke quickly, surprised to discover how much I wished he were.

"He must be wonderin' where you are." The old woman left the statement in the air so long it dried into a question.

"Yeah, how 'bout we tell him you're gonna stay a little while longer?" Brer said.

My skin prickled. I hadn't been aware of the twins moving, but suddenly there they were, right behind me, as if soundlessly rolled into position by dolly.

"You got a phone?" Brer tipped Melody off his lap and held out his hand.

Now I knew what was familiar about him. The white USA branding on his trucker hat—I'd seen it in the film *Breakdown*, a B movie if ever there was one. Naive East Coasters, Kurt Russell and his busty wife drive west to a new life. Before long they find themselves with car trouble in the middle of a place that looked an awful lot like this one. The wife gets snatched by sinister trucker J. T. Walsh, and poor, sweaty Kurt spends the next ninety minutes trying to wrest her back from Walsh and his cohort, a panoply of cunning sociopaths masquerading as dungaree-clad simpletons.

I thought about Mac. He'd be in his London office, sneakily checking the football scores, when he received the ransom call. "If you dare touch a hair on her head," I could hear him saying. He was prone to empire-style utterances when threatened, but he wouldn't have necessarily got the full picture. The Rubios, I suspected, were not the sort of people interested in either your hair or your head—it was the entire body they were after, preferably butchered into family-size portions and shrink-wrapped in a freezer.

"I should really be getting along," I whispered.

"Something wrong with my cooking?" Mother's chin shot up, revealing, to my astonishment, a profusion of overlapping warts covering her neck like roof shingles or bird feathers. I wrenched my eyes away and stared down at the stray apple pip on my plate. My stomach was sore. *I'm gonna die cos I ate pie*, I thought morosely.

Mac was forever telling me to be careful. Sometimes, when I looked at myself through his eyes, it seemed almost inevitable that I would come to a tawdry end, but I liked to think I could take care of myself. Once, overseeing work on the barn in the dead of winter, I'd had to talk down a crystal-meth head who'd wandered up the snowy drive barefoot and threatened to return after dark to party with me. "You're pretty," he'd said, eyes like bright moons; "I can sure think of things to do to you."

After he'd gone, I'd rung John for advice.

"It's easy girl. If he comes back, just hit him with a fire extinguisher."

"I'm sorry, what?"

"A fire extinguisher."

"Oh! Um, OK. But . . . where?"

"Right on the head."

"OK, but, like, how many times?"

"Until he's dead of course."

But this was different. There were six Rubios. Jolene might look as harmless as one of Bambi's woodland friends, but not the twins. Wasn't it said that in a fight, redheads counted for two each?

Once Mac had loved me enough to play the hero. I remembered the time we'd hiked across the plains searching for land on which to build the barn and been caught in a vicious storm. As lightning opened up craters all around us, he had pushed me to the ground and thrown himself on top of me. When the lightning stopped, the rain had come, unforgiving, apocalyptic. After that it was hail the size of Gobstoppers plummeting from the sky. I'd been heavily pregnant, ungainly as a piece of farm machinery; nevertheless, he'd scooped me up, soaking and shivering, and carried me across a flooding river only to be met by a bull on the other side, its eyes bloodshot and mad with fear. I'd been wearing a vintage rayon dress that afternoon, and the rain shrank it, comically fast. It clung to the mound of my belly, barely covering my knickers, and I'd stood there, my cap sleeve torn by barbed wire, face smeared with mud, a witless, gutless cut-rate Raquel Welch, wringing my hands while my newly minted One Million Years BC husband put his head down and charged the monstrous animal back.

I loved a white knight, who didn't? But my enjoyment of being mildly in distress probably made me less and less rewarding to save. Mac would be solicitous in his enquiries, of that I was sure. A daily phone call: *Good morning, Sheriff, any news?* Nevertheless, rescue from the Rubios would require ten constipating hours on a plane, a deadening four-hour layover in Denver, and two more on the Great Lakes puddle jumper (inevitably delayed), even before the long drive up to the barn. It was an awful lot of effort for a wife who favoured chopping vegetables over phone sex. Kurt's wife, I thought dismally—"five foot five, 115 pounds, three or four of that just pure tit"—had probably put out a lot more.

I stood up.

"Sit," scowled Brer.

"Go fetch the shrink-wrap," Mother ordered, and Jolene wordlessly lifted herself from her chair and lumbered, sweet and smiling, towards the kitchen.

I sank back down at the table feeling curiously other. My limbs were as liquid as mercury, but my brain was racing. Hemlock will do that to you. Wasn't it supposed to render its victims paralysed, yet hyperconscious enough to hear their own death rattle? *Who'd died of hemlock? Sophocles? Einstein? Errol Flynn? Concentrate*, I scolded myself. *Maintain the pretense of normality.* In dangerous situations normality was key, though good manners were sometimes a big help too.

"Oh, I'm sorry," I said pointedly. "How much do I owe you for the pie?" Jolene had not yet returned and this I took as a good sign. I stretched for my wallet. Perhaps the family was out of shrink-wrap, their chainsaw drained of gas, their freezer brimming with haunches of freshly slaughtered elk. Besides, if they needed money for a lawyer, might not ransom be all they had in mind?

Years ago, when I'd been in Yemen on a job for *Harper's Bazaar*, a restaurant owner confided that his family had been proactive in the kidnapping of tourists. "But we were very nice to them," he said almost wistfully. "We treated them with great respect, fed them like kings. If we were to kidnap you now, for example, I think you would enjoy it very much."

And I had a vision of staying on with the Rubios of my own free will, dancing barefoot with the ginger twins in the hills above the cabin while the relocated wolves howled in approval.

My wallet was empty. Strange. I could have sworn I'd had dollars when I left town. "Don't worry," I muttered, digging deeper to hide my embarrassment. "I have money here somewhere."

I felt the gentle scratch of Mother's nail on my arm. "Hey, girl, we don't need your money." She handed me the remainder of the pie, which Jolene had finished covering in aluminum foil. "If you're that hard up, take it for free. Ya look like you could use it."

My eyes went to the mirror behind her head. My hair needed a wash, and my eyebrows had bolted like broccoli florets. *Mirror, mirror*, I thought. There was nothing like solitary living to give even a moderately fair girl the veneer of crone. The warm pie felt comforting between my hands. The entire Rubio family was semi-circled around me now, more pitying than threatening.

"Thank you, that's really kind." I scraped back my chair. "It's so great you stayed open, especially with the storm and everything."

"What storm? There's been no storm." Brer said, and I followed his glance out the window. To my astonishment, the sky was a clear indigo.

Weather out here veered between extremes. Sometimes, noodling around in the barn, I'd hear rain drumming on the tin roof. I'd look out to see the landscape divided in two—a definitive line where the rain began and the sun shone bright. I'd stand on the deck with my arms stretched wide, one half of me becoming increasingly cold and wet, the other half burning. I still wasn't sure which I preferred.

Mother was looking at me strangely. "Passing through or not, be careful for when the snows do come," she warned. "A person can get isolated up there in the mountains. Loneliness plays tricks. You wouldn't be the first to get yourself lost for good."

"That's sensible advice," I said. "I won't forget it."

As the door of the café blew shut behind me, the newsprint wolves shifted restlessly. The neon light in the window flashed once then switched off. I walked slowly back to the truck, feeling like a fool, a silly fantasist. I turned on the ignition, laying the pie carefully on the passenger seat. Ahead the road was empty, the night so clear I could see the opaque veil of the Milky Way leading me home.

I pressed my foot to the accelerator. It would be nine p.m. by the time I made it to the barn. In England that was four a.m. in the future— as good a time as any to call Mac.

"I came looking for you, and you are mine." He'd once read Yeats to me as I fell asleep under his arm. "You are mine until the whole world is burned out like a candle that is spent." Again, I felt a catch in the back of my throat. I'd make it sound casual, obviously, but I needed to check—you know—the thing about what he'd save in the fire.

No matter how hard we tried...

What do you **WANT** ?

We ended up in the same place...

What do **YOU** want?

Perhaps we just needed the other to be less like the person we fell in love with and more like ourselves.

The idea came after yet another row. The kids and I should go away for a bit. For me and Mac maybe our only chance for a future was to minimize damage to each other in the present.

I wish I had found a way to explain it better.

Things I didn't know how to say

Instead I sold it as an adventure. For the kids
- to see the world differently. For me, to look for
a new project. I hoped that Mac would somehow
instinctively understand what was really going on.

But how could he?

So, I made plans. Jesse and Sam would stay in the care of their step-father and father. Giacomo had remarried. A gentle lady who rocked beige clothes and tan shoes and cooked beautiful pasta.

I left for the West feeling like the worst married person ever.

So here we are, under four feet of snow.

For Finn and Mabel, it was an adventure.

And for me?

One night I dreamt a mountain lion
appeared to me

I knew this mountain lion. I'd seen her
prints in the morning snow.

I followed her up the mountain
to a cave hidden in the rocks.

I wasn't afraid. I knew who she was.
She'd walked alongside me for years
this cat.

And if she was watching over my
family I was looking out for hers,

mother to mother, two secret
solitary animals aligned.

Now I felt the sharpness of her whiskers as they nudged my hand — as though she had something important to show me. She veered off towards the creek.

But ignoring me,

she began to daub mud onto her body
with her paws,

painting herself with big dark spots.

Until she morphed into an altogether
more primitive beast,

An animal I knew well, a creature I'd
been keeping at bay for way
too long a time.

THE BORDER

PROWL

The back of John's pickup smelled of rust and mouldy hay. Late March and the desert air was chilly, but I liked writing in the pickup and had taken to stationing myself there at first light with coffee and a notepad. Upstairs on the top floor of John and Emily's funny tower house, Mabel and Finn lay sprawled across the bed in a starfish of arms and legs. School started early in the canyon, and I wondered vaguely about waking them for breakfast, but it was so quiet, so pin-drop quiet, that I put off the moment a little longer.

We'd been out West nearly three months now. Mostly homeschooling up at the barn isolated by snowdrifts and power cuts, but twice a week commuting down to John's farm in the canyon, where Finn was enrolled in a tiny school on the edge of the Navajo reservation. Mabel spent her days, dazed with love, trailing John's foreman, Jesús, as he fed the goats and lambs, while I loafed around eating Emily's leftovers and trying to shake an apathy that hung off me like old skin.

You don't have to know what you're escaping from to become a fugitive. This, scribbled across the top of my pad. A single line, the *only* line of a new project. I'd handed in a book, but there had been no word back, and I'd yet found nothing to replace the intensity of working on it. I'm usually happiest in a place of transition, but waiting is an uneasy space to inhabit. I felt stuck in limbo, and limbo was a dangerous place for me.

A discarded newspaper lay under the hay. Idly, I dragged it out as the black-and-white remnants of night lifted. The sun rose in glorious

Kodachrome, a thin red line on the horizon, hardening ground and sky into separate worlds. A headline caught my attention—HUGE SURGE IN BORDER FATALITIES—and I scanned the story quickly. Borders were all anyone was talking about that drought-ridden spring. It was the ten-year anniversary of Operation "Hold the Line", Bill Clinton's butchly named US–Mexico border initiative, which had lowered the numbers of illegal crossings by exponentially beefing up manpower and technology. It was, according to the mainstream press, *Good job! Well done!*

This local paper, though, was telling a different story. Over the last decade the figure for people dying while attempting to cross had risen fivefold, and as I finished the article I felt it—the almost painful twinge of curiosity.

I knew a little about the border from Jesús, whose trajectory to US citizenship had included multiple crossings back when it was easy. After the line tightened he'd been forced to choose one country over another. On his final journey, he had curled himself around the engine of a truck whose battery had been removed and ingeniously rigged up beneath the vehicle to make space for him. He survived the burns and the discomfort, but coming through LA the smog had nearly asphyxiated him.

I glanced at the fugitive line in my notepad and for a moment glimpsed an upside-down symmetry. It takes an impressive leap to parallel an impecunious migrant struggling north with a white woman drifting in the opposite direction, but I saw in it, if nothing else, a mad irony.

Borders have always struck me as conceptually flawed divides. If the lottery of birth is already difficult enough to accept, how odd that maps and deeds drawn hundreds of years before should further denote our identity.

I shifted round to face south, remembering the dream about the mountain lion. How afterwards I'd woken, restless, to the dark of night and stepped outside feeling hungry for something I hadn't yet identified, something that lay beyond the shadow of the mountains.

I'd been to Mexico only once—to a resort where milky tourists turned pink on the beach and were secretly relieved to find English translations on the restaurant menu. It had been a lovely holiday but a long time ago. This was happening now, and the contradictory reports were so disturbing. The border was less than a day's drive away. What was really going on down there?

The children were ecstatic at the prospect of unlimited Kool-Aid and tortilla chips in Jesús's care. John needed no persuasion, and Emily had several days holiday coming to her, so the three of us headed down to southern Arizona to find out.

IF IT AIN'T WHITE, the flyer for the Ku Klux Klan said, IT AIN'T RIGHT. The piece of paper had snagged on the spur of a barbed-wire fence. We'd stopped randomly to stretch our legs, and there it was. Unsettled, we looked around at the emptiness of the desert. There was no sign of life unless you count a toothy gopher, and no checkpoint or law enforcement except for the single strand of wire which appeared to constitute the only physical divide between earth's most prosperous nation and one of its largest third-world countries.

It was the first of several border trips, each going in a little deeper. The conflicting reports both turned out to be accurate. In closing off the revolving door to the United States, the Clinton blockades had indeed lowered the official stats of illegal crossings, but the unintended effect had been to drive people deeper into the Sonoran Desert, North America's very own Sun's Anvil, 120,000 square miles of broiled wasteland. Aside from the heat and natural dangers were the human ones:

US Border Patrol, smugglers, Mexican police, bandits, and California Minutemen, a group of self-styled vigilantes for whom keeping migrants on the right side of the line had become a rewarding, year-round sport. If, at government level, immigration was a high-stakes game of polemics and economics, down at the Mexican border it was a different kind of game, one that came with the loaded dice of rape, robbery, violence, and murder. The Border Patrol hated illegals. The Mexican police hated the Border Patrol. Smugglers hated the Mexican police while the California Minutemen just hated everyone.

All in all, this low-intensity conflict perfectly matched what was going on inside my head—it took about seven seconds before I was hooked and not much longer than that to convince myself that it was my job and my job alone to highlight the plight of the illegal immigrant. It was unconscionable that so many people were dying, and I attached myself to the cause as though by umbilical right.

Enough daydreaming in trucks, scrabbling in my imagination for stories that had little bearing on real lives. People craved the truth. Journalism was the preserve of the serious, the resourceful, and the professional, and on these grounds there seemed no reason to assume I'd be anything other than excellent at it.

I would make that border crossing myself, I was soon announcing to anyone within earshot. I would highlight the perils migrants faced—write a story so powerful that it would change the way governments thought—and in the process, I privately reasoned, my own escape, my fugitive time, would be validated.

Friends openly laughed. "You? In the desert? Attempting to locate north?"

"Plus, it's a felony," Mac said drily, when I proposed the idea over the phone. "Try to imagine life, if you can, in a small, wretched cell without the range of ingredients required to make a club sandwich."

Undeterred, I e-mailed publications across America. Their editors also laughed—at least, when I heard nothing back from them, I can only assume they did—a thin, wry choke into their pastrami sandwiches.

These resounding endorsements should have been a heads-up that perhaps I wasn't entirely qualified for the job, but despite plenty of practice, I've never learned to deal elegantly with humiliation. So I did what anyone would have done on discovering that no one was the slightest bit interested in commissioning their five thousand words on the subject. I commissioned myself to write a hundred thousand instead.

All of which is how, several months later, with the children safely back in London, I found myself perched on a bale of compressed Guatemalan ponchos with John and Emily in the airless confines of a market stall in the town of Nogales.

Nogales is a hub of illegal immigration. Rising out of the shimmer of the desert, straddling the border, it is bisected by the wall, a green corrugated fence that curves up and over the hilly contours of the city like a dragon's tail, relegating its northern half to the United States while sweeping its pesky southern districts back into Mexico.

The American side, generously described by *The Rough Guide* as a "dreary little community," is a welter of generic fast-food joints, four-dollar-a-day parking lots, and drab houses crowded one against the other like Monopoly pieces. Nogales, US, is where everyone is trying to get to.

Nogales, *Mexico*, from where everyone wants to escape, acts as a vast open-air prison, a holding bay of first-time offenders, recidivists, and lifers, the last earning their living aiding and abetting the first two. Colourful, unstable, simmering with tension; just talking to people there was to plug a finger into an energy force field. It crackled through me like static—all the hope, ambition, determination, and anticipation. There was no more apathy. Nogales, Mexico, was where I came back to life.

Driving into the Mexican side from the US is painless. No one stops you, and if anyone does, your passport is given the most cursory of glances. Mexico welcomes all. Crossing back is another matter. There are checkpoints and interrogations and little mirrors on sticks—and that's if you're white and have valid ID. For an illegal immigrant, crossing in a town has become nigh on impossible. John, Emily, and I were in the market stall on the Mexican side to negotiate a desert crossing, which typically involved a thirty-mile trek through the Sonoran Desert—location of the greatest number of deaths. But from what? Bad guys, bad luck, or bad geography? To figure it out, we'd resolved to follow the same path as any migrant arriving in town. First task was to find a smuggler, or, as they are less fondly termed, a *coyote*, and ours was running nearly an hour late.

Earlier that morning an American woman had banged on our truck window while we were stopped at a red light. "Help me, please," she begged. "My car got stolen!"

She extended her hand for money, revealing stale sweat marks on the underarms of her cheesecloth smock. Nobody told her it wasn't safe to park her car over the border, she said, tearing up—she was just like us, day-trippers, here for the souvenirs.

I felt bad. She was around the same age as Emily and me, but she looked rough—hair tangled as thicket, a rip in her shorts.

"My purse was in there," she went on. "ID too. You gotta help me, I got no way of getting back over."

"Sure," John said mildly. "Hop in, girl, we'll take you to the consulate."

"No! No consulate, mister, I need to get back to my kids." She aimed a quivering lip at Emily and me. "I need money."

"Money will do you no good," John said. "You need papers."

"No, mister," she wheedled. "Please, just a few dollars."

"I got this, John." I thrust a handful of singles towards her.

"That it?" The woman looked at the creased bills in disgust. "That the best you can do?" A gob of spit flew through the air and landed on my cheek. "Fuck you, bitch."

"Fuck you too!" I retorted, indignant.

The woman had barely completed her fig sign before John's hand shot past me and grabbed her wrist through the window.

"You want more money?" He turned her arm to reveal the Morse code of needle scars on her inner elbow. "Introduce us to your dealer first."

While John escorted the junkie to her crack house, Emily and I went for coffee.

"Wouldn't take much," Emily mused, watching them go. "No car, money, ID. We'd be begging on streets after a week or two."

"Speak for yourself." I knew John would do better at the crack house on his own, but I was peeved not to be going with him. In the grip of a charged impatience, all I wanted was to push out to the edge of everything I was familiar with and keep on going after that.

"Think he'll be OK?"

"John?" I said, distracted. It was the woman I felt sorry for. Of all the marks in town she'd tried to scam a seasoned opportunist. We'd needed a smuggler and John must have calculated junkie to dealer to smuggler as the fastest route. Sure enough, he returned an hour later with the information that a blow job cost twenty dollars, an eight ball of crack sixty, and our meeting with the coyote was scheduled for three p.m., later that day.

It was now four o'clock, and the tiny covered market stall was sweltering. In my backpack, the light of my disk recorder flashed, dutifully collating audio, but small talk with the coyote's advance party had dried up, and what to make of the visual? The sizzling brute guarding the stall's makeshift entrance had a pistol shoved down his shorts and skin as pitted as an ostrich's. Acne, I thought vaguely, or chicken pox. The other two, their hair greased into tiny samurai man buns, were sporting a range of scars along with menacing stares that might have been perfected in henchmen's finishing school. Despite their bad rap, most smugglers, so we'd been told, were ordinary guys taking advantage of market opportunity. But there were exceptions. We had given ourselves up to chance and been rewarded with three utterly stereotypical heavies out of some filmmaker's imaginary Mexico and I felt an odd sense of detachment. If these men weren't real, then how could the situation be dangerous? Instead of keeping my wits about me, I was beginning to zone out in the heat, wondering whether Ostrich had grown to look mean after years of intimidation or whether he'd been born that way and pigeonholed into his career accordingly. "I'm sorry, *hijo*", I imagined his father saying, handing him a serrated knife tied with a big red bow and gently turning him to the mirror. "This face is good for one thing and one thing only." There was little subtlety to the samurai either, with their intimate language of tattoos and polished blades creviced within the folds of their clothes. You'd think that in this company, an ex-soldier and a doctor would have been exceptional choices of companion—but only in the event that one of these men spontaneously went into labour or required an emergency hysterectomy. Still, any doctor is a good doctor, particularly given Emily's healthy dose of medical callousness. Once, after too much tequila, she had pulled me close to her. "Ya know," she began in her Charleston accent—but instead of the profound statement about our friendship I'd been expecting, she came out with, "people say such *stoopid* shit when they die." Another time she rang me from a cadaver convention in Seattle and announced that she was standing in a room full of vaginas carved from their bodies. "Such cuties," she'd said dreamily, "just lyin' there all alone on big ol' velvet cushions."

As for John, if the basic training of Great Britain's special forces includes the removal of a person's eye with a toilet plunger it should be interesting to see what damage he could inflict with the rainbow-coloured threads of a poncho. He might these days be in the relatively civilized business of farming, but John remains an unpredictable lunatic with a propensity for improbable stories. And he was spinning one right now to Ostrich about the three of us being stuck in Mexico on the wrong side of line and law.

His sweat glands appeared to have taken on the role of Pinocchio's nose. With every lie, the damp circles under his arms spread further across his shirt until they began converging on his breast like two oceanic plates. Still, I was admiring his chutzpah. His tale of betrayal and redemption was so captivating I was beginning to wish I'd written it myself.

"So, you see, we just want to get back to the Estados Unidos," he finished.

"But no passports, huh?" Ostrich said.

"No passports."

The Mexican border is a place where shifty empathises with shifty. All you need is a compelling reason for not taking your chances at a customs checkpoint. Fortunately, the script of the town was so familiar that our guides were happy to supply the storyline themselves. "Sure, sure," Ostrich nodded. "So you got busted, I guess?"

"Look, I'd rather not go into this."

"We get it, we get it, but dope, right?"

John adopted a pained expression, which somehow managed to imply that, yes, wasn't it always dope that brought a good man down? "Plus, there are some other things—"

"Ah, sure . . . other things." The wider of the samurai nodded. "I guess you kill someone, huh?"

John's lips tightened, the very picture of a man determined to reserve his rights.

"Killing someone . . . ," the other one reflected with nostalgia. "Yeah, that's a bad rap."

"A very bad rwap," John agreed amiably.

The Mexicans did a discreet double take. No one is inclined to believe that a man who can't say his *r*'s can be much of a threat, which makes John's speech defect one of the most dangerous things about him. If his innate Englishness had thrown them, his r's threw them further.

"OK, OK," Ostrich said. "So you I get, but the women?" All of a sudden he was staring at Emily and me. A contemptuous stare that implied that if we couldn't muster our own bad rwap, then what respect could possibly be due us?

And for the first time, John wavered.

"Hey! *Juan es mi marido*," Emily jumped in, her Spanish fluent and emotive. "*Él es mi amor*, and I will never leave his side, *entiendes*?"

Suddenly I felt sad. It was true; John and Emily were devoted to one another, while Mac's and my relationship had become a union of two puffer fish, sharp mouthed—each of us doubling in size to keep threats at bay. I wondered about plagiarising Emily's story. *Hey! I too amo Juan. We all amamos each other, entiendes*? But what if the Mexicans didn't understand my pidgin, audiotape Spanish? What if they thought we were weird, or practising Mormons? I imagined playing the family angle—*Hey! I am the sister of Juan, and I amo him deeply!*—but this made me sound like the expendable spinster aunt. Still, Ostrich was waiting, and for a moment I became my eight-year-old self again, trapped at one of my parents' cocktail parties. *Panic, freeze, blurt.*

"I hit a man with a fire extinguisher," I said.

Ostrich blinked. "A fire extinguisher?"

"*Correcto.* On his head."

The samurai looked deeply impressed.

"How many times?" Ostrich asked.

Out of the corner of my eye I could see John shaking his head wearily.

"Until he was *muerto* of course," I replied smoothly.

Just then, a fourth man stepped through the poncho curtain and the backs of all three henchmen snapped straight. All oiled hair and manicured nails, the Mexican oozed authority that was further evidenced by his pristine cowboy hat, and the starched jeans held to hip by the sort of extravagant belt buckle George W. Bush liked to be papped in at his Texas ranch. On our long-awaited coyote there was not a drop of perspiration. His coolness was unsettling. If his sidekicks presented as cookie-cutter villains, this was something to be grateful for. Their warning was writ bold on the package. El Chuché, as the smuggler introduced himself, was beautiful, but a coiled tightness suggested that the more scrupulous his handshake, the wider his circle of power; and the more deferential his head tilt towards Emily and me, the more women he'd dragged through life by the hair.

"So," he addressed John, "you wanna get back to the United States."

"Yes."

"I can't help all of you." He flicked a glance our way.

"How much do you charge?"

"Eighteen hundred dollar per person."

John whistled. We'd talked to enough people to know that fifteen hundred dollars was the going rate. "And for that you can get us to a safe house? Keep us out of the way of the Border Patrol, the *bandidos*?"

"Not all of you."

"Why not?"

The samurai were beginning to fidget like children.

"Bring the women," El Chuché said, his smile soft, "and it will be bad for them."

I caught the flash in John's eye. I knew what he was thinking. He was thinking of ditching Emily and me. He was thinking it would be faster and safer without us. He'd taken a dislike to Chuché, but instead of finding a more palatable smuggler, he was toying with "turning" Chuché and his men "around"—his pet phrase for doling out some beastly if unspecified justice to those he believed deserved it. I glared at him, because we had agreed: it was all of us or none.

"You don't need to do the crossing to get the story," Mac had said. "You can just interview someone who's made it over. You do understand that's how journalism works, don't you?"

Yes, I understood. But we were ready to go, with press permissions from the US Immigration and Naturalization Service stamped and folded in my pocket. Moreover, the riskier El Chuché made the crossing sound the more I felt the hypnotic lure of danger. I couldn't wait to touch it, singe my fingers against the heat of it. Window-shopping the experience was of no interest, and in this John and I were the same. Together we could be reckless—his natural bent and mine creating a momentum that tended to override common sense. Nevertheless, a pipette-size drop of reality was beginning to break through. What was our cut-off line? Should things turn bad—and Chuché was virtually promising they would—at what point would we call in the Border Patrol? There would be others in our group. What would we say to them when the cops came whirring? *Guys! We're not actually part of the problem, just here to report it. But hey, good luck in the slammer, and keep in touch!*

It was a given that John would use his gun on anyone threatening Emily or me, but there would be others in peril—desperate people whose main preoccupation was survival, as opposed to a fatuous self-imposed deadline. Was John to be the protector of all, and if so, how representative of a true crossing would such potential complication be? Then again, weren't complications precisely what we were hoping for?

My head can be a dimly lit room at times, but even I could see that the story's success was entirely predicated on the crossing's failure.

I didn't care. My other self was out now and as ravenous as a jungle beast.

If you go, my glare back to him said, *I go too*, and he'd read my message as easily as I'd read his.

"I'll worry about the women," he was saying to Chuché, "and you worry about the crossing."

"How do I know I can trust you?" Chuché asked.

As if by stage prompt—a sharp click as the disk in my recorder came to an end. The machine purred softly, rewound, and stopped.

I held my breath. I knew it was idiotic to have brought it, but embedded in my ego was still the grandiose conviction that this crossing would prove to be not only a good story but the kind of Pulitzer Prize–worthy story that would have the brightest and best of newspaper editors gibbering with regret for their failure to commission it. Accuracy was fundamental, and without contemporaneous notes I'd have screwed it up before I'd begun. I snatched a quick look around the stall. No one had noticed. Smiling broadly, I thrust my hands into my backpack and began sifting through the flotsam and jetsam of old receipts, antacids, tampons, lidless ChapStick, and an arsenal of cracked, bleeding pens. *Find recorder, snap open, insert new disk.* More smiling, this time aimed specifically at Chuché. *Maintain beatific expression somewhere between gratitude at his cooperation and respect for his manly dominance.*

Hell, the disk wouldn't go in. Why wouldn't it? Ah, it was still in its wrapping, that's why. Blindly I searched for some fissure or tab. A mosquito settled on my leg and ogled me with nasty compound eyes. John was bargaining Chuché down on price, and I was missing crucial dialogue. In desperation, I jammed my entire head into the backpack and began nipping at the disk, corn-on-the-cob style. It was a fiddly little sucker, and if the market stall was steamy, it was a polytunnel inside the backpack. After a prolonged struggle I forced the disk in and triumphantly pressed the play button, but as I came up for air, I realised negotiations had stopped and every eye had swiveled my way.

John liked to say that his favourite thing was to be in a crowded bar when the room suddenly went quiet. I got it. In those moments anything can happen and life truly is a surprise. This moment was not quite like that. It was more like I'd taken a long time to tell a uniquely unfunny joke and now the whole dinner party was unsure how to respond. All four Mexicans were giving me the evils. Emily was staring at me in utter stupefaction, while John's look loosely translated to *If these guys don't kill you now, look forward to me doing it later.*

"What's she got in there?" El Chuché asked, and for the first time it struck me that this meeting might not end well.

This was not yet the Mexico that rolled a father's severed head through the high school gym until it came to rest at the feet of his own child, the Mexico where, if you so much as looked sideways at the cartels, they suspended you over the I-19 with your entrails dangling.

That Mexico was coming and it was coming soon, but Ostrich was coming even sooner. Inside my backpack, the traitorous eye of my recorder glowed red.

Do something, a voice in my head instructed, and do it now.

"*Agua!*" I blurted, extricating a crushed water bottle from the bag. I pantomimed extreme thirst and threw El Chuché a filthy look, as though he were the asshole barman who'd been ignoring my custom all night.

Ostrich backed off, but the tenor of the meeting changed abruptly.

"You pay me the money now," Chuché said. "Up front."

"Forget it," John snapped, before adding, more placatingly, that being English, we could decide nothing before a nice cup of tea and some quiet time in our hotel.

"Then we come to your hotel with you," Chuché said. "Help you decide."

So it was a forced march through the labyrinthine corridors of the market. A samurai each for Emily and me, John sandwiched between Ostrich and El Chuché. Past tin pails of bright marigolds, a donkey turd the size of a Christmas pudding, stands of painted wooden wrestlers, and a dove pecking at ruined fruit in a wheelbarrow, until finally we were ducking through a low stone doorway and into the glare of the sun.

Outside, the pavement was glossy from rain, the sky a sandblasted white. Streets were empty, but this was not siesta time in Nogales. The town thrummed with activity: I could feel its beat in the air like the wings of a thousand black moths. If the bisecting of Nogales is reminiscent of Cold War Berlin, the town's culture is closer to Bogart's Casablanca, bursting at the seams with gamblers and refugees. There was a frisson, a tangible prayer, as decks were shuffled, cards were dealt, and bets laid down for the night to come.

"Four thousand dollars for all of you," El Chuché said. "And I want my money now."

" I don't think so." John shielded his eyes from the sun.

"We gotta be sure you can pay. Where is your hotel?"

Ah, but we did not have a hotel this side of the border. On neither side did we have four thousand dollars locked into a mini-safe. Whatever the coyote equivalent of doing the washing up when you couldn't pay your bill, I suspected Emily and I were too long in the tooth for it.

"Here's what you can be sure of," John said; "we'll pay you after, not before."

"Then you come with us." El Chuché struck quickly at John's elbow, locking his arm, and from Emily came a gulp, so small and discreet it might almost have been classed as a hiccup.

Though I desperately want to be perceived as a brave person, the truth is that I'm anything but. Once, to my eternal shame, I sought refuge on Mac's head, when our Jet Ski capsized near a school of orcas in Panama. In my terror, I swear I must have convinced myself that his bald patch was a nice rock, and not even his pitiful drowning gurgles convinced me to abandon land for that tooth-infested sea. Since then my biggest fear is of being outed. *You know what you are?* Gary Cooper saying as he runs me out of *High Noon*'s Hadleyville: *Yer yella!*

Not so Emily. While training for her medical degree in New York, she famously scared off an approaching assailant on the subway by smiling coyly, then squeezing her trainers together until the fresh blood from the ER pooled onto the floor. But even Emily was jittery at the manhandling—not for herself, predictably, but for John.

"We can't let this happen," she whispered, as Chuché and Ostrich began muscling him down the street. "We can't let them take him."

"Of course not," I responded fiercely, wondering what on earth to do about it.

But in front of us, John had already stopped. "Right, that's enough." He planted his legs wide. "Here's how this thing is going to work. We'll go to our hotel on our own and contact you when we're good and ready. You got that, old chap?"

I watched him uneasily. *"Old chap" was not good. John shaking off Chuché was not good.* In the face-off between Mexico's chic violent type and our own trim articulate killer, it was hard to know who was the most intimidating. The truth is that inside every soldier is a monster on standby, ready and willing to go from zero to ten in a heartbeat, and once the pin was out of John's grenade it led to complication and—quite often—jail time.

John's hands, though scarred and twisted, were moving fast. Before we knew it, he had executed some clever military manoeuver and Emily and I were magically in his grip. Almost as one, the four smugglers stared at him with cartoon indignation, as though he'd done the Road Runner equivalent of running rings around them and leaving them tied back to back with a rope. Chuché, recovering first, took a step forwards.

John pushed his face into the Mexican's until the brims of their hats kissed.

"We're good, you and me," he said tightly. "Understand?"

There is a nuanced vibe that passes between men who acknowledge each other as peers. Chuché made a steadying gesture—the kind you might make to a horse rearing up in front of you—and backed off slowly.

"Walk," John instructed me and Emily in an undertone, "and don't turn around."

"OK," I whispered, "yes," then, aware of the Mexicans' eyes on our backs, "Walk where?"

"Truck," he said curtly. "Lead on, girl."

OK, truck was good. Inside the truck's glove compartment was
John's oily Smith & Wesson. Heading there was a sound idea. At least,
God help me, it would have been had I only been able to remember
where I'd parked it.

Mortifyingly, an hour or so before we were due to meet the smugglers, I'd lobbied for a quick shopping trip. "I want to get a set of those
earthenware bowls, John," I'd cajoled him. "You know, the ones Emily
cooks with?"

"What, *now* you turn all Suzy Homemaker?" he'd teased. "All
right—meet us at the west entrance of the market but leave passports
and wallets in the glove compartment. We can't have 'em on us."

*Copy that, John. Bit late for meeting, though—trouble identifying west
entrance of the market. Park truck, copy. Lock wallets and passports in
glove compartment, copy, copy.*

"Right or left?" John said, as we reached the end of the street.

Finding my way back from anywhere unfamiliar is like waking from
a dream. The harder I try to summon the details, the further they slide
from my grasp. Through all the years I've known John, I've played
down my disability, aware of what a stinging disappointment it made
me as an accomplice. Now, realising we'd exited the market from a
different archway I faltered. Chuché's menace was nothing compared
with John's scorn.

"Come on, girl," he pushed.

"Left?" I hazarded.

"You're sure."

"Positive," I said miserably.

June in Nogales. The hottest hours of the day had passed, nevertheless,
my cheeks were on fire. It took another scrabble board of streets before
John cottoned on to what I already knew.

"You've lost the truck," he said flatly.

"Lost . . . as in with our money and ID's inside?" Emily said.

I hung my head—my professional credentials? More Pink Panther's inspector Clouseau, than Edward R. Murrow.

Emily sighed. "We should split up and take a grid of streets each."

"Excellent idea." I set off, eager for redemption.

"Oh not you, girl," John said, seizing me around the waist and wrestling me to the ground much in the way he did to my kids when they were cheeky. "You, my little flowerpot, will stay right here till we get back. And I do mean, *right here.*" Then he and Emily, chortling, took off in opposite directions.

I picked myself up and stepped into the cool dustiness of a bar, but there wasn't a coin in my backpack. Tap water on the border tended to be served with parasites instead of ice, so I slumped back against the outside wall under a government sign depicting a woolly sheep with a warning bleat coming out of its mouth. DON'T FOLLOW THE FLOCK. BEWARE THE COYOTES!

My ankle, damaged long ago from a car accident, was puffy from the heat. I levered off a shoe, then threw down my cap and ran a hand through my hair. My fingers encountered something soft and sticky— chewing gum, from off the wall behind me.

Nice. I yanked at it crossly. A section of hair came away in my hand.

Oh, real pretty. Now the constellation of mosquito bites on my arm began to itch. I closed my eyes.

The air smelled of sagebrush cut with rust. Across the road a door slammed. A woman in a rah-rah skirt sauntered down her front steps in stilettos. I recognised her immediately. She was togged up in the same cheesecloth shirt as earlier, but it was now knotted at the waist. She loitered on the street, casting her eye over the evening as if deciding how to play it. It was only a matter of time before she saw me. As she took in the sweat rings, the bird's-nest hair, and the bleeding insect bites on my arm, I got a stretch of lip that definitely couldn't be mistaken for a smile.

Divided by the road, we gazed at each other.

She had me, no question. She crossed, walked straight on up, dragged something out of her back pocket. I knew what was coming. A pause that felt like an eternity before she dropped it: a single peso. I watched the coin spinning in the sunlight before it landed in my upturned hat with a *thunk*.

"Cunt," she said.

I was about to agree with her, when suddenly I remembered who I had become. A different spirit, a darker beast. And now I'd given in to that person, it would take a lot more than name-calling to bring me back.

I pocketed the coin, raised golden eyes to hers. "You've no idea." I bared my teeth, and she skittered away.

Tomorrow suddenly felt open-ended. Unmarked ground waiting to be explored.

Tomorrow I would do better.

DEAR DAVID GILMOUR

I met Vicente where I met everyone in Nogales, Mexico: loitering by the wall. He'd been following me for a while by then, and though I was pretending to check out the inscriptions on the crosses nailed to the corrugated iron, I'd noticed his two paces to my one every time I shuffled along. He was nearly caught up, so I turned, a move he correctly took as a cue for introductions.

"What you doin' here, lady?" he crooned.

"Who, me?" I shrugged, fake coy. "Nuthin'."

"Tsk, tsk, tsk . . ." He shook his head. "This is not a good place for nuthin'."

He had a shrill voice, all orchestral highs and lows, as though it had tried breaking during puberty, only to have his hormones bail out on him before the job was done.

I pressed my back to the wall, absorbing the heat off the metal. I liked it here, I told him, and it was no lie. I'd been slipping in and out of Nogales for over a year now, and I found the town as beautiful as it was disturbing. It was late afternoon. A flash of monsoon had washed the lethargy from the day and left a flicker of tension on the evening to come.

"No, you don't understand." He was a nondescript man, with an earnest face and plaintive brown eyes. There were few tourists in this town, he went on to explain, and people were watching. He, Vicente, was concerned for my safety. How he would hate for me to be set upon by thugs and muggers. "There are many of them out there," he said, his eyes flicking left and right and coming to land on an innocent postal box. "Many, many," he repeated sternly. "I don't want you to get into no trouble."

"Me neither," I told him. Trouble, we went on to agree, was a nasty business. Then we lapsed into silence to further contemplate this truth. We were stalling. It was the game. Nogales small talk, a little *amuse-bouche* before we progressed to the main course of business.

His was not the first advance I'd had that day, but I'd taken a speed-dating approach to the others. I blew off the first purely on the basis that his skin smelled chemical. The second had eyes that mirrored dollar signs when he looked into mine. But for all its dubious characters, there is chivalry to be found in Nogales and Vicente had a thread of it. My task for the afternoon? Find a fixer. And though this one may not have been exactly what John and I were looking for, it would soon be dusk, I was desperate to pee, and for what he considered a truly bargain rate, Vicente was prepared to put himself forwards as my guide—my shepherd against the marauding *lobos*. Vicente knew this town, and what was it exactly I was after? Spices? Some plastic Tupperware for my shiny U-S-of-A kitchen?

"Come on, tell Vicente," he wheedled, as though I were withholding my most shameful secrets on his Freudian couch. What would I like to do and where was it precisely I'd like to go?

"Down the tunnels, please," I told him.

"Here in Nogales?" He feigned innocence. *Dear God, there's always one*, his reproachful look implied. *The end-of-shift passenger who demands to be taken over the Brooklyn Bridge during rush hour, no change for a tip.* "Which tunnels you mean?"

I revealed the roll of dollars in my hand, a skill absorbed from countless reruns of *Starsky & Hutch*.

"Ah, *sí, sí, those* tunnels," he acknowledged, as though hoping I'd been referring to an infinitely more upmarket variety with fine dining and valet parking thrown in.

"Sure, I know where *those* tunnels are. Vicente knows where is located everything in this sweet *ciudad*!"

"And you'll take me? Me and my friend John?"

It's obvious he'd rather do anything else. Nevertheless, times are hard here in Nogales, city of hope and splintered dreams. In everybody's sweat are small beads of desperation. So yes, Vicente would take us through the drug tunnels to the US. "But!"—he raised a finger—not before proving his credentials as a moral and trustworthy man. "A good Mexican," he clarified, and to that end he hauled me along the street, randomly accosting locals on the way. Here, an old woman spit-roasting her sweet corn with the enthusiasm of an organ grinder. Outside the Santa Crista pharmacy it was the turn of a blind man selling trays of sunglasses, and had I not protested Vicente would have put the question to the mongrel pooping disconsolately into the gutter. "Who am I?" he demanded of everyone. "Tell her who I am!"

"Why," they said, looking bemused, "you are Vicente, of course!"

"Yes, I am Vicente"—he puffed out his chest—"and I am a family man!" He slid out a photograph depicting a fright of sultry teenagers pouting at the lens. "Are these not my daughters?" he demanded. "Well?"

"Indeed they are," all chorused obediently, including the blind man, who really couldn't have known whether he was being shown a family photo or the Shroud of Turin.

"You see!" Vicente crowed. "So now I trust you, and you trust Vicente! *Welcome to the machine!*"

"Huh?" I said.

* * *

The Alubia was a dingy local bar that, over the last eighteen months, had become a default office for John and me. Emily was back home in Colorado, delivering twins on the reservation, but John was at a corner table, sketching faces in his leather-bound pad, three beers already sudsing on empty by his elbow. Although I no longer felt like the peashooter John had brought along to the gunfight, it was still with some relief that I presented Vicente before bolting to the lavatory, where a hooker was douching her *panocha* at the tiny hand basin, her white stiletto balanced against the wall and a teeny-weeny leopard-skin purse chained to her wrist. By the time I returned, John was drumming his fingers on the table in a manner that suggested Vicente was in danger of losing an eye. John does not take kindly to men referring to themselves in the third person, but in the same way that people feel compelled to pass on their handyman however mediocre his services, I was determined that Vicente should be our guy. "Oh, sure, there are many dangers down the tunnels," he was boasting. "But it's OK because Vicente is brave. Vicente has been gifted with a pair of *cojones* the size of a Bengal tiger!"

It would be hard to find a worse person to play the testosterone card with than John, given his military background and love of an unnecessary fight, but he'd always had a soft spot for a fellow exaggerator. A fee was agreed upon, and the deal was done.

Ever since my father told me that alligators roamed the New York subway, I've been intrigued by the idea of creatures and people living beneath our feet, in heating shafts, under bridges, in the transit spaces of airports and cinemas. These are the homeless, the outsiders—people who don't belong, relegated to spaces that don't exist and making a life in conditions unthinkable for the rest of us. A tunnel connecting two cities on opposite sides of a line felt like the ultimate in-between space. The limbo of limbo, the nowhere of nowhere, a deeper form of exile. Many of Nogales's tunnels had been requisitioned and remodeled with almost comic-caper genius by the town's cartels. Others, though, were home to the town's border orphans, "tunnel kids," who, on a diet of paint thinner and attitude, reputedly earned a living by charging a fee for passage from one side to the other.

The tunnel Vicente had selected for us began a quarter-mile from the wall. Even though in a year's time it would be blocked off, secured by Homeland Security and fitted with sensors and cameras, it was, for now, Vicente promised, safe as socks.

"Actually, this is a really shitty part of town," our cabbie contradicted, pulling up. "So I wait here for you."

"That's good of you," John told him, "but we don't know how long we're going to be."

"Meter's off, man." The driver crossed his arms and killed the engine. "I wait for you anyway."

The tunnel itself was a concrete pipe about five feet high accessed by an entrance ramp sprinkled with garbage. The bunch of giggling schoolgirls at the bus stop opposite seemed impervious to the smell, but then this was Nogales's special blend Chanel No. 5, and it would have been hovering in the air since the day they were born.

"Good-bye, blue sky," Vicente sang with feeling.

I'd been thinking much the same. The day was flawless, the sun warm as wax against my skin. By comparison, the mouth of the tunnel seemed a whorl of loneliness, and for some reason "good-bye, blue sky" began repeating in my head like an earworm. Suddenly my brain locked onto why: "Welcome to the Machine," "Goodbye Blue Sky." Song titles, both of them.

"Pink Floyd, Vicente?" I said.

Vicente perked up, the guy on a painful first date who had finally found common ground.

"You heard of them?" he asked eagerly. "They're an English band, you know. The drummer is English, the guitar player is English, the lead singer is—"

"Yes, Vicente, er . . . I've heard of Pink Floyd, thank you."

Vicente looked crestfallen, and I felt bad. "You think they'll be people down there?" I asked.

Even if the tunnel wasn't cartel, chances were we'd still be traipsing uninvited through somebody else's hallway, and this one could have been housing any number of life's outcasts. The tunnel kids had a reputation for toughness, often beating up and robbing their customers, irrespective of whether or not their fee got paid. Rates for passage varied, depending on which Central American country the immigrants hailed from. Hondurans, we'd been told, came in for a particular drubbing.

"Maybe," Vicente admitted. "Yes, it's just possible there might be, well, you know, one or two people down there."

"And what if one of them tries to mess with us?"

"Ah, no worries. Vicente will show them who's boss." He drew himself up, managing to look about as macho as a snow globe. "It is Vicente's job to protect you."

This got a snort of laughter from John, twenty feet away, but I couldn't help but like Vicente. Back in London he'd be slipping his business card into letter boxes. *House needs a fresh coat of paint? Vicente's brushstrokes are straight and even! Ask anyone, even if they're blind! Especially if they're blind!*

"You can trust Vicente in a bad situation," he said. "This I swear on the life of my daughters." It was true he had yet to let us down, but the tunnels made him nervous. It had taken him three days to find one he was OK with, and now, as we stood shilly-shallying aboveground, he'd attached himself to my side like Velcro, more for his own protection, I suspected, than mine. John was already heading down the ramp as though on a walkway to the city's most prestigious social gathering, while inside the cab, the driver was furiously gesticulating at us to come back. So, purely to avoid being named and shamed, the motivation for almost every dubious decision I ever make, I sucked in a deep breath and stumbled down into the gloom.

The smell sharpened. I opened my mouth to call for John and tasted sewage. Thirty feet in, the ceiling of the pipe began to lower. A whispery scuttle of insects and a new smell—urine on the ferment—before the darkness, too bitter for our torches, swallowed everything.

It was hot in the tunnel. A truck rumbled overhead, and my coward's stream of consciousness switched on. *What if it was carrying an oversize load? One of those trucks hauling other trucks? What if the ground gave way, the pipe shattered?* It was monsoon season, and I worried about rain, the churning waters of a flash flood, *the suffocating, lung-bubbling death to follow.* Fuck John! Where was he? And what was Vicente mumbling on about?

"Run, rabbit," I heard him say.

"What? Where?" I peered into the dark. There were no rabbits—a savagely mutated rat maybe. A blast of subterranean air hit me. I caught a skein of cigarette smoke and, irrationally, had an image of John ahead, debonair as Gatsby, unsoiled in white shirt and tan trousers. Then I saw him, squatting on his haunches, talking to two boys slouched against the curve of the pipe, cocooned in filthy clothes. As we approached, they turned old-men eyes our way. One of them was cradling a Saturday night special—a small, sixty-dollar pistol. *Ha!* I thought, *John's gun is bigger,* then felt ashamed. They were just boys, not much older than Jesse or Sam.

Cálmate, John was instructing them. "We're here looking around, understand?"

They nodded, wary—mouths split narrow as we passed. John, once again, disappearing ahead. Behind us, the boys imitated his accent and laughed.

An eternity of seconds, then a low feral sound echoed around the concrete walls. A tentacle of fear stirred in my stomach. "John!"

Another moan, though animal or human, it was hard to say.

I clutched at Vicente. His eyes looked like peeled eggs in the dark. "Run, rabbit, run," he recited. "Dig that hole next the sun."

Instinctively, I corrected him: "Dig that hole, *forget* the sun." Then my foot skidded on something—a moon of soured milk from a busted carton.

"John!" I yelled.

Something snapped under my shoe—a spent hypodermic, and now I could identify John's voice mingled with a Spanish-speaking one, angry and swearing.

"Come on!" I dragged at Vicente, but he had his fingers stuck in his ears, like a child who's being told about his parents' divorce. "Run rabbit, run rabbit," he recited over and over, speeding up like a record cranked from thirty-three rpm to forty-five. I thumped him, and he started—not, as it happens, unlike a rabbit. He looked at me unseeingly, eyes bulging, teeth grinding, and then—before I could stop him—turned tail and scampered back the way we'd come.

For a minute I stood in the echoey quiet, bogged down by garbage, trapped by fear. As much as I'd have liked to follow Vicente, I couldn't abandon John. Truly I wanted to, but I couldn't. Instead I descended into slo-mo, my body's entirely unhelpful response to danger. It was a strangely detached state, a mixed-genre feeling, as though I were a pleasantly stoned hippie who'd been accidentally dropped into a horror flick directed by Arlo Guthrie. *So, hey, uh . . . looks kinda like John's dead or being set upon by, like, giant evil creatures or something! Bummer, man. Wonder if I should lend a hand?* But even as I peered around, a thunder of feet, more shouting, closer this time—and here was John, barreling down the tunnel and, for some inexplicable reason, grinning broadly.

"Run!" he yelled.

Vicente rested his tiny gerbil *cojones* on a stool in the relative safety of the Alubia. He dragged on a bottle of beer, avoiding my eyes.

"So what's with this Pink Floyd thing, Vicente?"

"*Qué?*" He gazed with intense curiosity into the middle distance. Mistaking this for a come-on, a woman nursing the dregs of a tequila gave him the eye. He flushed and looked away.

"Pink Floyd songs brings good memories to Vicente. Many beyooodiful memories of childhood." He drank and I sighed. Off the agenda, apparently, his failure as my protector. I still didn't know exactly who or what had happened down there. John hadn't been sure himself. In the dark, it had been no more than knees and arms and elbows—the limbs of phantoms living fragments of lives. This was not Vicente's worry, though. Far as he was concerned, we crawled, we saw, we ran. Deal done, tip expected.

"Maybe you think it's easy living on this side of the line," he said defiantly. "*Each day closer to death . . . just little bricks in the wall.*" He made a Shakespearean gesture through the Alubia's window towards the actual wall, then slammed his bottle onto the bar.

"Steady on, old boy," John said gently. "We've got your back."

Vicente was not to be quieted. "Roger Waters, Nick Mason, they're OK, man, they're great, but David Gilmour is Vicente's hero, you know?" He laid his head in his hands. "I swear by the Virgin of Guadalupe and all her sister saints, if I ever got to meet Dave Gilmour, man . . . that would be like, well—that would be the best thing that could ever happen to Vicente." His eyes moistened.

"Yeah, well." I choked down a slightly unkind laugh. "Good luck with that, my friend."

Back in my own city, London—a good town, a nice town, where for some the living is easy, especially in summertime—Mac and I were at a party for a restaurant on the river. People had gathered on the wharf under the cottony haze of sunset, all manner of nice, interesting people, chatting and eating delicious things, and I should have been out there too. Instead, I'd found the only liminal space possible under the circumstances, the ladies' room, where I was crouched on a closed loo seat feeling disconnected, feeling other. Transition between home and away was always a question of untangling my own hopelessly knotty lines. I should have been happy, but I was unable to track back to any emotion other than confusion. I couldn't explain this love affair with the border, other than I'd lost sight of home—not the immeasurable sweetness of my children, never that—but home as in the entity Mac and I had created between us. Stepping into the lives of others made it easy to put my own life on hold, and even as I stared at my reflection in the cubicle mirror, the wall behind me morphed into the shimmer of desert. I turned slowly to find I was standing on the brink of it, vast, uncompromising, and utterly compelling.

Outside I snatched a drink off a tray, and that's when I saw him. No more than three feet away, his back to the viscous, greasy flow of the Thames. *Live! In person, breathing in the air, right here, right now, on the light side of the moon.*

David Gilmour.

I was staring, moronically staring, and backing away too, some sort of ghastly grimace on my face. Famous people belong in their world and I in mine, and any question that we might have to share a realm is horrifying. But . . . but . . . it seemed so disloyal to Vicente. That tear-jerker speech had got to me—of course it had. So I firmed up my own teeny tiny *cojones* and approached.

Back on the border a few weeks later—this time without John, to do a ride-along with the Border Patrol—all I cared about was finding Vicente. His cell phone had been disconnected, so it was back to the sweet corn lady, the blind man with sunglasses, and the pooping mongrel. I left messages with them all, even the dog: I would wait for Vicente every day between six and eight p.m. outside the Santa Crista pharmacy.

This was my first time solo, but Nogales is a generous town. It had taken me in and shown me its secret places. Here, in this warren of barriers, walls, and checkpoints, paradoxically, I felt free.

After a third fruitless evening of waiting, I fell in with a gaunt man who loped up out of nowhere to scold some *federales* for hassling me about filming in the street.

When one of the cops turned pettish, the man grabbed my arm and said, "I'll take her," as though offering shelter to a skanky kitten who would otherwise have been humanely put down. He guided me through the traffic with all the assiduousness of a lollipop man at a school crossing, signaling an obliging driver here, acknowledging the hoot of a horn there. I didn't ask where we were going, but turned out to be his home—a park bench. From behind a shrub, he produced a plastic sandwich baggie containing his worldly goods: his ID papers, which had been nibbled by a mouse, a harmonica, and a faded picture of his wife holding a tiny baby.

"Is she here, too?" I questioned, tentatively.

He gave me a look of distaste, as if to say, *You think I'd drop an uncut diamond like her into this pile of dung?* Then, indicating my camera,

asked whether I would like to hear his story. But I was storied out. I'd
heard so many in the past few days that they'd merged into one long
dissertation of misery. When I suggested meeting for breakfast the
following morning, his face contracted. "You're not hungry now?" he
asked, and I felt like the world's biggest shit.

"This is the first restaurant I've eaten in for three years," Gabriel
confided from our corner booth, and I could well believe it. His skin
was translucent, his eyesight too poor to read the menu. I ordered him
the highest-protein dish I could find, but he wasn't happy—the *señora*
must not pay! And I was unable to make him comfortable until I hit
on the idea of showing him a forged BBC press pass I'd brought along
as a last-resort get-out-of-jail-free card.

"The British government will pay for both our dinners!" I told
him. "Drinks too!"

Gabriel stroked the laminated card in wonder while I made a big
show of switching on the camera. I was doubtful of getting much. His
inability to grasp the difference between *yes* and *no*, combined with a
habit of dropping his *t*'s, made understanding his English a guessing
game somewhere between Pictionary and charades.

Gabriel's story was one of family separation. He'd sneaked into the
United States, got married, had a kid, racked up a few unpaid parking
tickets, and ultimately run foul of the government's retrospective "three
strikes, you're out" policy. Deported, he'd paid a smuggler, got caught,
and tried again, this time under his own steam. Lost in the desert he'd
collapsed, waking only when someone stamped on his arm.

He put down his harmonica and, reaching for my hand, guided my
forefinger over a pebble of bone sticking out of his wrist at a queasy
angle.

"Will you try again?" I asked him.

"No, but I can."

Yes, he wants to cross, but he can't.

"I can' cross because of this."

"Your hand?"

"No. And because of this." Now he was dragging up his nylon shirt.

I shoved my plate aside. Running vertically from lower abdomen to breastbone was a scar so thick and ragged it looked as though it had been made with a harpoon.

"Jesus, Gabriel, what happened to you?"

"Cops," he shrugged. "Mexican."

"The cops did that to you?"

"No." He shook his head vigorously in the affirmative.

There had been two of them, one who stamped on his wrist, the other his head. When he came to, they told him he owed them money for saving his life. But no worries! This was his lucky day! Did he not know that he could pay his debt by having his *riñón* removed, and the good news was that he'd still have fifty bucks left over to send to his family?

"A *riñón* is a kidney, right?"

"No," he said emphatically.

"Are you sure?"

"I am sure," he said, looking doubtful.

I pushed harder. Gabriel became muddled and even more so when I started barking body organs at him in an attempt to guess which one, precisely, had been removed. *OK, so liver? Spleen? Rhymes with "queen"? One syllable? Two?*

Suddenly I caught sight of my reflection in the mirror behind him. Gonzo babe, the glittering, ugly face of hypocrisy. Although, right then and there, I would have done anything, taken on every branch of Homeland Security to piggyback Gabriel over the line and reunite him with his wife—at the same time, God help me, the organ I most wanted him to be missing was the biggest badass organ he owned. Had he hauled up his shirt to reveal the pulsing, hemorrhaging void where his heart had once been, I still can't guarantee I'd have been happy.

I felt a shift in my own heart, a soft click onto some higher setting of shame I hadn't known existed. It didn't matter how many nights I spent pacing my hotel room with men like Gabriel haunting the periphery of my consciousness. On ride-alongs with the Border Patrol, out with the repulsive California Minutemen, it was the same. A thrilling game of "catch me if you can." And if the poor bastards we rounded up were photogenic—as in, roughed up a little—it was all good copy.

Was this what my other self became when unchecked? *Tell the story*. Wasn't that what it was about? But I knew that any halfway decent impulse of mine was poisoned by a desire to walk on the wild side and "find" myself amongst lost people and lost causes. I couldn't help Gabriel and I couldn't help me. Suddenly I felt complicit in the crime that had been perpetrated on him. What was the point of observing pain if you were unable to provide a salve? I could come here and steal as many stories as I liked, and this was all I could give in return? A Mr. Rancheros steak with a side basket of tortillas?

Still, with the aid of Gabriel's napkin and a pen, we did, in the end, establish that, yes, of course, it was a kidney that had been ripped out of him.

Gabriel tipped back in his chair. "Kidney, yes," he agreed with a satisfied smile.

"Yes, kidney. Good," I said, feeling sick.

The following morning, having given up all hope of finding Vicente, I bumped into him on the street. To say he was astonished was an understatement. He fell about my neck and clasped me in a hug that felt more like a Rolfing technique. This was nothing to his reaction when I whipped out the Pink Floyd CDs. Wordlessly, he turned the cases over in his hands. *To Vicente*, David Gilmour had scribbled in elegant pen, *love David.*

Vicente slowly traced a finger over *David*, then the word *love*, and without warning burst into tears. When he demanded I go with him to meet his friends, I wasn't keen. I was still feeling raked over from supper the previous night, my emotions as bare as a tree that has shed its last leaf.

After Gabriel and I were done eating, he had escorted me to the wall. On the way, I'd tried to give him what cash I had on me. He refused. I shoved it into his shirt pocket. In exchange he fumbled his harmonica into my hands.

"No." I brushed it away, mortified at the idea of accepting what constituted 30 percent of his sum possessions. "You'll play again one day."

But he shook his head. When the moment had come for me to walk through the pedestrian turnstile to the US there was such a tornado of rage spinning round my head that I'm pretty sure I was shaking more than he was. Tunnels, airports, borders. I'm fascinated by these spaces because I can move freely across their divides, but what thrills me is the thing that would ultimately kill him.

The morning I bumped into Vicente, I'd been hoping for an arm-shot of normalcy—shopping, calling the children—but now he was dragging me past the toy emporium, past a shop of forlorn bridal gowns waiting for Miss Right, through the bright tumult of the flower markets, until a long flight of steps nearly finished him off. At the bottom he leaned against a pair of ornate gates, panting noises coming out of his chest as if from a faulty air-con unit. A man in dark glasses unwound the heavy chain, and suddenly we were in a basement room lit by a few bright coins of sun. From the corner came the sound of muffled crying.

No, I thought, *no, no, no.*

My eyes adjusted. Three men were sitting around a table, united, apparently, by some dreadful collective misery.

Oh, dear Lord. I shot Vicente a furious look.

"Ah, *sí*." He made an unnecessarily dramatic sign of the cross. "Today, death is with us."

One of the men sniffed obligingly.

"Well, yes, so sorry." I backed swiftly out of the room, wondering whether it would be tacky to ask about cabs. Vicente grabbed my hand.

"*Mis hermanos*," he addressed the men solemnly. Eyes turned— puffy, red-rimmed. My embarrassment at interrupting some family mourning intensified when Vicente suddenly raised my arm as though I'd won Olympic gold. "This is the writer I was telling you about, remember?" he said. And for a wildly uncomfortable moment, I thought I was going to be called upon to say a few words.

"Now, when I first tell you about her," he scolded, "you don't believe Vicente. You say Vicente is on drugs, that he gets *hiiiigh*." He yanked my arm up again. "But here is proof!"

The men acknowledged me courteously.

Undeterred, Vicente ratcheted up his performance. "So on this terrible day of sadness"—he produced the CDs from his pocket with a magician's flourish—"Vicente has brought a *milagro*! *That means miracle*," he whispered in my ear.

More watery smiles. Vicente sighed and handed around the cases. Finally, as it dawned on them what was written there, I heard sharp intakes of breath, followed by much whooping and backslapping, all of which Vicente absorbed, the smile of the vindicated on his face.

Still, while I'm as giant a fan of the Floyd as anyone, while David Gilmour's signature was beyond cool, these guys were treating me as if I'd just patented a cure for the common cold.

"What's going on, Vicente?"

Vicente stared at me, then slapped the side of his head. "She doesn't know!" he squawked. "She doesn't know!"

A newspaper was shoved into my hands. A full-page, grainy black-and-white picture. A familiar face. Donkey jacket, collar turned up. *Muerto!* The headline screamed. *Syd Barrett es muerto!*

I sat down. It was too much. Some sort of hoax. What does coincidence become when it's impossibly unlikely?

"You remember Syd Barrett?" Vicente asked.

Founding member of Pink Floyd. Well, yeah, kind of. I remembered hearing a story that he'd once stuck crushed quaaludes on his head before a concert and then stood immobile, neither playing nor singing, while they melted into his scalp under the heat of the stadium lighting.

"He was some kind of crazy diamond," said one of the other guys, shaking his head in admiration. "You know, without Syd Barrett and his poor messed-up soul, man, there wouldn't be no album *Wish You Were Here.*"

"Yeah, *shine on*, brother," Vicente said solemnly, producing a lit candle from God only knows where. "We will never forget you."

The irony. Oh the irony. Not so much the bittersweet serendipity of my timing, but the fact that while I was crying over Gabriel and the other pitiful stories generated out of this strip of land, these guys were mourning a sixty-year-old eccentric Englishman who'd lived in Cambridgeshire.

Vicente made introductions: Bashful Esteban. Jaimé, who was dressed like a geography teacher in a minor public school. The big weepy lunk was Jorge, a Mexican Lennie Small. "We used to be one more, you know," Vicente said. "Little guy with an *órgano bucal*. He wasn't so skilled, but he put his heart into it."

Esteban picked up his guitar and the mood brightened. Jaimé sat down next to him, and began plucking at his own strings in duet, while Jorge slammed his hands on the table in a magnificent effort at syncopation. They were good—properly good. Somehow, amidst this cache of talent, Vicente had landed himself the job of lead singer. I would love to report that when he opened his mouth out poured the burbling haiku of doves, but even lubricated by beer his voice sounded like peppercorns jumping on a hot skillet. "All in all," he croaked, as the party moved outside and began to attract a crowd, "we're just little bricks in the wall."

And I remembered.

A year earlier—concert in Hyde Park for Live 8, and though at least a dozen other bands were playing to save the world, I hadn't known a soul who wasn't there for Pink Floyd. It was late in the evening and the sky was shuddering with storm. Nobody cared, everybody was high on the waiting—twelve hours and then some—punch-drunk on emotion, swaying through the lulls between acts. But then the air tautened. A lone stagehand trailed out wires, a rumble built. NO MORE EXCUSES! flashed across the backdrop in liquid light. Two hundred thousand people roared into the starless night, as pink pigs drifted through the sky and the opening beats of "Breathe" electrified London.

Sometimes in Nogales, I'd screw up my eyes against the light and there was the dragon's tail of the actual wall, dark green, trenched into the ground. It was not made of bricks or even of metal. It was made of . . . well, if we're honest, it was made of lazy thinking. Remove the political posturing, kill the fear. Wasn't the jigsaw of Mexico and the United States always a good fit? One mass block of workers staring at one giant JOBS AVAILABLE sign?

Esteban had been strumming his own tune for a while, something quiet and melancholy. "This is for our fifth band member," he said. "The one who never came back."

"What happened to him?"

"He was our Syd Barrett, you know? Doomed." Esteban formed a chord, hit it once.

"Hey," I said, and admittedly I was feeling pretty maudlin when this idea hit me. "Let's record a message to David Gilmour! You know, with the camera! Get him to come and play a gig out here!"

The boys looked at me.

"You can get a message to him?" Jaimé asked.

"I dunno." I shrugged. *Maybe*, I thought. And if so, then maybe here was something I could do. Something I could give.

Dear Bella, Gilmour's note accompanying the CDs had read. *Hope this does the trick.* And I too, just like Vicente, had traced my finger over the inscription.

"Sure, why not?" Vicente coughed a few seeds out of his craw, then positioned himself in front of the camera, CDs clutched to his chest. "Hey, David!" he shouted. "I don't know what to say. You are a great musician . . . maybe the greatest in the world. Thank you, and that's all!"

"Hey, David Gilmour!" Jaimé nervously adjusted his shirttail. "You're the king of the enchiladas. You're like the biggest fuckin' tamale of all. You touch my heart. You touch me in here, you know?" He thumped his chest.

Jorge's turn. He stood, arms dangling uselessly by his sides. "I dunno how to start," he mumbled.

"Just do it, man." Esteban stopped playing. "He'll hear you no matter what you say."

"Pretend you're writing him a letter," I told him. My own accompanying note would have to be handwritten, of course. *Dear Mr. Gilmour. Dear David.* Fuck. Awkward.

"I can't write," Jorge said.

Up on the street, the last of the concert crowd had dispersed. The sun was dropping in this way station, this holding bay of dreamers. Time for business. Esteban was an electrician who dealt drugs. Vicente was a tourist guide who peddled information. Jaimé taught twelve-year-olds and moved guns. And Jorge? Big, soft Jorge? Well, who knows? Everybody in this town held down two jobs, but the one that put food on the table always began at dusk.

"OK, well, I jus' wanna say one last thing." Vicente had taken the microphone again. "David . . . I hope you live a long time. I hope you die good. I hope you don't lose all your money or ever have to be separated from your loved ones."

Don't die young, don't die bad, don't die poor or lonely. A message of luck summing up the collective fear of Nogales. Summing up everyone's fears, I guess. I switched off the camera.

Back in London, I spliced my footage together and sent it off with a note that I drafted at least a dozen times, but which eventually began: *Dear David, kind of a funny story for you . . .*

And then I waited.

I get it. Music is a beautiful plague, contagious and airborne. It pays no lip service to borders, to closed doors or minds. It connects those small cells of Jaimés, Estebans, and Vicentes everywhere. It connects us all. Spin the globe and stick in a pin. Up in Greenland, fishermen are sitting around ice holes humming songs from *Ummagumma.* Russian gem dealers grunting "you crazy diamond" are flying their Cessnas over the mines of eastern Siberia. In London hospitals, anaesthesiologists are softly crooning "Comfortably Numb."

The music belongs to them as it belongs to every one of us. I understand that Nogales's number-one Pink Floyd Fan Club is not unique, but it was unique to me.

So I'll go on waiting and I'll go on hoping. I have no doubt that you'll come round in the end, David, because when you think about it, it's only the teeniest, tiniest of fix-its. *A border town, a desert sky, and one last, great gig to play beneath it.*

SECRET LIFE

In the Los Angeles Hertz parking lot, there was but one solitary vehicle left: a gleaming black Lincoln Continental with souped-up masculinity lights and seats upholstered in an animal skin that looked suspiciously like that of the endangered snow leopard.

I checked the plates against the key fob in my hand.

The rep on the ground was a skinny kid with chin fuzz and a sloppy relationship with his chewing gum.

"Hey!" I waved him over.

"Hey to you, lady customer!" His Hertz uniform shirt, unironed and unbuttoned over a Mickey Mouse vest, was hanging loose as he was.

"I don't get it," I said, gesturing to the Lincoln. "What's this?"

He consulted his clipboard. "This is your vehicle, ma'am."

"It can't be!"

"Why?" He glanced up. "You book something else?"

"Well, yes! I asked for nothing flashy or expensive-looking. An inconspicuous car. You know, the kind of car no one could pick out in a police line-up."

"Inconspicuous, huh?" He patted the pimpmobile affectionately. "Oh, this ol' cough machine'll blend in anywhere."

I took in his nut-brown legs, the surf shorts across which a cavalry of sea horses, snouts raised, was gamely charging. "Forgive me for asking, but do you actually work here?"

"You betcha!" He flicked his name badge. RUDY, HERTZ EMPLOYEE OF THE MONTH.

263

"OK, well, Rudy. I can't take this car."

"Sure you can. This is one classy ride. A classy ride for a classy dame!"

I sighed. "Don't you have something else?"

For a moment I was hopeful that an actual directive was running through Rudy's head. *Find this customer the car she wants!*

"Look, I'm heading down to Tijuana," I told him. "I need something low-key, you know?"

"Low-key or fancy schmancy"—Rudy spat his gum into a pot housing a cactus—"you cannot take this vehicle into Mexico."

"But I always take my car into Mexico."

"Not *rentals* you don't. The border is like the carjacking capital of the world."

"Oh, don't worry. I'll put it in a proper parking lot."

"You're kidding, right?" Rudy peeled a fresh stick of gum from his pack and compressed it between his teeth. "Parking lots are basically carjackers' showrooms. Tijuana is like the Bermuda Triangle of rental vehicles."

"Is this some funky way of getting me to sign up for the extra insurance?"

"Listen, lady customer." He jangled the keys down into my hand. "Whatever you smoke is fine by me, but know this fun fact: with Hertz, your insurance runs out at the line."

There's no excitement like the vibe of a new city. Knowing nobody, everything to learn before familiarity comes like a photograph slowly revealing itself in developing fluid. I had no good reason to go to Tijuana. After a couple of years, the material I'd been collecting had more or less formed itself into a novel, but the idea of wrenching myself out of a world I'd been so happily lost in was unthinkable, and

I'd been seeking out travel pieces and any other snippets of work that kept me close to the line. First Emily and then even John had gone back to their normal lives, so I'd asked my only LA friend, Casey, a heavily tattooed film executive, to come with me. By the time we hit San Diego we were both exhausted from a sneezing fit brought on by the Lincoln's hairy interiors and nauseated from gobbling five pounds of dates purchased from a Vietnam vet in the festering heat of Salton City.

"Are we nearly there?" she whined.

"Can you die from too many dates?" I whined back.

"Must we really park this side and walk over?"

"Just keep your eye out for the exit, OK?"

"Which exit?" She lifted her head from the map just as we sped past the turn-off ramp signposted LAST EXIT TO US!

Immediately, another sign, this one flashing across the freeway in warning neon: TO MEXICO ONLY! And before I could even consider making an illegal U-turn, we found ourselves trapped in the gridlock of a dog-barking, temper-fraying, agent-shouting, trunk-searching, multiple-lane checkpoint.

"Oh crap," Casey said.

Driving in and out of small border towns is fun, it's buzzing. Twenty minutes of queuing and plenty of ways to pass the time. There's always some poor bastard on hand to soap your windshield or gargle with gasoline and set his mouth on fire for your entertainment. Street kids hawk noxious-coloured sweeties from trays slung around their necks. Velour towels printed with lurid images of the Last Supper are on sale and all this under the roving eye of the Mexican police, who lounge against the cement divide, chain-smoking and keeping watch for a pretty girl to hassle.

Tijuana takes itself a lot more seriously. California's port of entry to Mexico is the busiest land port in the world, with twenty million cars and over fifty million people crossing every year. When, ninety dreary minutes later, Casey and I were finally waved past the barrier, we were aghast to see that the queue back to San Diego was at least a hundred and fifty cars and still growing.

"Over there!" Casey pointed at a crude PARK HERE sign. I hesitated. "The Bermuda Triangle of cars," Rudy had said. But we had only this one day, and to waste half of it tailbacking in traffic was out of the question.

In the razed wasteland of the parking lot, an old man pushed stiffly off the steps of a trailer and made his way towards us, limping mildly. "Twenty dollar," he announced, casting a shrewd eye over the Lincoln as if already weighing up whether to sell it by the yard or the pound.

As the old man took the bill I noticed the scar in the centre of his palm—a small welt circling soft, purplish skin. I'd seen this crucifixion scar before and knew it to be some kind of rite of passage between prison inmates. Without thinking, I reached out and touched it, and his hand closed round my finger like a Venus flytrap.

The attendant's eyes were cloudy, the colour of a glacial lake. And even though I had yet to ask the question, he nodded, an imperceptible yes.

Alfredo was seventy-two, he told us, holding his little white moustache to the vent blowing cool air from the Lincoln's dashboard, a retired coyote recruited at thirteen by two Artful Dodgers. Smuggling had been the job of his dreams. Money, kudos, adrenaline—everything a bored street kid could ask for. After a while, though, and much to his dismay, his sense of morality kicked in. Witnessing the rape and robbery of his charges was scary and sad, he said, directing us through his old beat with directional shifts of his forefinger. Here were the shallows of the sea, the culs-de-sac that never truly dead-ended. "The pores in America's skin," he called them.

He got married. After the birth of his daughter he refused to bring across any more children. He worried that some of the men he was helping into America were scavengers, animals, but how was anyone supposed to tell the difference? In the garden of good and evil, the boots of all men left the same tread. As the years passed, he lost faith in people, so he began smuggling drugs instead and wound up where he was always going to wind up.

In prison he lifted a copy of *Lines and Shadows* off the library trolley. Joseph Wambaugh's novel detailed a crime task force sent to patrol the no-man's-land between Tijuana and San Diego—not to apprehend the thousands slipping into the United States, but to stop those who preyed on them. Alfredo had been profoundly shamed. "I done so many bad things," he said. "God knows I did."

The last time he went to prison he promised his family he would leave them alone. "And I've kept my word." His little girl would be grown up by now, an American citizen, living a new life on the other side of so many divides.

"Why don't you try to find her?"

"She's in San Diego. She knows I'm here."

"Maybe she wants you to make the first move?" I was having difficulty squaring Alfredo's image of himself as redemption-unworthy sinner with the regretful philosopher in our front seat. It was neither bad luck, bad geography, nor bad guys that killed most people—it was bad education. And what if Alfredo's daughter hadn't understood that?

"We could go to San Diego, bring her over to you," I offered, beginning to write a heroic role for myself in Alfredo's tale. I conjured up a pitch-haired girl, looking out of a small adobe house somewhere in the burbs.

"She'll find me if she wants to," Alfredo said stubbornly." He pressed his forehead to the window and stared at the metallic blur of traffic. "There is so much wanting in this city," he said softly. "It eats away at your soul."

For weeks after returning to London, I paced the cage of my office, unable to settle into a routine. Even as I guiltily closed my door against the clomp of my own daughter's feet on the stairs, I was thinking about Alfredo's. His acceptance of loneliness as her punishment for him made me sad. If a parent loves a child unconditionally, shouldn't that child try to absolve the parent of crimes committed? Wasn't it OK to fuck up a little if you loved a lot? And so I fretted about Alfredo, with his secrets branded into the palm of his hand. When the time had come for Casey and me to cross back over that day, he'd taken us to a track on the outskirts of town. "Follow it to the end," he'd instructed. "Give the man twenty dollar and tell him your friend Alfredo sent you. Avoid the queue, you know?"

A ping of his seat belt and he'd been gone.

But the real reason I was fractious was that I'd run out of excuses to ship myself back to the border. The novel was written. There were no more free travel passes from magazines. I couldn't even lose myself daydreaming. With other books, the world created had been a place that obeyed no space-time laws. There were no limitations on how often I could visit. But the world of the border was not mine. The lives of those who revolved around it would continue on without me and I would have done anything to get back there. It took me a while to figure out there was only one way: lift the story off the page and find it a new creative medium.

With that in mind, I posted the thing off to an LA film agent named Sylvie. Despite having zealously revised the final manuscript, I added a note peppered with phrases like "work in progress" and "super-early rough draft." If you're English, to be seen to try and then fail remains one of life's greater humiliations. Should anyone denounce your work as a piece of poop, better it be poop dashed off in a matter of hours. So low were my expectations that when, sometime later, a triptych of unpronounceable surnames flashed up on my mobile, I nearly hit the decline button.

To be clear, this isn't one of those stories with a blockbuster ending—nevertheless, a few phrases sank in. *Great work! Quite some interest!* To me, naturally, the exclamation marks said it all. Prone to the scepticism that is yet another cornerstone of the English national psyche, by the time this Sylvie person and I had wrapped up our conversation I had her pegged as an incorrigible bullshitter. With each ensuing phone call, particularly those in which she had something positive to report, I imagined her as an increasingly repulsive type of Hollywood monster. Still, by the time I'd agreed to come to LA and was waiting for my bag at the luggage carousel a few months later, I can't pretend I wasn't excited. I was beginning to see a future of script meetings and highly paid consultant work. Then a text from Sylvie pinged onto my phone. "Sorry! Manuscript escaped," it read.

Escaped? Sure. No doubt some insider's euphemism for total loss of interest.

"Bummer," I texted back.

"Stand by," came the reply.

LA terrifies me. It might be a town for dreamers, but it's not a town to be dreamy in. I had no idea how to stand by there.

I called Jerome, an agent/manager whose number I chanced upon in my contacts list.

"Fabulous!" he roared. "Let's hook up." And minutes later we were being escorted to his table in Chateau Marmont. I was coming down with a heavy cold, while Jerome appeared to be soaring on a marathon high. He buzzed through a virtual poppy field of hallucinatory topics before landing on Hurricane Katrina. "I was there, you know." He dropped his head into his hands. On the second day, he'd looked out of his hotel window and seen an alligator tearing into a dead body. "*A dead body! A gator!* Jesus Christ," he groaned. "I'm so messed up, baby."

I discreetly ordered myself a hot whiskey and lemon.

"You should get that remade," he said suddenly. "I'm thinking snakeskin."

"What?"

"Your watch strap. It's fraying."

"Oh." I looked down at my wrist.

"I have a friend at Hermès who owes me."

"I'm good, thanks."

"You're so grounded," Jerome's voice cracked. "You're one of my favourite people."

We'd met only twice before, and both times I'd suspected him of bitter misogyny. I covered his hand awkwardly, but even this small act was enough to breach his own internal levees, and he broke into sobs, pooling snot onto the sesame bun of his cheeseburger.

The waiter was seating a table close to us—a sleek-looking black dude and his blonde, meerkat-pretty girlfriend. Jerome, nose and eyes miraculously dry, swiftly levitated out of his seat, smoothed his leather pants, and introduced himself with greased confidence, pressing a business card on the guy—a famous rapper—and bullet-pointing his fully inclusive agent/managerial service. "Don't be a stranger, man," he said brightly, before returning to his seat and resuming his crying jag.

If this was the agenting flip side to Sylvie, it was doubly harrowing. The evening served as a timely reminder that, for me, LA was no Kansas. I decided to escape to the relative safety of Tijuana to see whether I could find my old friend Alfredo and talk him into a reconciliation with his daughter.

"Yeah, forget the film thing—wild goose chase—but what about a documentary?" I e-mailed Casey, seeing a less lucrative but equally happy few years of shooting, editing, and indie film festivals. Wasn't Alfredo's story of love lost and quest for forgiveness universal? "I mean, how far are any of us from losing our own families?" I pushed.

"I'm in," Casey replied.

This time we did it smart. Nose in the map. Eye on exits. We parked on the US side and walked over the arched pedestrian crossing to Alfredo's lot. In the whacked-out trailer that constituted an office, a young woman with crimped hair greeted us as though we were a pair of dykey bounty hunters, and only then did I remember that Alfredo was on parole.

"Check out this photo," I said to her. "See Alfredo smiling, arm round my shoulders? We're good friends, understand? See this camera?" I hoisted the rented Nikon onto the counter as though I actually knew how to use it. "We're here from LA, as in *Hollywood*—to film Alfredo's story and—ya know—maybe pay him a little something for his trouble."

We weren't lying. Her production company might be interested, Casey had said. Get Alfredo on film and they'd take a look.

Crimped girl was new in the car-parking business, she informed us, wincing at a broken nail. Sorry, but she barely knew this person, Alfredo.

She *was* lying, so we refused to leave, slouching against the watercooler, lighting up cigarettes and flicking them disdainfully aside in a manner that we very much hoped implied that we were, after all, ruthless bounty hunters, until finally, much to our satisfaction, she picked up the phone and spoke in rapid-fire Spanish.

"So, in a café half a mile from here," she said, hanging up, we were to meet a friend who would fix us up with Alfredo, who, by the way, "was known as *El Duck*."

"*El Duck!*" Casey and I exchanged surprised glances. "*Muchas gracias*, you're so super helpful."

"You're so super welcome!" she smiled sweetly. "Have a great day."

In the café, a septuagenarian with the erect posture of a cowboy sat at a table eating *huevos a la mexicana,* tethering and cutting the eggs with meticulous use of his knife and fork. I thought about breakfast back in London and Mabel's best-loved joke.

"What'll you have?" asked the mom, idly picking her nose.

"Two boiled eggs," yelled her daughter. "You can't get your finger in those."

A man slid into our booth. Smoothly attractive, a raspberry birthmark over one eyebrow. "You wanna find the Duck? *Bueno*. Follow me."

We followed, up and down the tourist estuaries flowing off Avenida Revolución, until we arrived at the steps of a modern church.

"Wait here," he said.

We waited. The air smelled of fried oil. My stomach rumbled. After a while a man stopped to admire Casey's arm tattoos.

"Hey, cool *frijoles!*"

"Oh, yeah, you like my beans?"

"I love them. You get 'em in prison?" He sized her up. Copper hair, five foot eleven, Casey is three parts iron warrior to one part smart-ass.

"Prison? Sure, why not."

"Two cute *palomitas* in Tijuana, huh? Who are you really: FBI? CIA? INS?"

"I make films, and my friend here is a writer."

"A writer? No kidding." His eyes stayed glued to Casey. "But you make movies, huh?"

"Yeah, but I used to be a cook." She lifted the hem of her shorts. "See, I have an onion!"

"Cebolla," the guy breathed, crouching down to examine her thigh.

"Hey, if you like vegetables, check out this bad boy."

At the sight of the broccoli on her ankle, the man nearly swooned. What are the odds, I thought, a touch peevishly, of running into a fresh-produce fetishist in Tijuana? I'd had an ankle incident in Nogales a while back, but it hadn't been quite so flattering. John and I had been sitting in a restaurant when a man, flanked by a couple of bodyguards, snaked in and sat down at the table next to us. He was cartel royalty, in clinking gold jewelry and Cuadra stingray boots. He ordered food, lit a Montecristo, his eyes roving lazily around the room until they came full circle to me. A smile glimmered on his face—the sort that glimmers on the face of a hyena when it spots a wounded impala. He blew out a cloud of smoke and then, without dropping his gaze, reached slowly under the table and seized my bare leg.

John stiffened. He hadn't had a good fight for days, but as the man's enormous digits attempted to close around my ankle a look of shock and disappointment crossed his face. *Calves like pistons! Bail bonds-woman boots!* He let go as though he'd been bitten by a deadly insect and, apologizing, left shortly afterwards.

"Hey," I said to Casey. "Ask your veggie friend if he knows El Duck."

The man looked taken aback. "Sure, everybody knows him."

"You know where we can find him?"

"Nobody *finds* El Duck. If he wants you, he'll find you first." He shoved his hands into his pockets and hurried off down the street.

Eventually a brown Cadillac drew up, chassis low to the ground. The driver leaned over and sprang the door. "Get in," he said.

"Where are you taking us?" I demanded. "You'll see," he replied, and I was reminded of a hitchhiking incident in England while I'd still been at school.

A girlfriend and I had been trying to get home after an all-night party in the country. We hadn't been waiting long before a car slowed. Bearded driver, mid-level company executive, document bag stuffed with reports which he tipped off the passenger seat to make room for me. My girlfriend passed out in the back, leaving conversation to me, but the man seemed content with pleasantries. I rested my head against the window and thought about the boy who had kissed me.

"After all, one good turn deserves another, don't you think?" The man was speaking, and I must have murmured some agreement. Even through the fog of my hangover, the statement seemed fair. "Good," he said, "so will you play with me?" His voice had turned so creepily childlike that I twisted my head in his direction. He indicated his penis, lying forlornly against his trouser thigh like a dying earthworm in urgent need of resuscitation.

"Ugh, no!" I said, too revolted for tact.

He flushed with anger and, fumbling his dick inside his zipper, snapped on the car's central locking.

"Just let us out," I said, feeling the claw of my girlfriend's hand at the back of my neck, "and we won't tell."

"Oh, but you will tell," he replied. "So I can't let you out."

I tried talking him down. Told him we had no intention of calling the police. He took a slip road off the motorway. My limbs prickled with fear. "Where are you taking us?" I demanded.

"You'll see," he said. The road was deserted, bordered on either side by dense woods. I shut my eyes and saw a fairy's grave of moss and bluebells, two girls lying face down, their pale legs crisscrossed by lines of blood.

"Let us go!" I ordered, "or bad things will happen to you!" And maybe the voodoo edge to my voice spooked him, because he swerved onto the verge.

"All right, go on then, get out," he screamed, as though we were a pair of raccoons at his garbage.

It wasn't until he drove off that I noticed the baby seat strapped into the back of the car, a pink pacifier attached to it by a ribbon. I don't think I had any idea before then, any idea at all, of the double lives people led.

I wound down the window as Tijuana passed in a mellow abstract of people, traffic, and houses. Double lives, two selves, twin towns. Mac thought I was in LA eating egg-white omelettes with Sylvie. Sylvie thought I was "standing by" with Jerome. Jerome was most likely on another impressive bender. It didn't matter. I felt happier than I had in months. I had a purpose, a plan, and nowhere else to be— if there was a better feeling in the world, I'd yet to experience it.

The driver stopped and spat us out into some kind of *barrio*. The air smelled furtive and sour. A dog with accordion ribs was moseying towards us, scabrous ears twitching. The camera was heavy, and its size rendered us so conspicuous that even the cockroaches were throwing us sideways looks. We agreed not to be fazed. Clearly Alfredo was more than just the regretful old felon we'd originally thought, but it seemed inconceivable that the old man had not spent as much time worrying about me as I had fretting about him. We'd swapped confidences that day, stranger status permitting its own intimacy.

"I know we're not fazed or anything," Casey said, "but what's with all the mystery?"

"Hell I know." I hoisted the camera onto my other shoulder. "But it's all good material, right?"

"Only if we find him."

"Oh, we'll find him," I said. My phone began vibrating. I could just make out Sylvie's disembodied voice over the static on the line. "So, Shar Leaves just put a call into my office!" she said.

"I'm sorry?"

"She loves the story. She wants to be part of the project."

"Uh, great!" I made an effort to match Sylvie's tone, which fell within the pleased spectrum. "I thought the manuscript had escaped or something?"

"Yes, I know." Sylvie's voice was barely audible. "Warn her brothers!"

It crossed my mind that Sylvie might be mentally unstable or a glue sniffer. Now she was suggesting a meeting with a producer who knew all about "Shar Leaves's interest" and was therefore intending to reach out to "Salmon Cake." And with this last bewildering incongruity, the signal died.

A car eased along the curb, a plastic Virgin wobbling on its dashboard, and we were off again. Another street corner, another pointless rendezvous, and thus the pattern continued. For each new driver I produced Alfredo's soft creased photo and held it to my chest like a flak jacket. "We're friends, El Duck and us," and into the word *friend* I injected as much subtext as possible, to leave them in no doubt as to the shocking *mala suerte* that would befall them should we be harmed in any way. Nevertheless, the afternoon was running on, and we'd eaten nothing all day.

"God almighty, who *is* this Alfredo dude?" Casey whispered.

I didn't know, but what kind of secret life must he have, that it should be so encoded and protected? Whoever he was, I couldn't shake the feeling that El Duck held the answers to everything. "One thing for sure," I said. "I'm going to hunt him down as if he were last edible fowl on a ruined earth."

"Man, are you stubborn," Casey said.

"If you don't mind," I muttered, "I prefer tenacious."

"*Chicas!*" Our next driver whistled through his teeth. "*Mensaje* for you: El Duck is ready to meet."

I brightened, hankering suddenly for a shower and a calming shot of tequila. If Alfredo was on parole, then that parole was surely being spent in a neoclassical mansion draped in bougainvillea and staff. Alfredo, resplendent in warlord chic, would open his world up to the camera. "I've been a foolish, stubborn *anciano*," he would confide. "but now, *mi guerrero* Bella, I need your help bringing my daughter home."

"Told you," I whispered to Casey, sliding the Alfredo photograph to the driver through the scratched Plexiglas divide. "Hey, *somos amigos*, you know?"

"Yeah, yeah," the driver said, bored. He stopped the car. "The Duck will meet you here."

"Here?" I pressed my nose to the window. "Are you sure?"

We were back where we had started, at the walkway to the United States, less than a quarter-mile from Alfredo's parking lot.

"You're kidding," Casey said.

"Enter the bridge from the south," the driver directed. "Stop at the halfway point, and in six minutes El Duck will approach."

Six minutes. I checked my watch as we hoofed it along the walkway. It was rush hour, and commuters streamed around us like sockeye salmon heading upriver. I craned my neck, looking for Alfredo's dinky paper hat. Suddenly a man jumped out of the flow, grabbed our elbows, and pulled us to the side.

"Hello," he said, smiling. "I am El Duck."

He was fortyish or so, wearing a crazy Hawaiian shirt with ALOHA printed across his chest.

"No," I stammered. "No, you're not!"

I said that because he was absolutely not the Duck.

"Oh, I'm the Duck all right," he said, the lines of his smile beginning to flatten. "And now I'm here, why don't you tell me what business you have with me?" He took my elbow. "Because if you're wasting my time . . ."

I wrenched my arm away. Wasting his time? *His* time? I'm sorry, but how *dare* he? We'd been dicked around for hours. Dicked and Ducked. *Ducked and fucked!*

"Hey, take it easy, *muchacha*!" He bent down quickly and, standing up again, pressed something sharp into my hand.

I stared stupidly at the broken tortoiseshell links, then dropped to the ground and scrabbled about for the watch face, but it was gone. Stricken, I pressed back against the wall and touched a finger to the links, time telescoping backwards. Finn's football triumphs, Jesse's first girlfriend, the letter from Sam's school advising us that he'd bought a pet tarantula—in the last few years I'd been away for all of them. I'd been on the road, too, when Mabel had rung to wish me happy birthday a few days earlier.

"Papa got you a cool present," she said.

"Ooh? What?"

"It's a surprise."

"Tell me at once."

"It's a picture with a message."

"Oh." I hesitated. "What kind of message?"

"OK, wait." She put the phone down and through the line I heard the receding clomp of her school shoes. When she returned she was breathing heavily.

"'She was beautiful in the way that forest fire is beautiful.'"

"What?"

"That's the message on the picture. 'She was beautiful in the way that forest fire is beautiful.'"

"Oh."

"It's sort of an embroidered thingy. Papa's going to give it to you when you get home."

"Oh." I felt a seismic shift in my heart.

"Mum?"

"I'm here, my sweetie."

"When *are* you coming home?"

Tears pricked my eyes.

The Mexican was frowning at me. "What's going on?"

I glared back. "What do you mean?"

"Why are you here?" he said. "What do want? What is it you're looking for?"

I opened my mouth but nothing came out. All those questions I had studiously avoided dealing with. I didn't need a watch to tell me time was running out—that my temporal swag was all used up. I looked at the people as they continued to stream by, a river that never stopped flowing. I think I was there because there everybody was in flux, everybody was searching for something. We were all fighting against the current to get back home.

I tried to explain.

But the Duck who turned out not to be the Duck did not appear moved. He was, in fact, laughing. "Oh, *Dios mio*," he said. "*Dios, Dios,*

Dios mio." He pulled a handkerchief from the pocket of his jeans and blew his nose.

"It's not funny!"

"Oh, but it is. It's a beautiful thought, but you're telling it to the wrong person. On the grave of my dead mother, you are not looking for the Duck."

"Yes, I am," I said stubbornly, and perhaps a bit tenaciously, too.

"So, what does he look like, this Duck of yours?"

For the last time I pulled out the photograph of Alfredo and smoothed over its exhausted creases. "We're friends!" I said, weakly, but only because by then the line was pure reflex. One look at Alfredo's toothy smile and the fake Duck was off again.

"You know this guy?"

"I know him. Now, ask me how I know he's not the Duck."

"How do you know he's not the Duck?"

"Because he's the *Goose!*" And now he was laughing so hard he was folded like a bent playing card.

"The Goose," I repeated flatly.

"The Goose." Casey began to smirk.

"Goose, Duck, you got your birds mixed up, *querida*. You got your eggs all scrambled."

The inside of my head was beginning to feel like a blast furnace. "So, if you're El Duck," I said slowly, "where is El Goose?"

"*El Ganso?* Ah, yes, so sorry for the inconvenience. I'm afraid he's out of town right now."

In LA, I met Sylvie for breakfast. She, too, was not who I thought. She was clever and lovely and, as I would soon discover, brimming with patience, loyalty, and the moral fortitude of Gandhi.

Once I recovered from the shock, we settled down to talk.

"So, the manuscript," she said.

"Yes."

"The line was terrible when we spoke, but you got the gist of it, right?"

"I think so," I answered carefully.

"I'm sorry about it getting out, but somebody passes it on when they're not supposed to and, before you know it, it's everywhere."

"No worries," I said.

"Well, as I mentioned, Charlize loved it. She called the office to tell me."

Shar Leaves. I nodded, as if I knew what she was talking about. "Yes, I remember you saying something about that."

"She's under contract with Warner Brothers. They're going to make an offer."

Warn her brothers. I laid down my fork.

"And the guy from Paramount I told you about? He's been talking to Sam and Kate."

Salmon Cake. I dimly remembered that, too.

"You know," Sylvie said, "as in a directing/starring thing?"

"Of course," I whispered. "That's wonderful."

"There are others, too, so we should talk about how you want to play it."

"What do you mean?"

"Well, you can take the best offer and walk away, or, if you want to stay involved, I can negotiate something else."

"Walk away?"

"Yes," Sylvie said.

I tried to hold on to the noise of the restaurant, the burble of deal-making, the clink of cutlery, but my mind kept drifting back to Tijuana, back to the pedestrian bridge. For a moment I couldn't figure out which was real, Hollywood or the border—until I remembered that in some form, both were fantasies.

Walk away. Could I? Would I?

On the bridge I'd asked El Duck whether Alfredo had made it over to the other side. He shrugged. "People give up hope," he'd said. "They go back to prison. They die."

No, I'd thought. No.

I understood then why I spent so much time lost in imaginary worlds. I wanted things for people that the real world couldn't give them.

There was only one way I could walk away from the border, and that was not to be scared for the people I cared about—to make sure they were safe. And for them to be safe, I had to bring them home.

And so as Sylvie talked, I conjured up the bright coins of light in the basement of the Pink Floyd Fan Club. Vicente and the guys strumming and setting up speakers, when suddenly the door opened and their missing band member finally walked in—Gabriel, with the harpoon scar, his *órgano bucal*, and the ID papers that a mouse had nibbled. And if Gabriel and his harmonica could be brought home, then so could all the others—the tunnel kids, the splintered families, all the hopeful, the lonely, and the exiled. And what of Alfredo, El Goose, wily old smuggler? Maybe he had failed or ended up back in prison, but I prefer to believe he nailed that one last crossing, that he found a way to the other side. Once again, I pictured a street in the San Diego burbs, an adobe building in a handkerchief-size yard, a raven-haired girl—and Alfredo, waiting in the shadows, smiling his secret smile.

But to bring everyone home, I knew I had to bring myself home first.

I thought about Mac and the message of love I needed to embroider on a picture for him. I shut my eyes and heard Mabel clomping up the stairs in her school shoes, and instead of closing my office door, I imagined clearing the space in my head I knew she needed to fill with all the stuff she was learning.

"You don't have to decide right now," Sylvie was saying. "Take as much time as you need."

"It's OK," I told her. "I'm good." As we clinked glasses, I noticed the band of pale skin on my wrist where my watch had been. The rest of my arm was sunburnt, covered in the muddy brown spots of freckles. I thought about dabbing the edge of my napkin in my water glass and rubbing them off, but I didn't want Sylvie to think I was weird, so I decided to wait until I got on the plane.

HOME

FUSS FUSS

Dad coughs a lot on the evening of his birthday. Ask which birthday, and I'd have to say it's his thirty-seventh, though you should know he's been thirty-seven for a few years now. Nevertheless, a great deal of effort has gone into making tonight special. Family is here. Friends have made the long journey. On the dining-room table sits a roast lamb with every conceivable trimming, and even if it's true that Dad would have preferred Frosties and cream, he's happy, he's fine. He catches my eye. An hour later, when he collapses, everyone assumes he's trying to get out of making his thank-you speech. We all know he's not above that kind of thing.

Two days later he spikes a temperature of 105 and goes berserk. Pneumonia, the hospital says. He's gone for broke and caught it in both lungs.

Idiot.

I blame the tweed coat. It retains water. He really shouldn't sleep in it so often.

As soon as my mother gives me the go-ahead, I drive down from London in the gloom of a midweek afternoon. On the motorway, I'm pulled over by a policeman. I'm driving erratically, he tells me. "You're all over the place."

I'm not bothered. I'm excellent with sheriffs. "I'm sorry," I whisper—then, *momentum dramaticus* as I raise anguished eyes to his—"but my father is dreadfully ill. I must get to the hospital." The policeman lets me off with sympathetic words. As he dissolves into the flash of his rotating lights, I cackle with laughter. Sucker. My father can't be that ill. Nobody's father is that ill at thirty-seven.

I find Dad's ward easily enough. Nurse Jummy is on duty. I count the braids in her hair while she talks on the phone. "Cholecystectomy," she's saying. "Conversion to open . . . yes, yes, definitely necrotic."

An old man floats by on a gurney, a water-lily of urine flowering on his blanket. "Nurse," he cries plaintively. "Nurse, nurse . . ."

Jummy consults her chart. "Your father is in the last cubicle but one."

I set off through the muttering, coughing, snoring, and weeping. Fragments of families perch on chairs next to beds, gingerly patting blanketed mounds or spooning goo into mouths that open and shut like hinged trapdoors. I walk, slower and slower, then stop. This is a geriatric ward! How dare they put my father here, in this circus of old, this...this *freak* show of senectitude! I storm back.

"I want him moved," I tell Jummy. I make a real fuss.

"Come with me." Jummy pushes back her chair. At the end of the ward, she rakes back the pleated curtain then stands aside. I freeze, speechless. My father is no longer thirty-seven. Not even close. He is the oldest man in the world. He is Father Time, and everything adult about me falls away. I want to scream and shout. I want to throw myself to the floor and drum my fists into the ground. When did this happen? How did I not notice? A small part of me holds out for mistaken identity, a doppelgänger playing a mean trick. "What have you done with him?" I want to rage at this chalk-like stranger in his bed. Where is my real father? The one wearing the smoking jacket, the one with the sardonic look in his eye—the one radiating health and humour.

His eyelids flutter open. "Pa?" I say, and the years and decades crash down around me like falling buildings. I'm overcome by the sort of helpless feeling you get when a skunk has died under your floorboards.

It's not the lungs I'm worried about. It's the age thing that is beyond my reach.

"Hello, Dau," he manages.

His voice sounds single strand. Pneumonia, the doctors had explained, equals too little pressure in the lungs, equals too few pulses of air into the vocal tract—equals an ant trying to make himself heard at a heavy-metal rock club.

He tires easily. I don't stay long. "Keep the engine running," he says as I get up to leave, and I think, *No, not that. Say anything but that.*

I stumble back through the ward and out into the corridor. At the elevator I can't make sense of the up and down symbols. The anger building inside me is so strong it bolts me to the floor. I stand, digging my nails into the flesh of my palm, waiting for it to subside.

"You all right?" an orderly asks. He gives me an Extra Strong Mint out of his pocket. I want to tell him about the anger, that it's a sickness in its own right—that I need emergency treatment there and then, but he's already moved off to be kind to someone else.

In the car park I smoke three cigarettes, one after the other, watching their red tips burn in the dark. *Yes, I know. We're all on the same road.* But this is not going to be the last stop on my father's journey. Not this place of self-defeat and shuffling regret.

Under the awning of the bus stop opposite, a huddle of disaffected youths are sucking on roll-your-owns and kicking around a beer can. I stare at the pebble-dash of the hospital wall. An ambulance draws up. I grind out my butt. The whole night smells of my fear.

Keep the engine running, I tell myself. *Keep it fucking running.*

Outside the glass doors of the airport, the world awaits. It's ten years earlier, another of Dad's thirty-seventh birthdays. The Venture car-rental lady is initializing our paperwork. I glance out at the fierce western sky, the alloy sun. The arctic whiteness of early morning has burnt off but Dad is never warm. My mother, born in Africa, hates the heat. My father, raised in England, can't stand the cold. He hunkers deeper into his tweed coat. He slept in it last night. It's January, and in John's tower room in the canyon, the heating had been on the blink.

"Coldest few hours of my life," Dad said cheerfully. "It's a miracle I survived."

In the car, an "authentic forest" air freshener hangs from the mirror. Rental lady explains the radio, the fog lights, then, uncertain of the power structure between Dad and me, dangles the keys neutrally. Dad takes them. I once drove him the wrong way around a roundabout and he's never allowed me to forget it. Rental lady shoots me a look of gender empathy, then hands me her business card as a booby prize. "Any problems . . ." she says.

"Let's make rules," I say to my father, as he tosses our cases into the trunk.

"Goody." He produces a fluff-covered lemon sherbet from his pocket and pops it into his mouth. "I love rules."

"No advance bookings, no chains. Seedy motels only."

"Agreed. If the decor's in any way tasteful, we'll leave instantly."

"Any room rate we pay over forty-nine dollars will be considered a failure."

"You're so damned classy, Dau, I can't stand it."

"No fixed route."

"Goes without saying. Itineraries are dreadfully bourgeois."

"And last but not least, we're not allowed to fill up the car unless the warning light is flashing."

"I'm surprised you felt that was even worth mentioning."

I look at the backdrop of mountains, the ridge of mesa, the road stretching ahead into the high desert. "You know, Dad, two people who like to flirt with disaster, no idea where they're going or why? This might not end well."

"Perhaps it's not supposed to," he says.

Monitors beep, medical charts flutter, pens click, machines pump, Dad sleeps.

The walls of his cubicle are shiny cream. Dozens of coats of paint, each overlaying the one before and preserving between them last century's germs of this century's eradicated diseases. This hospital should be a museum. The Varnished History of Medicine.

The patients on exhibit scare me. I think they scare everyone. It's not that they're old; it's that they've moved into a realm of age where it's no longer possible to tell if they're male or female.

"Amiable-looking bunch," Dad says. "Don't you think?"

I crack out a laugh, but all I want is to get up from my chair, run at the wall, and do a backflip—just to prove I still can.

"So what happened, Dad? You know, on your birthday?" I ask this to make him feel bad. I know exactly what happened. The three of us—Marcus, Susie, and me—have gone over it ad nauseam with Mum. He'd felt ill for days, had a cough for weeks. Instead of taking himself to the doctor, he'd gone for a walk in the rain, shot pigeons, chopped down trees, driven the tractor, built a twenty-foot bonfire.

"You don't exactly sound in the peak of condition either," we tell Mum, when she herself breaks off to cough.

"It's nothing," she says. "Don't fuss."

In the Zuni reservation, the desert is as dry as a sore throat. The dogs are thin, the horses thinner. I am allowed the wheel only when Dad naps. For twenty miles there's nothing and then, *boom*—Dad's eyes snap open just as we're driving by a sign: WELCOME TO THE TOWN OF GALLUP.

"Wouldn't it be ironic if we met a cowboy here?" he says.

Dad's good at this, the art of waking up and making a lame quip that I will find very funny.

In the hospital, Dad's hearing aid sits on the side table next to his heavy black-rimmed glasses. He's worn these glasses all his life, and his face has formed around them.

I watch for the accordion rise and fall of his breathing. He's always slept like the dead. On his back, hands crossed benediction-style over his chest. I study the pores of his skin, the creases in his ear lobe, the pale veins threaded through his eyelids. Human markings that belong to time, like the rings within trees or the alternating colours of seashells.

How do you quantify the impact of the people you love on your life? Toss a pebble into the water and watch the ripples radiating outwards, each circle growing wider and wider. Toss in another pebble, then another, until the circles begin to overlap, the cause and effect of each action continuing on, seemingly forever, yet all connecting back to that one first throw. That's how the relationships of our lives are formed. Layer after layer of paint, hundreds of overlapping rings, infinite circles of love.

Boom! His eyes open. "Didn't anyone teach you it was rude to stare?"

"You look different without your glasses."

"Less Clark Kent, more Superman?" He drifts back to sleep.

I plug in my earphones. A slower clock ticks here on the ward of last rites. I read the newspaper, edit work, concentrate on nothing.

Boom! Dad wakes. "What's that you're listening to?"

"Music," I tell him. "I'm listening to music."

"Ah, so that's what it's known as. Do tell, is it a new thing?"

"Yes, and it's sort of interesting. How can I describe it—like noise, but with more of a tune."

"What a tremendous idea," he says. "I wonder if it will catch on."

Pneumonia kills the old, or so the doctor informs us. James Brown died of it, so did Fred Astaire, Gerald Ford, Raymond Chandler, Charles Bronson, and even Tolstoy, collapsing in a tiny Russian railway station, ever the victim of his wanderlust. In the weeks, then months between my father's drips and pills and different hospital admissions, I scour the Internet, zeroing in on images of lungs, darkly diffracted by disease, as though they're hiding a cure that only the intensity of my research will uncover.

"Your father's hopeless, a nightmare," Mum says. "He gets furious when I tell him to put on more clothes, furious when I try to get him to eat sensibly."

"Hopeless," we three children agree. Mum's cross, we're all cross, but sitting at the kitchen table, drinking tea, watching her hide her fear, comforts us. At seventy-eight, my mother is beautiful. I see that she's getting old, but she's getting old in a way that makes sense. At fifty she was fifty and at sixty she was ten years further on. My mother has always been grounded in time. All my life I've held on to her steadiness like a handrail on a listing ship.

"You talk to him," she pleads. "He listens to you lot. He's stubborn, your father. He's a stubborn old man."

This morning Dad sits still and upright in the armchair next to his bed, staring into the middle distance. His hair, his snowy-white Moses hair, has been neatly brushed in some indefinably wrong way,

presumably by a well-meaning nurse. This, too, makes me cross, so
I give him a lecture.

"You can't sit here all day! If you learned to use a computer, you
could watch movies. Listen to music. You could e-mail friends, buy
rare trees." I hear the sharpness in my voice. What I really want to say
is: *Don't do less. Don't diminish. Don't leave me.*

When I finish, he smiles faintly. "My darling Froggins." He cups
a hand to his ear. "I have no doubt that every word falling from your
lips is a wondrous pearl brought up from the bottom of the ocean. It's
just a great pity I can't hear them."

Touché. Dad has always been elegant in his deafness.

"So, what is it about the road?" I ask him. We're picnicking somewhere in Geronimo country. Giant saguaro cactuses dot the hills,
each one a sublime deformity. I'm dining on Cheez Doodles, and my
father is halfway through his second pack of Kraft cheese slices. He's
using cheese slices to wean himself off hot dogs. In the last three days
he's consumed twelve, all in a bun and not a mitigating vegetable in
between, "but boy, am I beginning to feel the pain," he says happily.
In England he lives on white food. Not the grated bones, raw dough,
and fruit mould diet of Erik Satie, but soft smelly cheeses, bread
spread thickly with clotted cream and sprinkled with sugar; brandy
butter by the serving spoon.

"What about the road?" he says.

"Why is it so addictive, do you think?"

Today the Arizona sky looks freshly painted. A lone rig streaks by,
all gleaming hubcaps and lug nuts. Dad watches it go. "The freedom,"
he says somewhat distractedly. "What's round the next corner. Not
knowing what you might find there."

"I know, I know. But what are we hoping to find?"

"That's the point. Could be anything. A sparkling valley of grazing elephants, a nice patch of green grass."

"That's it? That's what we base our dreams on? A nice patch of green grass?" There are times when I revert to the child with my father. The one who asks the same question a thousand different ways until she gets the answer she wants.

"If you don't believe it," he says, "why do you keep on going?"

"But what if there's nothing round the corner?"

"Just because you don't know what you're looking for doesn't mean to say you won't find it."

I scowl. *Don't be so reasonable, Dad, don't be so grown-up. Just tell me it's going to be OK, because that's all I want to hear.*

"I bet you there's nothing," I say, suddenly grumpy.

"Fine. If you're going to be difficult." He crumples the Kraft wrappers into his pocket and lopes off down the narrow track. I watch his sneakers kicking up dust behind him. I don't follow. I know what's behind that small hill he's heading towards. I've climbed so many like it—there's always another hill. But he's out of sight and the drumming of insects fills the void. From far away, I hear a shout.

"What?" I shout back.

"Come see for yourself!"

Around the corner, Dad's grinning. A llama stands ten feet away, an idiotic smile spread across its loopy, bulbous lips.

"Bet he thinks he's the master of the universe," Dad says.

"A llama? A nice llama? That's what's round the corner?"

"Ha! Fooled you," Dad steps aside to reveal a random gravestone. He indicates the inscription with a foppish bow.

GENE MCKLINTOCK
THE BUCK STOPS HERE

The jug of water by his hospital bed collects plankton on its surface. Dad does not drink water. Not in a restaurant, not in a desert, not if his life depended on it, which, ironically, it now well might. He claims to have nearly drowned as a child and it put him off, but the truth is he prefers vodka. I become fixated by the stagnant water, the stale air in the room, the varnished walls of germs. My father does not do well in stasis. Stagnant water kills people; flowing water creates life. *Quick, jump into the river, fight the current. Swim wherever you like but keep on going.*

Boom! "Very disconcerting all this staring," he says. "Anyone would think I'm a specimen, waiting for dissection."

"How you doing, Dad?"

"Happy as a clam."

"Did you sleep?"

"Well, since you ask. One of the other inmates tried to climb into my bed last night."

"Dad! No!"

"I can't tell you how alarming it was."

"Which one?"

Dad inclines his head towards the Nosferatu opposite, propped up against pillows, white and masticating.

"Christ, Dad."

"Yes, well, I must say, I was quite relieved when an orderly arrived to wrestle him back into bed."

"Did you complain?"

"I didn't want to antagonise him, but now you're here, perhaps I'll avail myself of the bathroom facilities."

He shifts himself to the edge of his bed. I help him on with his slippers. "Want me to come with you, Dad?" But even as I say it, I wonder: Could I do it? Could I take care of him? *Stroke the blankets, spoon the goo?*

"Certainly not. There are certain things—very few, mind you—that a man must do alone." He pushes to his feet.

"Sure you're OK?"

He steadies himself on the tent poles of the cubicle. "Damn you, Shackleton," he says valiantly. "I may be some time."

I watch him as he goes. My father, the most athletic man I know. He of the faultless hand-eye coordination; the father who taught me to hit a baseball like Babe Ruth; the man who plays tennis in cowboy boots, with a cigarette dangling from his mouth. He's walking so slowly.

Please, please, do we always have to do this? Watch the strongest people in our lives separate from us inch by inch?

Susie and I share a plastic carton of pineapple chunks in the hospital corridor.

"Remember when Granny died?" she asks. I nod. Brave, thrifty, *Out of Africa* Granny. She fought drought and locusts and veldt fires and died in her nursing home just shy of her hundredth birthday.

"Don't let us live that long," our parents begged the three of us afterwards. "Pills, vodka, blow to the head, we don't care—just kill us off, if it's all the same to you. We don't want to stick around that long. We don't want to be a burden."

But it's not all the same to us, thank you.

"Promise us," they kept on saying. "Promise us."

"Do look." Dad slows down somewhere outside San Francisco. "A hitchhiker! What say you we pick him up?"

"Must we?"

"Why not? Nice boyfriend for you."

"He looks rough."

"So would you if you'd been sleeping on the side of the road."

"Rough *and* smelly."

"No, I honestly think he might do for you." He slows the car. "You young people could have fun together."

The hitchhiker has dreadlocks made of caterpillar nests and a smile forged of opportunity.

"Ditch the old man," he murmurs to me in the Chips Ahoy aisle of the next gas station. "Let's you and I have some fun together."

I look at him with pity.

"So, what did you think of our new friend?" I ask Dad as we make our escape.

"Well, I'm fighting a natural aptitude to be critical, but I must say I didn't take to him as much as I'd hoped. You?"

"I've known barnyard animals more appealing."

"He didn't exactly look like the straightest arrow."

"Or the most informative book in the library."

"Or the cleanest napkin in the drawer. Plus, I couldn't help but notice, he had a hungry air about him."

"No kidding, like he was sizing me up for slaughter."

"You know," Dad says. "Considering you're my daughter, I should probably look after you a little bit better in future."

"Really, Dad? D'ya think?" I bat my eyes at him.

Ask me what we talk about on the road, and I'd have to say we never get much beyond frivolous. How exactly did Heinz start his baked bean empire? A rehash through the plot of some B-movie, and surely I remembered the myth of Orpheus and Eurydice? But sometimes I wait for him to ask: *Are you happy? Are you sad? Pleased with your life or disappointed?*

How bad does it have to get for him to ask, I wonder, and the idea makes me cross. I word and re-word the question in my head for ten miles before throwing it out there.

He looks startled. "I never think it's any of my business."

"But you're my father. Aren't you curious?"

"I assume you'd tell me if you wanted to."

"But because you don't ask, I figure you're not interested."

"My poor Frog," he says. "So terribly misunderstood." The conversation has made him feel bad, I can see that, but my latest burst of petulance is not over.

"I mean, don't you think there are things you should have warned me about?"

"Like what?"

"Like how easy it was to fuck up in life?"

"I thought you were plenty intelligent to work that out for yourself."

"You had a head start, you could have saved me some time."

"I'm sorry. I've been very selfish. I see that now."

We're both still joking—sort of. I've long accepted that our natural home is in the spaces between the lines, and so we drive on in silence.

A few miles later, a giant billboard looms on the freeway.

WEARIED BY LIFE? TURN TO JESUS.

"There you go." Dad squeezes my hand. "The answer for both of us."

"How did you do it, Mum?" I ask her. We're walking together along a beach in the Outer Hebrides, where for a while my mother walked the wild and boggy alone. Mum's hands are shoved deep in her pockets, the curve of her back dictated by the strength of the wind. I'm writing a book set on this island, a book set closer to home in so many ways, and I've been thinking a lot about my parents' marriage—its catastrophes and triumphs, the multiple lost and found of it over the years. How did she do it? I've seen how tough it is to construct a life, to lay down tracks to the future. I've seen the hard labour and the rock breaking. How does anyone have the tools to see it through?

"You just find them," she says.

"But after everything, Mum, are you happy, are you sad? Pleased with your life or disappointed?"

When she turns, the wind blows the structure of her sentence into fragmented words, but I catch its meaning.

"I spent a long time crossing through sad," she says, "but I got to happy in the end."

There is a routine to illness, a rhythm that accompanies it. Doctors swish in and out. Interns come and go. Orderlies say hi, and fish happens on Fridays. Dad knows the rota of every single nurse and the city and country in which each was born. His fellow patients are beginning to lose their spectral look. They're now other people's fathers or husbands. Today when I look at my own father's face, I see every age he's ever been, each decade overlaid, one on top of the other, just like the paint and varnish on the walls.

Boom! Dad's eyes open. "What are you scribbling in that notebook of yours?"

"Nothing." I lay down my pen. *Oh the unfairness of it. That I can't write him back to health and glamour.*

"Copying down all the clever things I say, I'll be bound."

"You haven't said a word for the last two hours."

"Nonsense, I was probably talking in my sleep." He turns to the nurse fiddling with his IV. "Tell my daughter she really shouldn't plagiarise my work."

And Nguyu smiles the smile I have seen a thousand women smile.

"Don't let him charm his way out of hospital," my mother says. "He's still way too ill, and you know he'll try."

"He won't. We won't let him," we chorus. Susie, Marcus, and me, we know the score. We call our younger half-sibs, Josh and Lally. We confer by phone or in waiting rooms or tramp through muddy winter fields in borrowed gumboots, tying small knots onto the end of one another's long-forgotten threads.

"Remember after that shitty boyfriend of yours left and I slept in your bed for a week?" I ask Susie.

"Remember when I tried to stop you taking all those drugs and sent you to a GP?" she counters.

"Remember when you thought Giacomo's father was coming to steal the children?" Marcus puts his arm around both of us. "You were in a terrible state. I was supposed to be flying to Uist, but I didn't go. I waited by the phone in case you called."

I turn to look at him. "Oh, Marky, I didn't know."

"I never told you," he said.

Over never-ending cups of tea, I look at my brother and sister huddled close around the kitchen table. Marcus buys and rebuilds struggling manufacturing companies. Susie is an ace adviser of the art world. Like me, they have their jobs, friends, kids, dogs, excitements, and disasters. We are no longer eldest, middle, and youngest child; we are just us, and we all agree. *Of course Dad cannot come home!* Apart from anything else, it wouldn't be fair on Mum.

"You look tired, Mum," Susie says.

"Yes, Mum," Marcus and I agree. "You really do."

"Fuss, fuss," she says, and we know better than to push it.

I don't tell her, though, that I caught sight of her the other day walking down the street in London. There was something about the way her hair was hairdresser-pretty, something about the way she carried herself, that had me swerving the car over to a meter and shouting after a complete stranger. *Mum, no*, I think as I watch her make *pie of the cottage* and feed the dogs, *stay close, do not do this. Just as I'm spending more time with you and Dad, do not even think about getting ready to leave me.*

"Promise me," she says, sitting back down. "All of you. You know how persuasive he can be. He's not to come home until he's out of danger."

"Don't worry, Mum," we tell her. "We promise."

"Stop the car!" Dad says near Flagstaff.

"Why?"

"Just do it, but keep the engine running."

Worried he's ill, I pull off the road, but he leaps out, gazelle-like and waves down the car coming towards us.

"Dad, what on earth are you doing?"

"My good deed of the day. Watch."

The car stops. The driver looks like a gas/oil rep: maximum air conditioning, and briefcase from Office Depot.

"Just in case you were thinking of visiting the world's largest meteorite," my father tells him, "I'm here to let you know it's not worth it."

The gas/oil rep looks baffled, as well he might.

"Eighteen dollars each for what amounts to a large hole," Dad explains. "Honestly, I'd give it a miss if I were you."

"Well, thank you, sir," the rep says. "Appreciate it."

"See!" Dad says, after the rep's driven off. "I do believe he was genuinely touched."

"Oh, just get in the car, Dad," I sigh.

"You know something," he says a while later. "I'll cut off my pinky without anaesthetic if that car behind us doesn't belong to a sheriff."

My father thinks every car he sees contains a sheriff—just as every lightning-blackened tree on a hill is an Apache scout. Besides, I'm barely ten miles an hour over the speed limit.

Five minutes later a sheriff is knocking on the window.

"Told you so," Dad says, leaning over me as I wind it down. "Good afternoon, Officer. Are we in trouble?"

We're not in trouble; of course we're not. Man, woman, sheriff, horse—my father would charm a lightbulb if he thought it might help it to shine brighter. It's his means of communication with the world, and because the language of charm is universal, a speeding ticket is out of the question, just as our under-forty-nine-dollar motel room is always a shoo-in.

"Sir, is this your wife?" the sheriff asks.

"Good God, no!" Dad says. "I wouldn't be married to a nag like her. What's more, I regret to inform you, she's a terrible driver. I'd arrest her right now if I were you."

The sheriff looks as befuddled as the gas/oil rep.

"I can assure you," Dad says, "it's for her own good."

"I don't think that'll be necessary, sir."

"I blame myself," Dad continues. "The truth is I haven't always been a very good father to her."

I study my knees while the sheriff backtracks through his academy training for the correct response to unsolicited confessions of this nature.

"Move along," he says finally.

"Not a very good father, huh?" I start the engine. "That's one I've not heard before."

"Well, since you ask," he says, and for once there's no trace of pith in his voice, no sarcasm waiting in the wings. "I was never around all that much when you were little. And never when I should have been."

My daughterly jaw drops. *Seriously, Dad, seriously?* After all that we've come through, after all that we are as a family? *Absences mean nothing,* I want to tell him. *No more than empty air.*

"You think that's what counts?" I ask. "Minutes added up?"

"I think you know I love you," he says simply. "I just never knew if that was enough."

I look away.

Idiot father. It was always enough.

"Good news," Dad says brightly as I walk in. "Doctor God here says I can come home tomorrow."

A consultant stands at the foot of Dad's bed, talking with one of his underlings.

"That's right, you haven't met the new Doctor God yet, have you?" Dad says. "He visits obscenely early in the mornings but apart from that he's a most reasonable fellow."

Most reasonable means that he and my father have bonded over a species of tree found in the doctor's hometown of Jaipur. The doctor is homesick for Jaipur and very especially for this tree. My father, for many years an amateur tree expert and trustee of some famous public arboretum, has promised to help the doctor find a way to plant this tree in his own garden. After he's tracked down the seeds, he will drive halfway across England to a small shop in the backwoods of somewhere. He will adore doing this and will very likely ask me to accompany him.

I stall. "What happened to the other Doctor God?"

"He hasn't been around for a while. I have a horrible feeling he may have snuffed it."

I drag the new consultant away from his entourage. "How can coming home possibly be a good idea?" I hiss. With impeccable timing my father coughs, and I hear something stubborn in his chest—a squatter that knows its rights.

"Good grief, anyone would think she wasn't pleased." Dad is now addressing me through the doctor, sucking him into his conspiracy.

"Why on earth would I be pleased?" I don't just address the doctor. I take him out of the room and into the reception area, and though he is intimately acquainted with my father's notes, blast him with the whole history. *My father has not been suffering from a mere tickle of the throat! He's been in and out of hospital for months with pneumonia, with this incessant, terrifying, unyielding cough.*

Doctor God has eyes the colour of malt whiskey. He has been put on earth solely to make my father better. Part of me wants to give up the rest of my life to polish his shoes; the other half wants to take him out with a crowbar.

"You really think sending him home is a good idea?"

"Just for a day or two," the doctor replies gently. "It might do him good."

"Then you'd better sign the forms quickly, before my daughter starts grumbling again," Dad says on our return. "I don't know whether I mentioned it, but she's a terrible grumbler. Never stops." There is hurt behind the lightness.

"Dad," I falter. "It's freezing outside."

I know my father is going mad in here. That staying still, staying in one place, is the equivalent of death for him. But how can his beleaguered lungs withstand the booby trap of a frosty morning, the sneeze of a passer-by, or that coiled spore of the flu virus waiting for its chance? In the war of attrition that is old age, death always has the greater resources.

"Fuss, fuss," he says. "It's not like I haven't got a good coat."

"Of course he must come home," Mum says when I tell her about Doctor God's proposed bail. "Don't be so silly." She turns away so I won't see her tear up. "Besides, I miss him terribly."

I'm in the attic of my parents' house. There have been other nights like this, nights when I sleep in the comforting single bed with an electric blanket and the window grumbling in its frame. Except sleep is not what I do. At best it's a paddle through the shallows of an insomnia that Mum's pills, my pills, and even the illegally scored big-city Xanax don't touch.

Night is the time for demons of every sort, and after they've finished with me, I lie twitching, nauseated, unable to calm my mind.

How's your dad? I imagine friends asking, and to inoculate myself—to inject antivenin straight into my heart—I practise my response.

He's dead, I say. *I am broken.* Then I allow the pain to wash over me. I don't even try to measure its depth. *How will I ever surface? Who will I be without my father, and how much of me will he take with him when he goes?*

In real life, when friends ask me how he's doing, I give a tiny Gallic shrug. *You're sweet,* this shrug implies, *but we all go through the same thing sooner or later.* But what I'm really thinking is: *Fuck you! Don't nod your stupid head like that. You don't get it! Nobody has ever been through this! Nobody feels the way I do. Because Dad and me? We're different.*

"Road trip, Pa?"

"What? Now?" He looks at my brother and me in feigned surprise, even though he's out of bed, out of his hospital pajamas, ready and waiting in his tweed coat.

"Engine's running," I tell him.

"Always in a hurry," he says. "Hurry, hurry, hurry. Oh, well, if you insist."

Marcus positions a wheelchair in front of the bed.

"How exciting." Dad settles into it and sweeps the hem of his coat onto his knees. "Where are we off to?"

"Home," Marcus says.

The word floors him. He closes his eyes, then opens them again, sangfroid recovered. "I don't know if I've ever mentioned it before, but you're very unpredictable, the pair of you."

We stop at the pharmacy on the ground floor for Marcus to pick up Dad's prescription. Dad sits very upright. I study the familiar pattern of the tweed, the raglan shoulders, the curling frayed edges of those pockets from which, as a child, I used to steal quarters. I squeeze the handles of the wheelchair and dare myself to look down. I dread seeing anything old people–ish on top of Dad's head, a looming scalp under wispy strands or a patch of skin with hyperpigmentation—but it's all good. Dad has always had epically thick hair.

"How you doing, Pa?"

He considers. "Well, since you ask, I'm road testing a new emotion."

"How exciting. What is it?"

"I believe it's called gratitude."

It's a clear run home. The minimal traffic of the English countryside. I crank up the heating as we pass a market garden, then a long industrial estate encircled by barbed wire. Dad naps in the passenger seat. I look at his familiar profile, those hawkish cheekbones, nose from the Jewish side of the family, and inside my chest my heart feels loose and unstable, as though it's being held together with sticky tape.

As we were leaving the hospital, Doctor God had stepped out of his office. "Quick word?" he'd said, touching me on the shoulder.

"I'm afraid the pneumonia might just be a symptom." This from behind his desk.

"What do you mean?" In my pocket, my mobile was vibrating. *Susie.* I pressed decline. "A symptom of what?"

"I think there might be something wrong with his blood."

This is not OK. To hear that the thing that your father has been battling, the thing that has stolen his strength—nearly stolen his life—is merely a symptom of something worse?

"What do you mean? Give me a name. Give me a disease."

"Leukemia," Doctor God said. "But we won't know more until we do tests."

A pause.

"I'm sorry."

As I left his office, my mobile vibrated again. "It's about Mum's cough." Susie said, and as she began talking I felt something internal in me collapse, a structural part—the steel of me. I leaned against the glossy walls of the corridor for support. *Something has been growing inside our mother,* Susie appeared to be saying. *Something she'd decided not to tell us about until she was sure. Something she'd now had X-rayed and biopsied and found to be a tumour.* "Tell Marky," Susie said, "but obviously not Dad."

"Course," I said, although I can't be sure I said anything, because by that time the edges of my brain were burning, hot as a jet engine.

Idiot parents, we'd agreed numbly before signing off, *getting cancer on the same day.*

Boom! In the car, Dad's eyes snap open. "Cacophobia," he says. "What does it mean?"

"Fear of poo."

"Nope."

"Fear of dark chocolate."

"Don't be ridiculous." He looks out the window as the industrial estate recedes in a blur of smoke and light. "It means fear of ugly things. Isn't that wonderful? Isn't English the most wonderful language?"

My brother overtakes us in his dirt-streaked saloon. He hoots. I hoot back. Code for: *Don't panic, it'll be OK, we'll get through this, we'll figure it out.*

"Appalling drivers," Dad says, "the pair of you."

Marcus catches my eye as he passes. I clutch the steering wheel. Leukemia? Lung cancer? The words weigh down, heavy as iron girders. But even as my daughter heart is breaking, my child selfishness takes over. *No, this cannot be happening to me. I won't let it happen. We will go back to the beginning. I will write us all back in time. Back to Ninety-Second Street. Back to Papagoya and roast chicken picnics in Central Park.*

Blink, and we're there. I'm up in a tree, dangling thirty feet above the ground on the end of my father's hand. Above me, Dad is whistling. He leans against the tree trunk for support. He looks young. Thirty-seven-ish, I guess. His black hair edges the collar of his shirt. His jeans, cowboy hipsters, are just a little bit flared.

"Ready?" he calls, adjusting his grip. His fingers are made of willow, supple and strong. My limbs are Potty Putty—nevertheless, we're the same. Even as a child I know this. I've always known. It's like I grew out of his arm.

He begins to swing me from side to side. Slowly, then with increasing momentum. Above him the sky winks through the leaves, almost within reach, as tantalizing as space. "Be brave," he'd said earlier. "Who knows what you'll see from up there."

But I don't feel brave. I have never been brave.

"Ready?" he shouts.

Far below us, sitting cross-legged on the picnic blanket, Susie is drawing. My mother is reading *Here Comes Mumfie* to Marcus. I love the way she tells stories, and for a moment I ache to be down there too, curled up in her lap. My head to her heart. That feeling-safe feeling.

"No!" I feel the panic rising. "Not ready!"

Blink again, and I'm me watching that eight-year-old self, frozen between sky and ground. And suddenly I see it. The genesis of limbo. Caught between safety and curiosity, courage and cowardice, being told stories and taken places. Torn between conflicting desires and warring selves.

There it is, there's the moment.

For as long as I can remember, the opposing pull of home or away has been the central struggle of my life. It has split me in two. And those two selves I've imagined and reimagined, as twins, as spirit creatures, as tectonic plates, one constantly shifting underneath the other, subducting, grinding, creating friction, causing internal stress. I've blamed this for my own continental drift—across land, in and out of relationships, and over the course of careers. I've lived with the fear that disaster is inevitable, that the earthquake is coming and that when it does, my world will be annihilated.

Frantic, I kick my eight-year-old legs.

"Stop struggling," Dad warns. His hold on me begins to slip, but all I know, all I've ever known, is to kick harder.

Now, alerted to my fear, my mother pushes to her feet off the picnic blanket. She comes to stand underneath the tree and looks up, one hand shielding her eyes from the glare of the sun. Calmly she checks my likely trajectory, my fall from tree to ground, and moves into position. And, still twisting on the end of my father's arm like a paper streamer, I'm rotated out of the moment. My perspective shifts and once again I'm watching myself through the crystal ball of time, suspended midair between my parents, in the middle, where I belong. And as my father urges me on, as my mother gives me courage, I see the two combine to create that electrical jolt I have so often felt passing through me, that powerful surge of happiness.

And I wonder. With my lousy sense of maps and direction, is it possible I've got my inner geography all muddled, too? I keep forgetting that the earth is not flat. Its roads are not straight but looped around and around. What if my duality, the thing of which I am most afraid, is not a fault line but simply two points at opposite ends of a circle, each forever leading back to the other? This realisation makes me feel strong. Strong enough to be thrown, strong enough to fly, strong enough to keep going through the removal of my mother's lung, through the long years of my father's treatment to come.

And finally I stop struggling. "Ready," I shout. "I'm ready."

Dad resumes swinging, wider and wider. Counting three, two, one—then he lets go.

I soar, airborne—perhaps for a single second, perhaps decades— looking for a safe place to land and eventually I find one.

I snatch at the branch above him, gripping it with my claws and balancing with my tail.

"Made it!" I cry.

"Brilliant daughter!" Dad shouts back. "Now tell me what you see!"

Toss a pebble into the water. Isn't this how the relationships of our lives are formed? Your father helps you climb a tree. Your mother holds out her arms in case you fall. Every action, another pebble thrown, another circle created. The flight through the air, the joy you feel, the world you see from the top—every one a ripple, radiating out, growing wider, overlapping one another, connecting my whole life.

"Well?" Dad demands. "Tell me!"

I see what he's always hoped I'd see. What he and Mum have always wanted me to see. "Everything," I shout back. "I can see everything!"

*   *   *

In the car, Dad is looking at me quizzically. "Dreaming," he sighs. "Always daydreaming. What is it this time?"

I smile. "Just stuff. New York stuff."

"You're way too young to retreat into memory. Pull yourself together."

"Won't happen again."

"I should hope not. Memories are for people my age."

Is that true, I wonder, that memories should be saved for grown-ups? For when you're older and better able to ascribe meaning to them?

"Dad, do you remember taking us to see *Fantasia*?"

"*Fantasia* the movie?"

"Yes, one afternoon after school. You bunked off work. Turned up at the apartment out of the blue."

"Rubbish."

"We had to run all the way through the park to get to the West Side."

"You're making it up."

"What about *Airport '77*?"

He brightens. "Jacqueline Bisset, blown to smithereens in the loo?"

"Well at least you haven't got dementia. What about *Man in the Iron Mask*?"

"Masterpiece."

"We saw it together, remember? I was in labour."

He looks at me uncertainly.

"You were the only other person in the cinema. Right in the front row. I sat at the back and then I realised it was you."

Another blank look.

"Come on, Dad. I was having contractions. You held my hand and fed me popcorn."

He looks stricken. "I'd forgotten. It's too awful."

I reach for his hand.

"Don't get old," he says.

"I won't."

How do I tell my father he has cancer? That Mum does, too? How do I tell Mum about Dad? Breathe, I tell myself. Breathe. It's just another road trip, that's all, a different kind of journey.

"I've been thinking," Dad says.

"Oh?"

"Taking you to the movies? Coming back in the middle of the day like that when I should have been working. Holding your hand in labour, giving you half my popcorn . . ."

"Yes?" I say.

"Well, I think I must have been a terribly good father." He gives my hand another squeeze. "I have to say, you're really very lucky, you know."

DEMON

(THE RECKONING)

The sun has gone, the day long since faded. Outside the window, night presses against the glass. The air has the opaque, dreamy quality of a summer solstice. The moon, a crown of silver in the sky, casts light over papers strewn across the bed. Four a.m. and my demon comes, as I imagined he might.

Yes, we still see each other from time to time, my incubus and I, though it's fair to say that some of the heat has gone out of our relationship. Sometimes I wake to find his hand on my shoulder, before he slips away between the shadowy gaps of my sleep. Of late, he's even acquired a sense of humour—should one choose to call it that. Earlier this year for instance, as I felt his iron filings drain from my body, he touched the palm of my hand with his finger and said, "You do know I'm married, don't you?"

More recently he appeared to me no longer a collection of iron filings but made of flesh-coloured sandstone, and instead of a finger he had a rotating drill on the end of his hand, which he extended towards me. "Don't even think about it," I said scornfully and went back to sleep.

Only the next morning did the significance of this encounter occur to me. It was the first time I'd seen him not as an image in my head, not as a presence wrapped around my body, but as a "real" entity outside myself. Though in terms of recovery, arguably, we still have some way to go, I took this as a step in the right direction.

Before encountering him, I'd never considered myself an addict. Sure I smoked a little, chugged down the odd shot of tequila, and happily swallowed any pill slipped to me, but I could easily live without these things. Escape, solitude, wonder—these were the highs I craved. When I'm at home I love everything it represents, but sooner or later life becomes too comfortable, too predictable, and my fear of complacency sets in. After that I veer quickly from feeling safe to feeling edgy, unable to breathe, and finally so claustrophobic that I will do anything to break free, to experience the adrenaline and bliss of freedom. How uncannily like the pattern of my haunting.

Sometimes I think back again to that day at the Bronx Zoo when as a little girl I stood hypnotized as the cobra banged its head against the glass in its determination to escape. The following day it had. The glass was smashed and the snake gone. This had terrified me. The serpent had had me in its sights, with every intention of hunting me down.

I like to think that my shadow creatures are the mountain lion and the jungle cat, but perhaps in the end it's the snake I understand best. Now I realise it meant no harm as it slithered through the unfamiliar streets of the city, excitedly taking in the new sights and smells, revelling in its liberty and independence. How long, though, I wonder, before it tired of freedom in those unfamiliar streets? Before it curled up in an alley, cold and lonely, dreaming of a dead mouse and a dry cage? How long before it yearned to go back to the only place where things made sense?

A little perspective informs everything. Demons, addictions, obsessions don't always come out of a bottle. Home or away? I had avoided choosing between the two, preferring instead to inhabit the liminal spaces, the places between awake and dreaming, and there search out adventure and danger in worlds that were not my own. I'd driven my family crazy with this behaviour, until finally my confusion began manifesting itself in some sort of inhuman form. *Deal with me*, my demon had ordered. *I am your demon, and you need to pay attention, or I will paralyse you forever.*

So, I paid attention.

I'm piecing together a new story to tell myself. It's still a work in progress. Meanwhile I no longer wish to be rid of my incubus. His visits always come when I'm alone, thinking about embarking on something new, and they serve as a reminder not to mess too much with the balance of life—that it's OK to make my home in the middle, because from there, if I stretch hard enough, I can reach the furthest points of away. And that makes him a friend, not an enemy.

Besides, what's hidden deep inside us can also be the one thing that keeps driving us forwards. The thing that keeps us going.

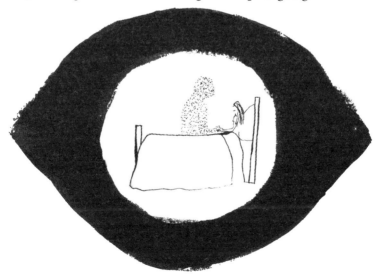

ACKNOWLEDGMENTS

I've heard tell of authors who manage to write books by themselves, but I needed a great deal of help from a good many smart people. Those collaborations, in their varying forms, were the happiest and most productive stages of what turned out to be a surprisingly long journey, and to all those who came on it with me, I owe a huge debt of gratitude.

My love and thanks to:

Mac: For understanding. For loyalty and sheer generosity of spirit, you are, quite simply, the best.

Sam: My brilliant and insightful boy, who was in on these stories from inception, and in reading them over and over, kept pushing me closer to their truth. Sam, apart from coming up with almost all the best lines, it's no exaggeration to say that without you this book would have ended up in a different place.

Jesse, Mabel and Finn: You are my Incredibles. For your iron support, relentless teasing and astute literary observations. I adore you #nowgotoyourroom, love your devoted 2%Mum.

My graphic memoir team, Kate, Amy, Daisy: For your creative ingenuity. Thank you for taking such an enormous leap of faith in working with me when it was obvious I didn't have the faintest idea what I was doing.

Kate Boxer: For your soup kitchen and fried cheese things. For my beautiful lions and demons and that portrait you did that makes me look like Steve Tyler on a really off-day. I love seeing the world through your eyes.

Amy Gadney: For your 'All at Sea Board Game' and for somehow making my prose look pretty. For always cutting through the nonsense and insisting that everything had to be hand-done and genuine. You also bake really good soda bread.

Daisy Sworder: For your exhaustive optimism and inspired ideas. For being able to do everything I can't and everything I can just that little bit better. I would be in the nuthouse without you, but then you know that already.

My revered and loyal editors: Elizabeth Schmidt at Grove Atlantic and Maria Rejt, at Mantle. I know this sounds oily, but I am proud to be published by you. Thank you for helping me make this book more of a silk purse than a sow's ear.

The Mantle and Grove teams: Josie Humber, Camilla Elworthy, Katie Raissian, Sal Destro and Gretchen Mergenthaler, Deb Seager and Justina Batchelor. For elevating patience and professionalism to an art form.

To Morgan Entrekin: You are the Zeus of publishers.

Ami Smithson: For your beautiful cover design which I love, love.

My wise London agent: Sarah Lutyens, whose uncanny resemblance to wise spectral agent, Sarah in the book is purely coincidental. Sarah, just so you know – you are almost always quietly right about everything.

My fearless US agents: Kim Witherspoon and Sylvie Rabineau, whose uncanny resemblance to fearless US agents in the book is unsurprising given it is a memoir. Thank you for not minding how babyish I am.

My friend of friends, John Sutcliffe: For our adventures. Wherever you're going, can I always come too?

To friends Colleen Woodcock, Stacey Workman, HC, KI, LW, and others whose names I've changed or in some cases omitted. You are all part of this story.

The Virginia Centre for the Creative Arts residency programme where this book was both conceived and completed.

My VCCA residency family: Thank you Bea Booker, Sheila Pleasants, Sarah Sargent, Carol O'Brien, Dana Jones, and Kimberley Stiffler – for feeding and watering me over the years. VCCA could not mean more to me in terms of support and inspiration.

My fellow residency fellows: A. K. Benninhofen, Julie Bloemeke, Tim Denevi, Paul Skenazy, Sandell Morse, Howie Axelrod, Frank Day, Agu, Alberto and oh so many others. For your thoughtful reads, friendship and superior skills at mixing cocktails.

Special thanks to Kristen Cosby: For helping me whip these stories into some kind of shape. You are an incredibly smart, generous and intuitive reader whose ruthless pen sharpened every line it touched.

Thank you too, to VCCA France, Moulin à Nef in Auvillar and the wonderful Tyrone Guthrie residency in Ireland.

To my Pollen family: Stellar sibs, Susie and Marcus #superglue. And also my beloved half-sibs, Josh and Lally. Thank God we're all in this together.

My heroic father. My mother became suddenly ill and died while I was on deadline for MMITIB. Thank you, Pops, for bullying me into picking up the manuscript and for keeping me at it all those days and nights in hospital when it was the last thing on earth I wanted to be doing.

And lastly to Mum … For teaching me about the things that really matter. For always giving me courage when I had none left. You were the invisible force behind these stories but now I see you on every page. You were, are, and will forever be, the most spectacular of mothers.